MTTC Social Studies
84 Teacher Certification Exam

By: Sharon Wynne, M.S
Southern Connecticut State University

DATE DUE

"..., while there's no reason yet to panic, I think it's only prudent that we make preparations to panic."

MANKOFF

XAMonline, INC.
Boston

To obtain permission(s) to use the material from this work for any purpose including workshops or seminars, please submit a written request to:

XAMonline, Inc.
21 Orient Ave.
Melrose, MA 02176
Toll Free 1-800-509-4128
Email: info@xamonline.com
Web www.xamonline.com
Fax: 1-781-662-9268

Library of Congress Cataloging-in-Publication Data

Wynne, Sharon A.
    Social Studies 84: Teacher Certification / Sharon A. Wynne. -2nd ed.
    ISBN 978-1-58197-970-1
    1. Social Studies 84.   2. Study Guides.   3. MTTC
    4. Teachers' Certification & Licensure.   5. Careers

Disclaimer:

The opinions expressed in this publication are the sole works of XAMonline and were created independently from the National Education Association, Educational Testing Service, or any State Department of Education, National Evaluation Systems or other testing affiliates.

Between the time of publication and printing, state specific standards as well as testing formats and website information may change that is not included in part or in whole within this product. Sample test questions are developed by XAMonline and reflect similar content as on real tests; however, they are not former tests. XAMonline assembles content that aligns with state standards but makes no claims nor guarantees teacher candidates a passing score. Numerical scores are determined by testing companies such as NES or ETS and then are compared with individual state standards. A passing score varies from state to state.

Printed in the United States of America   œ-1

MTTC: Social Studies 84
ISBN: 978-1-58197-970-1

About the Subject Assessments

Subject Assessment in the Social Studies examination

Purpose: The assessments are designed to test the knowledge and competencies of prospective secondary level teachers. The question bank from which the assessment is drawn is undergoing constant revision. As a result, your test may include questions that will not count towards your score.

Test Version: There are two sections of subject area assessments for social science tests in Michigan. Although both sections of the test emphasize conceptual comprehension, synthesis, and analysis of the principles of the social sciences, the major difference between versions lays in the *degree* to which the examinee's knowledge is tested.

Section 1- Basic Skills: This version requires basic skills in reading, writing and arithmetic is based on a typical knowledge level of entry level elementary education for persons who have completed a _bachelor's degree program_ in social science.

Section 2- Social Studies: This version requires a greater depth of comprehension in US History, world history, economics, geography, political science, anthropology and psychology. The social studies guide is based on a typical knowledge level of persons who have completed a _bachelor's degree program_ in social science.

Taking the Correct Version of the Subject Assessment: While some states other than Michigan offer just one test called a social science test, Michigan offers additional tests in Humanities, Political Science and Geography. However, as Michigan's licensure requirements change, it's highly recommended that you consult your educational institution's teaching preparation counselor or your state board of education's teacher licensure division, to verify which subject areas you should take. Not mentioned is a History test. If you plan on applying for a position in another state as well as Michigan consider a History option. XAMonline.com website can inform you what you need to do to become certified in any particular state.

Time Allowance, Format, and Length: The time allowance and format for Social Studies is that you will have about 4 hours to complete the test and the questions are presented in a 100 question multiple-choice format . The basic skills section includes multiple choice questions and a sample writing test.

Content Areas: The subject assessments test content categories are divided into 5 broad areas. The questions on the test are equally divided among the 5 broad areas, such that 20% of the questions pertain to each area.

Test Taxonomy: Both versions of the subject assessments are constructed on the comprehension, synthesis and analysis levels of Bloom's Taxonomy. In many questions, the candidate must apply knowledge of more than one discipline in order to correctly answer the questions.

Additional Information about the Michigan Assessments: The MTTC series subject assessments are developed by the *Michigan State Board of Education* of Lansing, .Michigan. They provide additional information on the MTTC series assessments, including registration, preparation and testing procedures, study materials such as topical guides that are about 25 pages of information including approximately 10 additional sample questions.

Topical guides versus study guides. The latest topical guide developed by the State of Michigan is presented below. The topics are in bold face type. The numbers following the competencies represent the interpretation of the major topics by the State of Michigan test preparation staff.

TABLE OF CONTENTS

Great Study and Testing Tips!

What to study in order to prepare for the subject assessments is the focus of this study guide but equally important is *how* you study.

You can increase your chances of truly mastering the information by taking some simple, but effective steps.

Study Tips:

1. Some foods aid the learning process. Foods such as milk, nuts, seeds, rice, and oats help your study efforts by releasing natural memory enhancers called CCKs (*cholecystokinin*) composed of *tryptopha*n, *choline*, and *phenylalanine*. All of these chemicals enhance the neurotransmitters associated with memory. Before studying, try a light, protein-rich meal of eggs, turkey, and fish. All of these foods release the memory enhancing chemicals. The better the connections, the more you comprehend.

Likewise, before you take a test, stick to a light snack of energy boosting and relaxing foods. A glass of milk, a piece of fruit, or some peanuts all release various memory-boosting chemicals and help you to relax and focus on the subject at hand.

2. Learn to take great notes. A by-product of our modern culture is that we have grown accustomed to getting our information in short doses (i.e. TV news sound bites or USA Today style newspaper articles.)

Consequently, we've subconsciously trained ourselves to assimilate information better in neat little packages. If your notes are scrawled all over the paper, it fragments the flow of the information. Strive for clarity. Newspapers use a standard format to achieve clarity. Your notes can be much clearer through use of proper formatting. A very effective format is called the *"Cornell Method."*

> Take a sheet of loose-leaf lined notebook paper and draw a line all the way down the paper about 1-2" from the left-hand edge.

> Draw another line across the width of the paper about 1-2" up from the bottom. Repeat this process on the reverse side of the page.

Look at the highly effective result. You have ample room for notes, a left hand margin for special emphasis items or inserting supplementary data from the textbook, a large area at the bottom for a brief summary, and a little rectangular space for just about anything you want.

3. Get the concept then the details. Too often we focus on the details and don't gather an understanding of the concept. However, if you simply memorize only dates, places, or names, you may well miss the whole point of the subject.

A key way to understand things is to put them in your own words. If you are working from a textbook, automatically summarize each paragraph in your mind. If you are outlining text, don't simply copy the author's words.

Rephrase them in your own words. You remember your own thoughts and words much better than someone else's, and subconsciously tend to associate the important details to the core concepts.

4. Ask Why? Pull apart written material paragraph by paragraph and don't forget the captions under the illustrations.

Example: If the heading is "Stream Erosion", flip it around to read "Why do streams erode?" Then answer the questions.

If you train your mind to think in a series of questions and answers, not only will you learn more, but it also helps to lessen the test anxiety because you are used to answering questions.

5. Read for reinforcement and future needs. Even if you only have 10 minutes, put your notes or a book in your hand. Your mind is similar to a computer; you have to input data in order to have it processed. *By reading, you are creating the neural connections for future retrieval.* The more times you read something, the more you reinforce the learning of ideas.

Even if you don't fully understand something on the first pass, *your mind stores much of the material for later recall.*

6. Relax to learn so go into exile. Our bodies respond to an inner clock called biorhythms. Burning the midnight oil works well for some people, but not everyone.

If possible, set aside a particular place to study that is free of distractions. Shut off the television, cell phone, and pager and exile your friends and family during your study period.

If you really are bothered by silence, try background music. Light classical music at a low volume has been shown to aid in concentration over other types. Music that evokes pleasant emotions without lyrics is highly suggested. Try just about anything by Mozart. It relaxes you.

7. <u>Use arrows not highlighters</u>. At best, it's difficult to read a page full of yellow, pink, blue, and green streaks. Try staring at a neon sign for a while and you'll soon see that the horde of colors obscure the message.

A quick note, a brief dash of color, an underline, and an arrow pointing to a particular passage is much clearer than a horde of highlighted words.

8. <u>Budget your study time</u>. Although you shouldn't ignore any of the material, *allocate your available study time in the same ratio that topics may appear on the test.*

Testing Tips:

1. Get smart, play dumb. Don't read anything into the question. Don't make an assumption that the test writer is looking for something else than what is asked. Stick to the question as written and don't read extra things into it.

2. Read the question and all the choices *twice* before answering the question. You may miss something by not carefully reading, and then re-reading both the question and the answers.

If you really don't have a clue as to the right answer, leave it blank on the first time through. Go on to the other questions, as they may provide a clue as to how to answer the skipped questions.

If later on, you still can't answer the skipped ones . . . *Guess.* The only penalty for guessing is that you *might* get it wrong. Only one thing is certain; if you don't put anything down, you will get it wrong!

3. Turn the question into a statement. Look at the way the questions are worded. The syntax of the question usually provides a clue. Does it seem more familiar as a statement rather than as a question? Does it sound strange?

By turning a question into a statement, you may be able to spot if an answer sounds right, and it may also trigger memories of material you have read.

4. Look for hidden clues. It's actually very difficult to compose multiple-foil (choice) questions without giving away part of the answer in the options presented.

In most multiple-choice questions you can often readily eliminate one or two of the potential answers. This leaves you with only two real possibilities and automatically your odds go to Fifty-Fifty for very little work.

5. Trust your instincts. For every fact that you have read, you subconsciously retain something of that knowledge. On questions that you aren't really certain about, go with your basic instincts. **Your first impression on how to answer a question is usually correct.**

6. Mark your answers directly on the test booklet. Don't bother trying to fill in the optical scan sheet on the first pass through the test.

Just be very careful not to miss-mark your answers when you eventually transcribe them to the scan sheet.

7. Watch the clock! You have a set amount of time to answer the questions. Don't get bogged down trying to answer a single question at the expense of 10 questions you can more readily answer.

THIS PAGE BLANK

SUBAREA I.   **HISTORICAL PERSPECTIVE**

Skill 1.1   **Demonstrate an understanding of the chronology, narratives, perspectives, and interpretations of major eras of U.S. history through Reconstruction.**

The Meeting of Three Worlds: Africa, Europe, and the Americas beginnings to 1620

The Age of Exploration actually had its beginnings centuries before exploration actually took place. The rise and spread of Islam in the seventh century and its subsequent control over the holy city of Jerusalem led to the European so-called Holy Wars, the Crusades, to free Jerusalem and the Holy Land from this control. Even though the Crusades were not a success, those who survived and returned to their homes and countries in Western Europe brought back with them new products such as silks, spices, perfumes, new and different foods.

New ideas, inventions, and methods also went to Western Europe with the returning Crusaders and from these new influences was the intellectual stimulation which led to the period known as the Renaissance. The revival of interest in classical Greek art, architecture, literature, science, astronomy, medicine and increased trade between Europe and Asia . The invention of the printing press helped to push the spread of knowledge and start exploring.

For many centuries, mapmakers produced maps and charts, which stimulated curiosity and the seeking of more knowledge. At the same time, the Chinese were using the magnetic compass in their ships. Pacific islanders were going from island to island, covering thousands of miles in open canoes navigating by sun and stars. Arab traders were sailing all over the Indian Ocean in their dhows. The trade routes between Europe and Asia were slow, difficult, dangerous, and very expensive. Between sea voyages on the Indian Ocean and Mediterranean Sea and the camel caravans in central Asia and the Arabian Desert, the trade was still controlled by the Italian merchants in Genoa and Venice. It would take months and even years for the exotic luxuries of Asia to reach the markets of Western Europe. A faster, cheaper way had to be found. A way had to be found which would bypass traditional routes and end the control of the Italian merchants.

Prince Henry of Portugal (also called the Navigator) encouraged and financed the Portuguese seamen who led in the search for an all-water route to Asia. A shipyard was built along with a school teaching navigation. New types of sailing ships were built which would carry the seamen safely through the ocean waters. Experiments were conducted in newer maps, navigational methods, and instruments. These included the astrolabe and the compass enabling sailors to determine direction as well as latitude and longitude for exact location. Although Prince Henry died in 1460, the Portuguese kept on exploring Africa's west coastline. In 1488, Bartholomew Diaz and his men sailed around Africa's southern tip and headed toward Asia. Diaz wanted to push on but turned back because his men were discouraged and weary from the long months at sea, extremely fearful of the unknown, and refused to travel any further.

The Portuguese were finally successful ten years later in 1498 when Vasco da Gama and his men, continuing the route of Diaz, rounded Africa's Cape of Good Hope, sailing across the Indian Ocean, reaching India's port of Calicut (Calcutta). Da Gama had proved Asia could be reached from Europe by sea.

Columbus' first Trans-Atlantic voyage was to try to prove his theory that Asia could be reached by sailing west. To a certain extent, his theory was true. It could be done but only after figuring how to go around or across or through the landmass in between. Long after Spain dispatched explorers and her famed conquistadors to gather the wealth for the Spanish monarchs and their coffers, the British were searching valiantly for the "Northwest Passage," a land-sea route across North America and open sea to the wealth of Asia.

Spain, France, and England along with some participation by the Dutch led the way with expanding Western European civilization in the New World. These three nations had strong monarchial governments and were struggling for dominance and power in Europe. With the defeat of Spain's mighty Armada in 1588, England became undisputed mistress of the seas. Spain lost its power and influence in Europe and it was left to France and England to carry on the rivalry, leading to eventual British control in Asia as well.

Spain's influence was in Florida, the Gulf Coast from Texas all the way west to California and south to the tip of South America and some of the islands of the West Indies. French control centered from New Orleans north to what is now northern Canada including the entire Mississippi Valley, the St. Lawrence Valley, the Great Lakes, and the land that was part of the Louisiana Territory. A few West Indies islands were also part of France's empire. England settled the eastern seaboard of North America, including parts of Canada and from Maine to Georgia. Some West Indies islands also came under British control. The Dutch had New Amsterdam for a period but later ceded it into British hands.

All three nations, especially England, the extended land claims partly or all the way across the continent, regardless of the fact that the others claimed the same land. The wars for dominance and control of power and influence in Europe would extend to the Americas, especially North America.

The importance of the Age of Exploration was not just the discovery and colonization of the New World, but better maps and charts, newer, more accurate navigational instruments, increased knowledge, and great wealth. New and different foods as well as items previously unknown in Europe were introduced. A new hemisphere became accessible as a refuge from poverty and persecution, and a place to start a new and better life. The proof that Asia could be reached by sea and that the earth was round; ships and sailors would not sail off the edge of a flat earth and disappear forever into nothingness.

Colonization and Settlement (1585-1763)

The part of North America claimed by France was called New France and consisted of the land west of the Appalachian Mountains. This area of claims and settlement included the St. Lawrence Valley, the Great Lakes, the Mississippi Valley, and the entire region of land westward to the Rocky Mountains. They established the permanent settlements of Montreal and New Orleans, thus giving them control of the two major gateways into the heart of North America, the vast, rich interior. The St. Lawrence River, the Great Lakes, and the Mississippi River along with its tributaries made it possible for the French explorers and traders to roam at will, virtually unhindered in exploring, trapping, trading, and furthering the interests of France.

Most of the French settlements were in Canada along the St. Lawrence River. Only scattered forts and trading posts were found in the upper Mississippi Valley and Great Lakes region. The rulers of France originally intended New France to have vast estates owned by nobles and worked by peasants who would live on the estates in compact farming villages--the New World version of the Old World's medieval system of feudalism. However, it didn't work out that way. Each of the nobles wanted his estate to be on the river for ease of transportation. The peasants working the estates wanted the prime waterfront location, also. The result of all this real estate squabbling was that New France's settled areas wound up mostly as a string of farmhouses stretching from Quebec to Montreal along the St. Lawrence and Richelieu Rivers.

In the non-settled interior areas were the French fur traders. They made friends with the friendly tribes of Indians, spending the winters with them getting the furs needed for trade. In the spring, they would return to Montreal in time to take advantage of trading their furs for the products brought by the cargo ships from France, which usually arrived at about the same time. Most of the wealth for New France and its "Mother Country" was from the fur trade, which provided a livelihood for many, many people. Manufacturers and workmen back in France, ship-owners and merchants, as well as the fur traders and their Indian allies benefited. However, the freedom of roaming and trapping in the interior was a strong enticement for the younger, stronger men and resulted in the French not strengthening the areas settled along the St. Lawrence.

Into the 18th century, the rivalry with the British was growing.. New France was united under a single government and enjoyed the support of many Indian allies. The French traders were very diligent in not destroying the forests and driving away game upon which the Indians depended for life. It was difficult for the French to defend all of their settlements as they were scattered over half of the continent. However, by the early 1750s, in Western Europe, France was the most powerful nation. Its armies were superior to all others and its navy was giving the British stiff competition for control of the seas. The stage was set for confrontation in both Europe and America.

Spanish settlement had its beginnings in the Caribbean with the establishment of colonies on Hispaniola (at Santo Domingo which became the capital of the West Indies), Puerto Rico, and Cuba. There were a number of reasons for Spanish involvement in the Americas:

- the spirit of adventure
- the desire for land
- expansion of Spanish power, influence, and empire
- the desire for great wealth
- expansion of Roman Catholic influence and conversion of native peoples

The first permanent settlement in what is now the United States was in 1565 at St. Augustine, Florida. A later permanent settlement in the southwestern United States was in 1609 at Santa Fe, New Mexico. At the peak of Spanish power, the area in the United States claimed, settled, and controlled by Spain included Florida and all land west of the Mississippi River--quite a piece of choice real estate. Of course, France and England also lay claim to the same areas. Nonetheless, ranches and missions were built and the Indians who came in contact with the Spaniards were introduced to animals, plants, and seeds from the Old World that they had never seen before. Animals brought in included horses, cattle, donkeys, pigs, sheep, goats, and poultry.

Barrels were cut in half and filled with earth to transport and transplant trees bearing:

apples	olives
oranges	lemons
limes	figs
cherries	apricots
pears	almonds
walnuts	

Even sugar cane and flowers made it to America along with bags bringing seeds of wheat, barley, rye, flax, lentils, rice, and peas.

All Spanish colonies belonged to the King of Spain. He was considered an absolute monarch with complete or absolute power and claimed rule by divine right, the belief being God had given him the right to rule and he answered only to God for his actions. His word was final, was the law. The people had no voice in government. The land, the people, the wealth all belonged to him to use as he pleased. He appointed personal representatives, or viceroys, to rule for him in his colonies. They ruled in his name with complete authority. Since the majority of them were friends and advisers, they were richly rewarded with land grants, gold and silver, privileges of trading, and the right to operate the gold and silver mines.

For the needed labor in the mines and on the plantations, Indians were used first as slaves. However, they either rapidly died out due to a lack of immunity from European diseases or escaped into nearby jungles or mountains. As a result, African slaves were brought in, especially to the islands of the West Indies. Some historians state that Latin American slavery was less harsh than in the later English colonies in North America.
Three reasons are given:

1. The following of a slave code based on ancient Roman laws;
2. The efforts of the Roman Catholic Church to protect and defend slaves because of efforts to convert them;
3. The existence of less prejudice because of racial mixtures in parts of Spain controlled at one time by dark-skinned Moors from North Africa.

Regardless, slavery was still slavery and was very harsh--cruelly denying dignity and human worth and leading to desperate resistance.

Spain's control over her New World colonies lasted more than 300 years, longer than England or France. To this day, Spanish influence remains in names of places, art, architecture, music, literature, law, and cuisine. The Spanish settlements in North America were not commercial enterprises but were for protection and defense of the trading and wealth from their colonies in Mexico and South America. The Russians hunting seals came down the Pacific coast, the English moved into Florida and west into and beyond the Appalachians, and the French traders and trappers were making their way from Louisiana and other parts of New France into Spanish territory. The Spanish never realized or understood that self-sustaining economic development and colonial trade was so important. Consequently, the Spanish settlements in the U.S. never really prospered.

The nation had only itself to blame for this. The treasure and wealth found in Spanish New World colonies went back to Spain to be used to buy whatever goods and products were needed instead of setting up industries to make what was needed. As the amount of gold and silver was depleted, Spain could not pay for the goods needed and was unable to produce goods for themselves. Also, at the same time, Spanish treasure ships at sea were being seized by English and Dutch "pirates" taking the wealth to the coffers of their own countries.

Before 1763, when England was rapidly on the way to becoming the most powerful of the three major Western European powers, its thirteen colonies, located between the Atlantic and the Appalachians, physically occupied the least amount of land. Nonetheless, the thirteen English colonies were successful and, by the time they had gained their independence from Britain, were more than able to govern themselves. They had a rich historical heritage of law, tradition, and documents leading the way to constitutional government conducted according to laws and customs. The settlers in the British colonies highly valued individual freedom, democratic government, and getting ahead through hard work.

The English colonies, with only a few exceptions, were considered commercial ventures to make a profit for the crown or the company or whoever financed its beginnings. One was strictly a philanthropic enterprise and three others were primarily for religious reasons but the other nine were started for economic reasons. Settlers in these unique colonies came for different reasons:

- religious freedom
- political freedom
- economic prosperity
- land ownership

The colonies were divided generally into the three regions of New England, Middle Atlantic, and Southern. The culture of each was distinct and affected attitudes, ideas towards politics, religion, and economic activities. The geography of each region also contributed to its unique characteristics.

The **New England colonies** consisted of Massachusetts, Rhode Island, Connecticut, and New Hampshire. Life in these colonies was centered on the towns. What farming was done was by each family on its own plot of land but a short summer growing season and limited amount of good soil gave rise to other economic activities such as manufacturing, fishing, shipbuilding, and trade. The vast majority of the settlers shared similar origins, coming from England and Scotland. Towns were carefully planned and laid out the same way. The form of government was the town meeting where all adult males met to make the laws. The legislative body, the General Court, consisted of an Upper and Lower House.

The **Middle or Middle Atlantic colonies** included New York, New Jersey, Pennsylvania, Delaware, and Maryland. New York and New Jersey were at one time the Dutch colony of New Netherlands and Delaware at one time was New Sweden. These five colonies, from their beginnings were considered "melting pots" with settlers from many different nations and backgrounds. The main economic activity was farming with the settlers scattered over the countryside cultivating rather large farms. The Indians were not as much of a threat as in New England so they did not have to settle in small farming villages. The soil was very fertile, the land was gently rolling, and a milder climate provided a longer growing season.

These farms produced a large surplus of food, not only for the colonists themselves but also for sale. This colonial region became known as the "breadbasket" of the New World and the New York and Philadelphia seaports were constantly filled with ships being loaded with meat, flour, and other foodstuffs for the West Indies and England. There were other economic activities such as shipbuilding, iron mines, and factories producing paper, glass, and textiles. The legislative body in Pennsylvania was unicameral or consisted of one house. In the other four colonies, the legislative body had two houses. Also units of local government were in counties and towns.

The **Southern colonies** were Virginia, North and South Carolina, and Georgia. Virginia was the first permanent successful English colony and Georgia was the last. The year 1619 was a very important year in the history of Virginia and the United States with three very significant events. First, sixty women were sent to Virginia to marry and establish families, Second, twenty Africans, the first of thousands, arrived, Third, most importantly, the Virginia colonists were granted the right to self-government and they began by electing their own representatives to the House of Burgesses, their own legislative body.

The major economic activity in this region was farming. Here the soil was very fertile and the climate was very mild with an even longer growing season. The large plantations eventually requiring large numbers of slaves were found in the coastal or tidewater areas. Although the wealthy slave-owning planters set the pattern of life in this region, most of the people lived inland away from coastal areas. They were small farmers and very few, it any, owned slaves.

The settlers in these four colonies came from diverse backgrounds and cultures. Virginia was colonized mostly by people from England while Georgia was started as a haven for debtors from English prisons. Pioneers from Virginia settled in North Carolina while South Carolina welcomed people from England and Scotland, French Protestants, Germans, and emigrants from islands in the West Indies. Products from farms and plantations included rice, tobacco, indigo, cotton, some corn and wheat. Other economic activities included lumber and naval stores (tar, pitch, rosin, and turpentine) from the pine forests and fur trade on the frontier. Cities such as Savannah and Charleston were important seaports and trading centers.

In the colonies, the daily life of the colonists differed greatly between the coastal settlements and the inland or interior. The Southern planters and the people living in the coastal cities and towns had a way of life similar to that in towns in England. The influence was seen and heard in how people dressed and talked. The architectural styles of houses and public buildings, and the social divisions or levels of society mimicked that of England. Both the planters and city dwellers enjoyed an active social life and had strong emotional ties to England.

On the other hand, life inland on the frontier had marked differences. All facets of daily living--clothing, food, housing, economic and social activities--were all connected to what was needed to sustain life and survive in the wilderness. Everything was produced practically themselves. They were self-sufficient and extremely individualistic and independent. There were little, if any, levels of society or class distinctions as they considered themselves to be the equal to all others, regardless of station in life. The roots of equality, independence, individual rights and freedoms were extremely strong and well developed. People were not judged by their fancy dress, expensive house, eloquent language, or titles following their names.

The colonies had from 1607 to 1763 to develop, refine, practice, experiment, and experience life in a rugged, uncivilized land. The Mother Country had virtually left them on their own to take care of themselves all that time. When in 1763, Britain decided she needed to regulate and "mother" the "little ones," to her surprise she had a losing fight on her hands.

Revolution and the New Nation (1754 – 1815)

By the 1750s in Europe, Spain was "out of the picture," no longer the most powerful nation and not even a contender. The remaining rivalry was between Britain and France. For nearly 50 years, between 1689 and 1748, a series of "armed conflicts" involving these two powers had been taking place. These conflicts had spilled over into North America. The War of the League of Augsburg in Europe, 1689 to 1697, also called King William's War. The War of the Spanish Succession, 1702 to 1713, known as Queen Anne's War. The War of the Austrian Succession, 1740 to 1748, called King George's War in the colonies. The two nations fought for possession of colonies, especially in Asia and North America, and for control of the seas, but none of these conflicts was decisive.

The final conflict, which decided once and for all the most powerful nation, began in North America in 1754, in the Ohio River Valley. It was known in America as the French and Indian War and in Europe as the Seven Years War.,. In America, both sides had advantages and disadvantages. The British colonies were well established and consolidated in a smaller area. British colonists outnumbered French colonists 23 to 1. Except for a small area in Canada, French settlements were scattered over a much larger area (roughly half of the continent) and were smaller. However, the French settlements were united under one government and were quick to act and cooperate when necessary. In addition, the French had many more Indian allies than the British. The British colonies had separate, individual governments and very seldom cooperated, even when needed. In Europe, at that time, France was the more powerful of the two nations.

Both sides had stunning victories and humiliating defeats. If there was one person who could be given the credit for British victory, it would have to be William Pitt. He was a strong leader, enormously energetic, supremely self-confident, and determined on a complete British victory. Despite the advantages and military victories of the French, Pitt succeeded. In the army he got rid of the incompetents and replaced them with men who could do the job. He sent more troops to America, strengthened the British navy, gave to the officers of the colonial militias equal rank to the British officers - in short, he saw to it that Britain took the offensive and kept it to victory. Of all the British victories, perhaps the most crucial and important was winning Canada.

The French depended on the St. Lawrence River for transporting supplies, soldiers, and messages-the link between New France and the Mother Country. Tied into this waterway system was the connecting links of the Great Lakes, Mississippi River and its tributaries along which were scattered French forts, trading posts, and small settlements.

In 1758, the British captured Louisburg on Cape Breton Island, New France was doomed. Louisburg gave the British navy a base of operations preventing French reinforcements and supplies getting to their troops. Other forts fell to the British: Frontenac, Duquesne, Crown Point, Ticonderoga, and Niagara, those in the upper Ohio Valley, and, most importantly, Quebec and finally Montreal. Spain entered the war in 1762 to aid France but it was too late. British victories occurred all around the world: in India, in the Mediterranean, and in Europe.

In 1763 in Paris, Spain, France, and Britain met to draw up the Treaty. Great Britain got most of India and all of North America east of the Mississippi River, except for New Orleans. Britain received from Spain control of Florida and returned to Spain Cuba and the islands of the Philippines, taken during the war. France lost nearly all of its possessions in America. India and was allowed to keep four islands: Guadeloupe, Martinique, Haiti on Hispaniola, and Miquelon and St. Pierre. France gave Spain New Orleans and the vast territory of Louisiana, west of the Mississippi River. Britain was now the most powerful nation

Where did all of this leave the British colonies? Their colonial militias had fought with the British and they too benefited. The militias and their officers gained much experience in fighting which was very valuable later. The thirteen colonies began to realize that cooperating with each other was the only way to defend themselves. They didn't really understand that, until the war for independence, setting up a national government, but a start had been made. At the start of the war in 1754, Benjamin Franklin proposed to the thirteen colonies that they unite permanently to be able to defend themselves. This was after the French and their Indian allies had defeated Major George Washington and his militia at Fort Necessity. This left the entire northern frontier of the British colonies vulnerable and open to attack.

Delegates from seven of the thirteen colonies met at Albany, New York, along with the representatives from the Iroquois Confederation and British officials. Franklin's proposal, known as the Albany Plan of Union, was totally rejected by the colonists, along with a similar proposal from the British. They simply did not want each of the colonies to lose its right to act independently. However, the seed was planted.

The War for Independence occurred due largely to economic and political reasons. By the end of the French and Indian War in 1763, Britain's American colonies were thirteen out of a total of thirty-three scattered around the earth. Like all other countries, Britain desired having a strong economy and a favorable balance of trade. To have that delicate balance a nation needs wealth, self-sufficiency, and a powerful army and navy. Colonies provided raw materials for the industries in the Mother Country, and a market for the finished products. Also a strong merchant fleet, would be a school for training for the Royal Navy and provide bases for the Royal Navy.

Between 1607 and 1763, the British Parliament enacted different laws to assist the government in achieving a trade balance. One series of laws required that most of the manufacturing be done only in England, prohibiting exporting of wool or woolen cloth from the colonies, and the manufacturing of beaver hats or iron products. The colonists weren't concerned as they had no money and no highly skilled labor to set up any industries, anyway.

The Navigation Acts of 1651 put restrictions on shipping and trade within the British Empire by requiring that it was allowed only on British ships. This increased the strength of the British merchant fleet and greatly benefited the American colonists. Since they were British citizens, they could have their own vessels, building and operating them as well. By the end of the war in 1763, the shipyards in the colonies were building one third of the merchant ships under the British flag. There were quite a number of wealthy, American, colonial merchants.

The Navigation Act of 1660 restricted the shipment and sale of colonial products to England only. In 1663 another Navigation Act stipulated that the colonies had to buy manufactured products only from England and that any European goods going to the colonies had to go to England first. These acts were a protection from enemy ships and pirates and from competition from European rivals.

The New England and Middle Atlantic colonies felt threatened by these laws as they had started producing many of the products already being produced in Britain. They soon found new markets for their goods and began what was known as a "triangular trade." Colonial vessels started the first part of the triangle by sailing for Africa loaded with kegs of rum from colonial distilleries. On Africa's West Coast, the rum was traded for either gold or slaves. The second part of the triangle was from Africa to the West Indies where slaves were traded for molasses, sugar, or money. The third part of the triangle was home, bringing sugar or molasses (to make more rum), gold, and silver.

The major concern of the British government was that the trade violated the 1733 Molasses Act. Planters had wanted the colonists to buy all of their molasses in the British West Indies but these islands could give the traders only about one eighth of the amount of molasses needed for distilling the rum. The colonists were forced to buy the rest of what they needed from the French, Dutch, and Spanish islands, thus evading the law by not paying the high duty on the molasses bought from these islands. If Britain had enforced the Molasses Act, economic and financial chaos and ruin would have occurred. Nevertheless, for this act and all the other mercantile laws, the government followed the policy of "salutary neglect," deliberately failing to enforce the laws.

In 1763, after the war, money was needed to pay the British war debt, for the defense of the empire, and to pay for the governing of 33 colonies scattered around the earth. It was decided to adopt a new colonial policy and pass laws to raise revenue. It was reasoned that the colonists were subjects of the king and since the king and his ministers had spent a great deal of money defending and protecting them (this especially for the American colonists), it was only right and fair that the colonists should help pay the costs of defense, especially theirs. The earlier laws passed had been for the purposes of regulating production and trade which generally put money into colonial pockets. These new laws would take some of that rather hard-earned money out of their pockets and it would be done, in colonial eyes, unjustly and illegally.

Before 1763, except for trade and supplying raw materials, the colonies had been left pretty much to themselves. England looked on them merely as part of an economic or commercial empire. Little consideration was given as to how they were to conduct their daily affairs, so the colonists became very independent, self-reliant, and extremely skillful at handling those daily affairs. This, in turn, gave rise to leadership, initiative, achievement, and vast experience. In fact, there was a far greater degree of independence and self-government in the British colonies in America than could be found in Britain or the major countries on the Continent or any other colonies anywhere. There were a number of reasons for this:

- The religious and scriptural teachings of previous centuries put forth the worth of the individual and equality in God's sight. Keep in mind that freedom of worship and freedom from religious persecution were major reasons to live in the New World.

- European Protestants, especially Calvinists, believed and taught the idea that government originates from those governed, that rulers are required to protect individual rights and that the governed have the right and privilege to choose their rulers.

- Trading companies put into practice the principle that their members had the right to make the decisions and shape the policies affecting their lives.

The colonists believed and supported the idea that a person's property should not be taken without his consent, a principle handed down from the treasured English document, Magna Carta, and English common law.

From about 1700 to 1750, population increases in America came about through immigration and generations of descendants of the original settlers. The immigrants were mainly Scots-Irish who hated the English, Germans who cared nothing about England, and black slaves who knew nothing about England. The descendants of the original settlers had never been out of America at any time.

In America, as new towns and counties were formed, representative government practices developed. Representatives to the colonial legislative assemblies were elected from the district in which they lived, chosen by qualified property-owning male voters, and representing the interests of the political district from which they were elected. Each of the 13 colonies had a royal governor appointed by the king, representing his interests in the colonies. Nevertheless, the colonial legislative assemblies controlled the purse strings having the power to vote on all issues involving money to be spent by the colonial governments.

In contrast, members of the English Parliament were not elected to represent their own districts. They were considered representative of classes, not individuals. If some members of a professional or commercial class or some landed interests were able to elect representatives, then those classes or special interests were represented. It had nothing at all to do with numbers or territories. Some large population centers had no direct representation at all, yet the people there considered themselves represented by men elected from their particular class or interest somewhere else. Consequently, it was extremely difficult for the English to understand why the American merchants and landowners claimed they were not represented because they themselves did not vote for members of Parliament.

The colonists' protest of "no taxation without representation" was meaningless to the English. Parliament represented the entire nation, was completely unlimited in legislation, and had become supreme; and the colonists were incensed at the English attitude of "of course you have representation--everyone does." The colonists considered their colonial legislative assemblies equal to Parliament, totally unacceptable in England, of course. There were two different environments of the older traditional British system in the Mother Country and in America new ideas and different ways of doing things. In a new country, a new environment has little or no tradition, institutions or vested interests. New ideas and traditions grew extremely fast pushing aside what was left of the old ideas and old traditions. By 1763, Britain had changed its perception of its American colonies to their being a "territorial" empire. The stage was set and the conditions were right for a showdown.

It all began in 1763 when Parliament decided to have a standing army in North America to reinforce British control. In 1765, the Quartering Act was passed requiring the colonists to provide supplies and living quarters for the British troops. In addition, efforts by the British were made to keep the peace by establishing good relations with the Indians. Consequently, a proclamation was issued which prohibited any American colonists from making any settlements west of the Appalachians until provided for through treaties with the Indians.

The Sugar Act of 1764 required efficient collection of taxes on any molasses that were brought into the colonies. It also gave British officials free license to conduct searches of the premises of anyone suspected of violating the law. The colonists were taxed on newspapers, legal documents, and other printed matter under the Stamp Act of 1765. Although a stamp tax was already in use in England, the colonists would have none of it and after the ensuing uproar of rioting and mob violence, Parliament repealed the tax.

Of course, great exultation, jubilance, and wild joy resulted when news of the repeal reached America. However, what no one noticed was the small, quiet Declaratory Act attached to the repeal. This act plainly and unequivocally stated that Parliament still had the right to make all laws for the colonies. It denied their right to be taxed only by their own colonial legislatures--a very crucial, important piece of legislation but virtually overlooked and unnoticed at the time. Other acts leading up to armed conflict included the Townshend Acts passed in 1767 taxing lead, paint, paper, and tea brought into the colonies. This really increased anger and tension resulting in the British sending troops to New York City and Boston.

In Boston, mob violence provoked retaliation by the troops thus bringing about the deaths of five people and the wounding of eight others. The so-called Boston Massacre shocked Americans and British alike. Subsequently, in 1770, Parliament voted to repeal all the provisions of the Townshend Acts with the exception of the tea tax. In 1773, the tax on tea sold by the British East India Company was substantially reduced, fueling colonial anger once more. This gave the company an unfair trade advantage and forcibly reminded the colonists of the British right to tax them. Merchants refused to sell the tea; colonists refused to buy and drink it; and a shipload of it was dumped into Boston Harbor--a most violent Tea Party.

In 1774, the passage of the Quebec Act extended the limits of that Canadian colony's boundary southward to include territory located north of the Ohio River. However, the punishment for Boston's Tea Party came in the same year with the Intolerable Acts. Boston's port was closed; the royal governor of the colony of Massachusetts was given increased power, and the colonists were compelled to house and feed the British soldiers. The propaganda activities of the patriot organizations Sons of Liberty and Committees of Correspondence kept the opposition and resistance before everyone. Delegates from twelve colonies met in Philadelphia September 5, 1774, in the First Continental Congress. They definitely opposed acts of lawlessness and wanted some form of peaceful settlement with Britain. They maintained American loyalty to the Mother Country and affirmed Parliament's power over colonial foreign affairs.

They insisted on repeal of the Intolerable Acts and demanded ending all trade with Britain until this took place. The reply from King George III, the last king of America, was an insistence of colonial submission to British rule or be crushed. With the start of the Revolutionary War April 19, 1775, the Second Continental Congress began meeting in Philadelphia on May 10th to conduct the business of war and government for the next six years.

One historian explained that the British were interested only in raising money to pay war debts, regulate the trade and commerce of the colonies, and look after business and financial interests between the Mother Country and the rest of her empire. The establishment of overseas colonies was first, and foremost, a commercial enterprise, not a political one. The political aspect was secondary and assumed. The British took it for granted that Parliament was supreme, was recognized so by the colonists, and were very resentful of the colonial challenge to Parliament's authority. They were contemptuously indifferent to politics in America and had no wish to exert any control over it. As resistance and disobedience swelled and increased in America, the British increased their efforts to punish them and put them in their place.

The British had been extremely lax and totally inconsistent in enforcement of the mercantile or trade laws passed in the years before 1754. The government itself was not particularly stable so actions against the colonies occurred in anger and their attitude was one of a moral superiority, that they knew how to manage America better than the Americans did themselves. This of course points to a lack of sufficient knowledge of conditions and opinions in America. The colonists had been left on their own for nearly 150 years and by the time the Revolutionary War began, they were quite adept at self-government and adequately handling the affairs of their daily lives. The Americans equated ownership of land or property with the right to vote. Property was considered the foundation of life and liberty and, in the colonial mind and tradition, these went together.

Therefore when an indirect tax on tea was made, the British felt that since it wasn't a direct tax, there should be no objection to it. The colonists viewed any tax, direct or indirect, as an attack on their property. They felt that as a representative body, the British Parliament should protect British citizens, including the colonists, from arbitrary taxation. Since they felt they were not represented, Parliament, in their eyes, gave them no protection. So, war began. August 23, 1775, George III declared that the colonies were in rebellion and warned them to stop or else.

By 1776, the colonists and their representatives in the Second Continental Congress realized that things were past the point of no return. The Declaration of Independence was drafted and declared July 4, 1776. George Washington labored against tremendous odds to wage a victorious war. The turning point in the Americans' favor occurred in 1777 with the American victory at Saratoga. This victory decided for the French to align themselves with the Americans against the British. With the aid of Admiral deGrasse and French warships blocking the entrance to Chesapeake Bay, British General Cornwallis trapped at Yorktown, Virginia, surrendered in 1781 and the war was over. The Treaty of Paris officially ending the war was signed in 1783.

During the war, and after independence was declared, the former colonies now found themselves as independent states. The Second Continental Congress was conducting a war with representation by delegates from thirteen separate states. The Congress had no power to act for the states or to require them to accept and follow its wishes. A permanent united government was desperately needed. On November 15, 1777, the Articles of Confederation were adopted, creating a league of free and independent states.

The central government of the new United States of America consisted of a Congress of two to seven delegates from each state with each state having just one vote. The government under the Articles solved some of the postwar problems but had serious weaknesses. Some of its powers included: borrowing and coining money, directing foreign affairs, declaring war and making peace, building and equipping a navy, regulating weights and measures, asking the states to supply men and money for an army. The delegates to Congress had no real authority as each state carefully and jealously guarded its own interests and limited powers under the Articles. Also, the delegates to Congress were paid by their states and had to vote as directed by their state legislatures. The serious weaknesses were the lack of power: to regulate finances, over interstate trade, over foreign trade, to enforce treaties, and military power. Something better and more efficient was needed. In May of 1787, delegates from all states except Rhode Island began meeting in Philadelphia. At first, they met to revise the Articles of Confederation as instructed by Congress; but they soon realized that much more was needed. Abandoning the instructions, they set out to write a new Constitution, a new document, the foundation of all government in the United States and a model for representative government throughout the world.

The first order of business was the agreement among all the delegates that the convention would be kept secret. No discussion of the convention outside of the meeting room would be allowed. They wanted to be able to discuss, argue, and agree among themselves before presenting the completed document to the American people.

The delegates were afraid that if the people were aware of what was taking place before it was completed the entire country would be plunged into argument and dissension. It would be extremely difficult, if not impossible, to settle differences and come to an agreement. Between the official notes kept and the complete notes of future President James Madison, an accurate picture of the events of the Convention is part of the historical record.

The delegates went to Philadelphia representing different areas and different interests. They all agreed on a strong central government but not one with unlimited powers. They also agreed that no one part of government could control the rest. It would be a republican form of government (sometimes referred to as representative democracy) in which the supreme power was in the hands of the voters who would elect the men who would govern for them.

One of the first serious controversies involved the small states versus the large states over representation in Congress. Virginia's Governor Edmund Randolph proposed that state population determine the number of representatives sent to Congress, also known as the Virginia Plan. New Jersey delegate William Paterson countered with what is known as the New Jersey Plan, each state having equal representation.

After much argument and debate, the Great Compromise was devised, known also as the Connecticut Compromise, as proposed by Roger Sherman. It was agreed that Congress would have two houses. The Senate would have two Senators, giving equal powers in the Senate. The House of Representatives would have its members elected based on each state's population. Both houses could draft bills to debate and vote on with the exception of bills pertaining to money, which must originate in the House of Representatives.

Another major controversy involved economic differences between North and South. One concerned the counting of the African slaves for determining representation in the House of Representatives. The southern delegates wanted this but didn't want it to apply to determining taxes to be paid. The northern delegates argued the opposite: count the slaves for taxes but not for representation. The resulting agreement was known as the "three-fifths" compromise. Three-fifths of the slaves would be counted for both taxes and determining representation in the House.

The last major compromise, also between North and South, was the Commerce Compromise. The economic interests of the northern part of the country were ones of industry and business whereas the south's economic interests were primarily in farming. The Northern merchants wanted the government to regulate and control commerce with foreign nations and with the states. Of course, Southern planters opposed this idea as they felt that any tariff laws passed would be unfavorable to them. The acceptable compromise to this dispute was that Congress was given the power to regulate commerce with other nations and the states, including levying tariffs on imports. However, Congress did not have the power to levy tariffs on any exports. This increased Southern concern about the effect it would have on the slave trade. The delegates finally agreed that the importation of slaves would continue for 20 more years with no interference from Congress. Any import tax could not exceed 10 dollars per person. After 1808, Congress would be able to decide whether to prohibit or regulate any further importation of slaves.

Of course, when work was completed and the document was presented, nine states needed to approve for it to go into effect. There was much discussion, arguing, debating, and haranguing. The opposition had three major objections:

1) The states seemed as if they were being asked to surrender too much power to the national government.
2) The voters did not have enough control and influence over the men who would be elected by them to run the government.
3) A lack of a "bill of rights" guaranteeing hard-won individual freedoms and l iberties.

Eleven states finally ratified the document and the new national government went into effect. It was no small feat that the delegates were able to produce a workable document that satisfied all opinions, feelings, and viewpoints. The separation of powers of the three branches of government and the built-in system of checks and balances to keep power balanced were a stroke of genius. It provided for the individuals and the states as well as an organized central authority to keep a new inexperienced young nation on track. They created a system of government so flexible that it had continued in its basic form to this day. In 1789, the Electoral College unanimously elected George Washington as the first President and the new nation was on its way.

Expansion and Reform (1801-1861)

Beginning with Washington's election to the Presidency in 1791 to the election of Abraham Lincoln in 1860, the United States expanded to the boundaries of today's 48 conterminous states. During that 69-year period, four wars were fought: the War of 1812 with Great Britain, the war with the Barbary pirates in the Mediterranean, the war with Mexico, and the Seminole wars in Florida. By 1860, the nation had had 15 presidents (Lincoln was the 16th), had greatly increased its area, established and strengthened the federal court system, saw the beginnings of and increased influence of political parties, the first and second U.S. banks, economic "panics" or depressions, the abolition movement, the controversies and turmoil leading to the Civil War. There were 33 states in the Union by 1860.

Territorial expansion began in 1783 with the signing of the Treaty of Paris ending the Revolutionary War. According to the terms of the treaty, the land gained by the Americans was all of the land between the Appalachian Mountains and the Mississippi River; from the Great Lakes to the Florida boundary. Nine additional states were formed from this area alone.

The next large territorial gain was under President Thomas Jefferson in 1803. In 1800, Napoleon Bonaparte of France secured the Louisiana Territory from Spain, who had held it since 1792. The vast area stretched westward from the Mississippi River to the Rocky Mountains as well as northward to Canada. An effort was made to keep the transaction a secret but the news reached the U.S. State Department. The U.S. didn't have any particular problem with Spanish control of the territory since Spain was weak and did not pose a threat. However, it was different with France. Though not the world power that Great Britain was, nonetheless France was still strong and, under Napoleon's leadership, was again acquiring an empire. President Jefferson had three major reasons for concern:

a. With the French controlling New Orleans at the mouth of the Mississippi River, as well as the Gulf of Mexico, Westerners would lose their "right of deposit" which would greatly affect their ability to trade. This was very important to the Americans who were living in the area between the river and the Appalachians. They were unable to get heavy products to eastern markets but had to float them on rafts down the Ohio and Mississippi Rivers to New Orleans to ships heading to Europe or the Atlantic coast ports. If France prohibited this; it would be a financial disaster.

b. President Jefferson also worried that if the French possessed the Louisiana Territory; America would be extremely limited in its expansion into its interior.

c. Under Napoleon Bonaparte, France was becoming more powerful and aggressive and this would be a constant worry and threat to the western border of the U.S. President Jefferson was very interested in the western part of the country and firmly believed that it was both necessary and desirable to strengthen western lands. So Jefferson wrote to the American minister to Paris, Robert R. Livingston, to make an offer to Napoleon for New Orleans and West Florida, as much as $10 million for the two. Napoleon countered the offer with the question of how much the U.S. would be willing to pay for all of Louisiana. After some discussion, it was agreed to pay $15 million and the largest land transaction in history was negotiated in 1803, resulting in the eventual formation of 15 states.

In 1804, the United States engaged in the first of a series of armed conflicts with the Barbary pirates of North Africa. The Moslem rulers of Morocco, Algiers, Tunis, and Tripoli, the Barbary States of North Africa, had long been seizing ships of nations that were Christian and demanding ransoms for the crews. The Christian nations of Europe decided it was cheaper and easier to pay annually a tribute or bribe. The U.S. had been doing this since 1783 with the beginnings of trade between the Mediterranean countries and the newly independent nation. When the rulers in Tripoli demanded a ridiculously exorbitant bribe and chopped down the flagpole of the American consulate there, Jefferson had had enough. The first skirmish against Tripoli in 1804 and 1805 was successful. In 1815, the payment of bribes to the rulers ceased after the War of 1812 ended. The Americans could trade and sail freely in the Mediterranean.

United States' unintentional and accidental involvement in what was known as the War of 1812 came about due to the political and economic struggles between France and Great Britain. Napoleon's goal was complete conquest and control of Europe, including and especially Great Britain. Although British troops were temporarily driven off the mainland of Europe, the navy still controlled the seas, the seas across which France had to bring the products needed. America traded with both nations, especially with France and its colonies. The British decided to destroy the American trade with France, mainly for two reasons: (a) Products and goods from the U.S. gave Napoleon what he needed to keep up his struggle with Britain. He and France was the enemy and it was felt that the Americans were aiding the Mother Country's enemy. (b) Britain felt threatened by the increasing strength and success of the U.S. merchant fleet. They were becoming major competitors with the ship owners and merchants in Britain.

The British issued the Orders in Council which were a series of measures prohibiting American ships from entering any French ports, not only in Europe but also in India and the West Indies. At the same time, Napoleon began efforts for a coastal blockade of the British Isles. He issued a series of Orders prohibiting all nations, including the United States, from trading with the British. And he didn't stop there. He threatened seizure of every ship entering any French ports after they stopped at any British port or British colony, even threatening to seize every ship inspected by British cruisers or that paid any duties to their government. Adding to all of this, the British were stopping American ships and seizing, or impressing, American seamen to service on British ships. Americans were outraged.

In 1807, Congress passed the Embargo Act, forbidding American ships from sailing to foreign ports. It couldn't be completely enforced and it really hurt business and trade in America so, in 1809, it was repealed. Two additional acts passed by Congress after James Madison became president attempted to regulate trade with other nations and to get Britain and France to remove all the restrictions they had put on American shipping. The catch was that whichever nation removed restrictions, the U.S. agreed not to trade with the other one. Clever Napoleon was the first to do this, prompting Madison to issue orders prohibiting trade with Britain, ignoring warnings from the British not to do so. Of course, this didn't work either and although Britain eventually rescinded the Orders in Council, war came in June of 1812 and ended Christmas Eve, 1814, with the signing of the Treaty of Ghent.

During the war, Americans were divided over not only whether or not it was necessary to even fight but also over what territories should be fought for and taken. The nation was still young and just not prepared for war. The primary American objective was to conquer Canada but it failed. Two naval victories and one military victory stand out for the United States. Oliver Perry gained control of Lake Erie and Thomas MacDonough fought on Lake Champlain.

Both of these naval battles successfully prevented the British invasion of the United States from Canada. Nevertheless, the troops did land below Washington on the Potomac, marched into the city, and burned the public buildings, including the White House. Andrew Jackson's victory at New Orleans was a great morale booster to Americans, giving them the impression the U.S. had won the war. The battle actually took place after Britain and the United States had reached an agreement and it had no impact on the war's outcome. The peace treaty did little for the United States other than bringing peace, releasing prisoners of war, restoring all occupied territory, and setting up a commission to settle boundary disputes with Canada. Interestingly, the war proved to be a turning point in American history. European events had profoundly shaped U.S. policies, especially foreign policies.

After 1815, the U.S. became more independent from European influence and was treated with growing respect by European nations who were impressed by the fact that the young United States showed no hesitancy in going to war with the world's greatest naval power.

The Red River cession was the next acquisition of land and came about as part of a treaty with Great Britain in 1818. It included parts of North and South Dakota and Minnesota. In 1819, Florida, both east and West, was ceded to the U.S. by Spain along with parts of Alabama, Mississippi, and Louisiana. Texas was annexed in 1845 and after the war with Mexico in 1848 the government paid $15 million for what would become the states of California, Utah, Nevada and parts of four other states. In 1846, the Oregon Country was ceded to the U.S., which extended the western border to the Pacific Ocean. The northern U.S. boundary was established at the 49th parallel. The states of Idaho, Oregon and Washington were formed from this territory. In 1853, the Gadsden Purchase rounded out the present boundary of the 48 conterminous states with payment to Mexico of $10 million for land that makes up the present states of New Mexico and Arizona.

In domestic affairs of the new nation, the first problems dealt with finances-- paying for the war debts of the Revolutionary War and other financial needs. Secretary of the Treasury Alexander Hamilton wanted the government to increase tariffs and put taxes on certain products made in the U.S., for example, liquor. This money in turn would be used to pay war debts of the federal government as well as those of the states. There would be money available for expenses and needed internal improvements.

To provide for this, Hamilton favored a national bank. Secretary of State Thomas Jefferson, along with southern supporters, opposed many of Hamilton's suggested plans. Later, Jefferson relented and gave support to some proposals in return for Hamilton and his northern supporters agreeing to locate the nation's capital in the South. Jefferson continued to oppose a national bank but Congress set up the first one in 1791, chartered for the next 20 years. In 1794,

Pennsylvania farmers, who made whiskey, their most important source of cash, refused to pay the liquor tax and started what came to be known as the Whiskey Rebellion. Troops sent by President Washington successfully put it down with no lives lost, thus demonstrating the growing strength of the new government.

The **Judiciary Act** set up the U.S. Supreme Court by providing for a Chief Justice and five associate justices. It also established federal district and circuit courts. One of the most important acts of Congress was the first 10 amendments to the Constitution called the Bill of Rights which emphasized and gave attention to the rights of individuals.

Under President John Adams, a minor diplomatic upset occurred with the government of France. By this time, the two major political parties called Federalists and Democratic-Republicans had fully developed. Hamilton and his mostly northern followers had formed the Federalist Party, which favored a strong central government and was sympathetic to Great Britain and its interests. The Democratic-Republican Party had been formed by Jefferson and his mostly Southern followers and they wanted a weak central government and stronger relations with and support of France. In 1798, the Federalists, in control of Congress, passed the Alien and Sedition Acts written to silence vocal opposition. These acts made it a crime to voice any criticism of the President or Congress and unfairly treated all foreigners.

The legislatures of Kentucky and Virginia protested these laws, claiming they attacked freedoms and challenging their constitutionality. These Resolutions stated mainly the states had created the federal government which was considered merely as an agent for the states and was limited to certain powers and could be criticized by the states, if warranted. They went further stating that states' rights included the power to declare any act of Congress null and void if the states felt it unconstitutional. The controversy died down as the Alien and Sedition Acts expired, one by one, but the doctrine of states' rights was not finally settled until the Civil War.

Supreme Court Chief Justice John Marshall made extremely significant contributions to the American judiciary. He established the foundation of the judicial system and the federal government. He started the power of judicial review; the right of the Supreme Court to determine the constitutionality of laws passed by Congress. He stated that only the Supreme Court had the power to set aside laws passed by state legislatures when they contradicted the U.S. Constitution. He established the right of the Supreme Court to reverse decisions of state courts.

After the U.S. purchased the Louisiana Territory, Jefferson appointed Captains Meriwether Lewis and William Clark to explorethe territory. The expedition went all the way to the Pacific Ocean, returning two years later with maps, journals, and artifacts. This led the way for future explorers to make available more knowledge about the territory and resulted in the Westward Movement and the later belief in the doctrine of Manifest Destiny.

The election of Andrew Jackson as President signaled a swing of the political pendulum from government influence of the wealthy, aristocratic Easterners to the interests of the Western farmers and pioneers and the era of the "common man." Jacksonian democracy was a policy of equal political power for all. After the War of 1812, Henry Clay and supporters favored economic measures that came to be known as the American System. This involved tariffs protecting American farmers and manufacturers from having to compete with foreign products, stimulating industrial growth and employment. With more people working, more farm products would be consumed, prosperous farmers would be able to buy more manufactured goods, and the additional monies from tariffs would make it possible for the government to make the needed internal improvements. In 1816, Congress not only passed a high tariff, but also chartered a second Bank of the United States. Upon becoming President, Jackson fought to get rid of the bank.

One of the many duties of the bank was to regulate the supply of money for the nation. The President believed that the bank was a monopoly that favored the wealthy. Congress voted in 1832 to renew the bank's charter but Jackson vetoed the bill, withdrew the government's money, and the bank finally collapsed. Jackson also faced the "null and void," or nullification issue from South Carolina. Congress, in 1828, passed a law placing high tariffs on goods imported into the United States. Southerners, led by South Carolina's then Vice-President of the United States, John C. Calhoun, felt that the tariff favored the manufacturing interests of New England. Calhoun denounced it as an abomination, and claimed that any state could nullify any of the federal laws it considered unconstitutional. The tariff was lowered in 1832, but not enough to satisfy South Carolina, which promptly threatened to secede from the Union. Although Jackson agreed with the rights of states, he also believed in preservation of the Union. A year later, the tariffs were lowered and the crisis was averted.

Many social reform movements began during this period, including education, women's rights, labor, and working conditions, temperance, prisons and insane asylums. But the most intense and controversial was the abolitionists' efforts to end slavery, an effort alienating and splitting the country, hardening Southern defense of slavery, and leading to four years of bloody war. The abolitionist movement had political fallout, affecting admittance of states into the Union and the government's continued efforts to keep a balance between total numbers of free and slave states. Congressional legislation after 1820 reflected this.

The **Industrial Revolution** had spread from Great Britain to the United States. Before 1800, most manufacturing activities were done in small shops or in homes. However, starting in the early 1800s, factories with modern machines were built making it easier to produce goods faster. The eastern part of the country became a major industrial area although some developed in the West. At about the same time, improvements began to be made in building roads, railroads, canals, and steamboats. The increased ease of travel facilitated the westward movement as well as boosted the economy with faster and cheaper shipment of goods and products, covering larger and larger areas. Some of the innovations include the Erie Canal connecting the interior and Great Lakes with the Hudson River and the coastal port of New York. Many other natural waterways were connected by canals.

Robert Fulton's "Clermont," the first commercially successful steamboat, led the way in the fastest way to ship goods, making it the most important way to do so. Later, steam-powered railroads soon became the biggest rival of the steamboat as a means of shipping, eventually being the most important transportation method opening the West. With expansion into the interior of the country, the United States became the leading agricultural nation in the world. The hardy pioneer farmers produced a vast surplus and emphasis went to producing products with a high-sale value. Implements as the cotton gin and reaper aided in this. Travel and shipping were greatly assisted in areas not yet touched by railroad or, by improved or new roads, such as the National Road in the East and in the West the Oregon and Santa Fe Trails.

People were exposed to works of literature, art, newspapers, drama, live entertainment, and political rallies. With better communication and travel, more information was desired about previously unknown areas of the country, especially the West. The discovery of gold and other mineral wealth resulted in a literal surge of settlers and even more interest.

Public schools were established in many of the states with more and more children being educated. With more literacy and more participation in literature and the arts, the young nation was developing its own unique culture becoming less and less influenced by and dependent on that of Europe.

More industries and factories required more and more labor. Women, children, and, at times, entire families worked the long hours and days, until the 1830s. By that time, the factories were getting even larger and employers began hiring immigrants who were coming to America in huge numbers. Before then, efforts were made to organize a labor movement to improve working conditions and increase wages. It never really caught on until after the Civil War, but the seed had been sown.

Following is just a partial list of well-known Americans who contributed their leadership and talents in various fields and reforms:

Lucretia Mott and Elizabeth Cady Stanton for women's rights

Emma Hart Willard, Catharine Esther Beecher, and Mary Lyon for education for women

Dr. Elizabeth Blackwell, the first woman doctor

Antoinette Louisa Blackwell, the first female minister
Dorothea Lynde Dix for reforms in prisons and insane asylums Elihu Burritt and William Ladd for peace movements

Robert Owen for a Utopian society

Horace Mann, Henry Barmard, Calvin E. Stowe, Caleb Mills, and John Swett for public education

Benjamin Lundy, David Walker, William Lloyd Garrison, Isaac Hooper, Arthur and Lewis Tappan, Theodore Weld, Frederick Douglass, Harriet Tubman, James G. Birney, Henry Highland Garnet, James Forten, Robert Purvis, Harriet Beecher Stowe, Wendell Phillips, and John Brown for abolition of slavery and the Underground Railroad

Louisa Mae Alcott, James Fenimore Cooper, Washington Irving, Walt Whitman, Henry David Thoreau, Ralph Waldo Emerson, Herman Melville, Richard Henry Dana, Nathaniel Hawthorne, Henry Wadsworth Longfellow, John Greenleaf Whittier, Edgar Allan Poe, Oliver Wendell Holmes, famous writers

John C. Fremont, Zebulon Pike, Kit Carson, explorers

Henry Clay, Daniel Webster, Stephen Douglas, John C. Calhoun, American statesmen

Robert Fulton, Cyrus McCormick, Eli Whitney, inventors

Noah Webster, American dictionary and spellers

The list could go on and on but the contributions of these and many, many others greatly enhanced the unique American culture.

In between the growing economy, expansion westward of the population, and improvements in travel and mass communication, the federal government did face periodic financial depressions. Contributing to these downward spirals were land speculations, availability and soundness of money and currency, failed banks, failing businesses, and unemployment. Sometimes conditions outside the nation would help trigger it; at other times, domestic politics and presidential elections affected it. The growing strength and influence of two major political parties with opposing philosophies and methods of conducting government did not ease matters at times.

As 1860 began, the nation had extended its borders north, south, and west. Industry and agriculture were flourishing. Although the U.S. did not involve itself actively in European affairs, the relationship with Great Britain was much improved and it and other nations that dealt with the young nation accorded it more respect and admiration. Nevertheless, war was on the horizon. The country was deeply divided along political lines concerning slavery and the election of Abraham Lincoln.

Although the 13 colonies won independence, wrote a Constitution forming a union of those states under a central government, fought wars and signed treaties, purchased and explored vast areas of land, developed industry and agriculture, improved transportation, saw population expansion westward, increased each year the number of states admitted to the Union . . . despite all of these accomplishments, the issue of human slavery had to be settled once and for all. One historian has stated that before 1865, the nation referred to itself as "the United States are ... ," but after 1865, "the United States is ..." It took the Civil War to finally, completely unify all states into one Union.

Westward expansion occurred for a number of reasons, most important being economic. Cotton had become most important to the people who lived in the southern states. The effects of the Industrial Revolution, which began in England, were now being felt in the United States. With the invention of power-driven machines, the demand for cotton fiber greatly increased for the yarn needed in spinning and weaving. Eli Whitney's cotton gin made the separation of the seeds from the cotton much more efficient and faster. This, in turn, increased the demand and more and more farmers became involved in the raising and selling of cotton.

The innovations and developments of better methods of long-distance transportation moved the cotton in greater quantities to textile mills in England as well as the areas of New England and Middle Atlantic States in the U.S. As prices increased along with increased demand, southern farmers began expanding by clearing increasingly more land to grow more cotton. Movement, settlement, and farming headed west to utilize the fertile soils. This, in turn, demanded increased need for a large supply of cheap labor. The system of slavery expanded, in numbers and in the movement to lands "west" of the South.

Cotton farmers and slave owners were not the only ones heading west. Many, in other fields of economic endeavor, began the migration: trappers, miners, merchants, ranchers, and others were all seeking their fortunes. The Lewis and Clark expedition stimulated the westward push. Fur companies hired men, known as "Mountain Men", to go westward, searching for the animal pelts to supply the market and meet the demands of the East and Europe. These men in their own way explored and discovered the many passes and trails that would eventually be used by settlers in their trek to the west. The California gold rush also had a very large influence on the movement west.

There were also religious reasons for westward expansion. Increased settlement was encouraged by missionaries who traveled west with the fur traders. They sent word back east for more settlers and the results were tremendous. By the 1840s, the population increases in the Oregon country alone were at a rate of about a thousand people a year. People of many different religions and cultures as well as Southerners with black slaves made their way west which leads to a third reason: political.

It was the belief of many that the United States was destined to control all of the land between the two oceans or as one newspaper editor termed it, "Manifest Destiny." This mass migration westward put the U.S. government on a collision course with the Indians, Great Britain, Spain, and Mexico. The fur traders and missionaries ran up against the Indians in the northwest and the claims of Great Britain for the Oregon country.

The U.S. and Britain had shared the Oregon country. By the 1840s, with the increase in the free and slave populations and the demand of the settlers for control and government by the U.S., the conflict had to be resolved. In a treaty, signed in 1846, by both nations, a peaceful resolution occurred with Britain giving up its claims south of the 49th parallel.

In the American southwest, the results were exactly the opposite. Spain had claimed this area since the 1540s, had spread northward from Mexico City, and, in the 1700s, had established missions, forts, villages, towns, and very large ranches. After the purchase of the Louisiana Territory in 1803, Americans began moving into Spanish territory. A few hundred American families in what is now Texas were allowed to live there but had to agree to become loyal subjects to Spain. In 1821, Mexico successfully revolted against Spanish rule, won independence, and chose to be more tolerant towards the American settlers and traders. The Mexican government encouraged and allowed extensive trade and settlement, especially in Texas. Many of the new settlers were southerners and brought with them their slaves. Slavery was outlawed in Mexico and technically illegal in Texas, although the Mexican government rather looked the other way.

With the influx of so many Americans and the liberal policies of the Mexican government, there came to be concern over the possible growth and development of an American state within Mexico. Settlement restrictions, cancellation of land grants, the forbidding of slavery and increased military activity brought everything to a head. The order of events included the fight for Texas independence, the brief Republic of Texas, eventual annexation of Texas, statehood, and finally war with Mexico. The Texas controversy was not the sole reason for war. Since American settlers had begun, pouring into the Southwest the cultural differences played a prominent part. Language, religion, law, customs, and government were totally different and opposite between the two groups. A clash was bound to occur.

The impact of the entire westward movement resulted in the completion of the borders of the present-day conterminous United States. Contributing factors include the bloody war with Mexico, the ever-growing controversy over slave versus free states affecting the balance of power or influence in the U.S. Congress, especially the Senate and finally to the Civil War itself

Civil War and Reconstruction (1850-1877)

The drafting of the Constitution, its ratification and implementation, united 13 different, independent states into a Union under one central government. The two crucial compromises of the convention delegates concerning slaves pacified Southerners, especially the slave owners, but the issue of slavery was not settled. Sectionalism became stronger and more apparent each year putting the entire country on a collision course.

Slavery in the English colonies began in 1619 when 20 Africans arrived in the colony of Virginia at Jamestown. From then on, slavery had a foothold, especially in the agricultural South, where a large amount of slave labor was needed for the extensive plantations. Free men refused to work for wages on the plantations when land was available for settling on the frontier. Therefore, slave labor was the only recourse left. If it had been profitable to use slaves in New England and the Middle Colonies, then without doubt slavery would have been more widespread. However, it came down to whether or not slavery was profitable. It was in the South, but not in the other two colonial regions.

It is interesting that the West was involved in the controversy as well as the North and South. By 1860, the country was made up of these three major regions. The people in all three sections or regions had a number of beliefs and institutions in common. Of course, there were major differences with each region having its own unique characteristics. The basic problem was their development along very different lines.

The section of the North was industrial with towns and factories growing and increasing at a very fast rate. The South had become agricultural, eventually becoming increasingly dependent on the one crop of cotton. In the West, restless pioneers moved into new frontiers seeking land, wealth, and opportunity. Many were from the South and were slave owners, bringing their slaves with them. So between these three different parts of the country, the views on tariffs, public lands, internal improvements at federal expense, banking and currency, and the issue of slavery were decidedly, totally different. This period of U.S. history was a period of compromises, breakdowns of the compromises, desperate attempts to restore and retain harmony among the three sections, short-lived intervals of the uneasy balance of interests, and ever-increasing conflict.

At the Constitutional Convention, one of the slavery compromises concerned counting slaves for deciding the number of representatives for the House and the amount of taxes to be paid. Southerners pushed for counting the slaves for representation but not for taxes. The Northerners pushed for the opposite. The resulting compromise, sometimes referred to as the "three-fifths compromise," was that both groups agreed that three-fifths of the slaves would be counted for both taxes and representation.

The other compromise over slavery was part of the disputes over how much regulation the central government would control over commercial activities such as trade with other nations and the slave trade. It was agreed that Congress would regulate commerce with other nations including taxing imports. Southerners were worried about taxing slaves coming into the country and the possibility of Congress prohibiting the slave trade altogether. The agreement reached allowed the states to continue importation of slaves for the next 20 years until 1808, at which time Congress would make the decision as to the future of the slave trade. During the 20-year period, no more than $10 per person could be levied on slaves coming into the country.

These two "slavery' compromises were a necessary concession to have Southern support and approval for the new document and new government. Many Americans felt that the system of slavery would eventually die out in the U.S., but by 1808, cotton was becoming increasingly important in the primarily agricultural South and the institution of slavery had become firmly entrenched in Southern culture. It is also evident that as early as the Constitutional Convention, active anti-slavery feelings and opinions were very strong, leading to extremely active groups and societies.

Democracy is loosely defined as "rule by the people," either directly or through representatives. Associated with the idea of democracy are freedom, equality, and opportunity. The basic concept of democracy existed in the 13 English colonies with the practice of independent self-government. The right of qualified persons to vote, hold office and actively participate in his or her government is sometimes referred to as "political" democracy. "Social" and "economic" democracy pertain to the idea that all have the opportunity to get an education, choose their own careers, and live as free men everyday all equal in the eyes of the law to everyone.

These three concepts of democracy were basic reasons why people came to the New World. The practices of these concepts continued through the colonial and revolutionary periods and were extremely influential in shaping the new central government under the Constitution. As the nation extended its' borders into the lands west of the Mississippi, thousands of settlers streamed into this part of the country. They brought with them ideas and concepts and adapted them to the development of the unique characteristics of the region. Equality for everyone, as stated in the Declaration of Independence, did not yet apply to minority groups, black Americans or American Indians. Voting rights and the right to hold public office were restricted in varying degrees in each state. All of these factors decidedly affected the political, economic, and social life of the country and these were focused in the attitudes towards slavery in three sections of the country.

The first serious clash between North and South occurred during 1819-1820 when James Monroe was in office as President and it was concerning admitting Missouri as a state. In 1819, the U.S. consisted of 21 states: 11 free states and 10 slave states. The Missouri Territory allowed slavery and if admitted would cause an imbalance in the number of U.S. Senators. Alabama had already been admitted as a slave state and that had balanced the Senate with the North and South each having 22 senators. The first Missouri Compromise resolved the conflict by approving the admission of Maine as a free state along with Missouri as a slave state. Thus the balance of power continued in the Senate with the same number of free and slave states.

An additional provision of this compromise was that with the admission of Missouri, slavery would not be allowed in the rest of the Louisiana Purchase territory north of latitude 36 degrees 30'. This was acceptable to the Southern Congressmen since it was not profitable to grow cotton on land north of this latitude line anyway. It was thought that the crisis had been resolved but in the next year, it was discovered that in its state constitution, Missouri discriminated against the free blacks. Anti-slavery supporters in Congress went into an uproar, determined to exclude Missouri from the Union. Henry Clay, known as the **Great Compromiser**, then proposed a second **Missouri Compromise** which was acceptable to everyone. His proposal stated that the Constitution of the United States guaranteed protections and privileges to citizens of states and Missouri's proposed constitution could not deny these to any of its citizens.

The acceptance in 1820 of this second compromise opened the way for Missouri's statehood--a temporary reprieve only.

The issue of tariffs also was a divisive factor during this period, especially between 1829 and 1833. The Embargo Act of 1807 and the War of 1812 had completely cut off the source of manufactured goods for Americans, so it was necessary to build factories to produce what was needed. After 1815 when the war had ended, Great Britain proceeded to get rid of its industrial rivals by unloading its goods in America. To protect and encourage its own industries and their products, Congress passed the Tariff of 1816, which required high duties to be levied on manufactured goods coming into the United States. Southern leaders, such as John C. Calhoun of South Carolina, supported the tariff with the assumption that the South would develop its own industries.

For a brief period after 1815, the nation enjoyed the "Era of Good Feelings." People were moving into the West; industry and agriculture were growing; a feeling of national pride united Americans in their efforts and determination to strengthen the country. However, over speculation in stocks and lands for quick profits backfired. Cotton prices were increasing so many Southerners bought land for cultivation at inflated prices. Manufacturers in the industrial North purchased land to build more plants and factories as an attempt to have a part of this prosperity. Settlers in the West rushed to buy land to reap the benefits of the increasing prices of meat and grain. To have the money for all of these economic activities, all of these groups were borrowing heavily from the banks and the banks themselves encouraged this by giving loans on insubstantial security.

In late 1818, the Bank of the United States and its branches stopped renewal of personal mortgages and required immediate repayment. The state banks were unable to do this so they closed their doors and were unable to do any business at all. Since mortgages could not be renewed, people lost all their properties and foreclosures were rampant throughout the country. At the same time, as all of this was occurring, cotton prices collapsed in the English market. Its high price had caused the British manufacturers to seek cheaper cotton from India for their textile mills. With the fall of cotton prices, the demand for American manufactured goods declined, revealing how fragile the economic prosperity had been.

In 1824, a higher tariff was passed by Congress, favoring the financial interests of the manufacturers in New England and the Middle Atlantic States. In addition, the 1824 tariff was closely tied to the presidential election of that year. Before becoming law, Calhoun had proposed the high tariffs in an effort to get Eastern business interests to vote with the agricultural interests in the South (who were against it). Supporters of candidate Andrew Jackson sided with whichever side served their best interests. Jackson himself would not be involved in any of this scheming.

The bill became law, to Calhoun's surprise, due mainly to the political maneuvering of Martin van Buren and Daniel Webster. By the time the higher 1828 tariff was passed, feelings were extremely bitter in the South, who believed that the New England manufacturers greatly benefited from it. Vice-President Calhoun, also speaking for his home state of South Carolina, promptly declared that if any state felt that a federal law was unconstitutional, that state could nullify it. In 1832, Congress took the action of lowering the tariffs to a degree but not enough to please South Carolina, which promptly declared the tariff null and void, threatening to secede from the Union.

In 1833, Congress lowered the tariffs again, this time at a level acceptable to South Carolina. Although President Jackson believed in states' rights, he also firmly believed in and determined to keep the preservation of the Union. A constitutional crisis had been averted but sectional divisions were getting deeper and more pronounced. The abolition movement was growing rapidly, becoming an important issue in the North.

The slavery issue was at the root of every problem, crisis, event, decision, and struggle from then on. The next crisis involved the issue concerning Texas. By 1836, Texas was an independent republic with its own constitution. During its fight for independence, Americans were sympathetic to and supportive of the Texans and some recruited volunteers who crossed into Texas to help the struggle. Problems arose when the state petitioned Congress for statehood. Texas wanted to allow slavery but Northerners in Congress opposed admission to the Union because it would disrupt the balance between free and slave states and give Southerners in Congress increased influence.

Others believed that granting statehood to Texas would lead to a war with Mexico. Mexico had refused to recognize Texas independence. For the time being, statehood was put on hold.

Friction increased between land-hungry Americans swarming into western lands and the Mexican government, which controlled these lands. The clash was not only political but also cultural and economic. The Spanish influence permeated all parts of southwestern life: law, language, architecture, and customs. By this time, the doctrine of Manifest Destiny was in the hearts and on the lips of those seeking new areas of settlement and a new life. Americans were demanding U.S. control of not only the Mexican Territory but also Oregon. Peaceful negotiations with Great Britain secured Oregon but it took two years of war to gain control of the southwestern U.S.

In addition, the Mexican government owed debts to U.S. citizens whose property was damaged or destroyed during its struggle for independence from Spain. By the time war broke out in 1845, Mexico had not paid its war debts. The government was weak, corrupt, tom by revolutions, and not in decent financial shape. Mexico was also bitter over American expansion into Texas and the 1836 revolution, which resulted in Texas independence. In the 1844 Presidential election, the Democrats pushed for annexation of Texas and Oregon and after winning, they started the procedure to admit Texas to the Union.

When statehood occurred, diplomatic relations between the U.S. and Mexico was ended. President Polk wanted U.S. control of the entire southwest, from Texas to the Pacific Ocean. He sent a diplomatic mission with an offer to purchase New Mexico and Upper California but the Mexican government refused to even receive the diplomat. Consequently, in 1846, each nation claimed aggression on the part of the other and war was declared. The treaty signed in 1848 and a subsequent one in 1853 completed the southwestern boundary of the United States, reaching to the Pacific Ocean, as President Polk wished.

The slavery issue flared again not to be done away with until the end of the Civil War. It was obvious that the newly acquired territory would be divided up into territories and later become states. Factions of Northerners advocated prohibition of slavery and Southerners favored slavery. A third faction arose supporting the doctrine of "popular sovereignty" which stated that people living in territories and states should be allowed to decide for themselves whether or not slavery should be permitted. In 1849, California applied for admittance to the Union and the furor began.

The result was the Compromise of 1850, a series of laws designed as a final solution to the issue. Concessions made to the North included the admission of California as a free state and the abolition of slave trading in Washington, D.C. The laws also provided for the creation of the New Mexico and Utah territories. As a concession to Southerners, the residents there would decide whether to permit slavery when these two territories became states. In addition, Congress authorized implementation of stricter measures to capture runaway slaves.

A few years later, Congress took up consideration of new territories between Missouri and present-day Idaho. Again, heated debate over permitting slavery in these areas flared up. Those opposed to slavery used the Missouri Compromise to prove their point showing that the land being considered for territories was part of the area the Compromise had designated as banned to slavery. On May 25, 1854, Congress passed the infamous Kansas-Nebraska Act which nullified the provision creating the territories of Kansas and Nebraska. This provided for the people of these two territories to decide for themselves whether or not to permit slavery to exist there. Feelings were so deep and divided that any further attempts to compromise would meet with little, if any, success.

Political and social turmoil swirled everywhere. Kansas was called "**Bleeding Kansas**" because of the extreme violence and bloodshed throughout the territory because two governments existed there, one pro-slavery and the other anti-slavery.

The Supreme Court in 1857 handed down a decision guaranteed to cause explosions throughout the country. Dred Scott was a slave whose owner had taken him from slave state Missouri, then to free state Illinois, into Minnesota Territory, free under the provisions of the Missouri Compromise, then finally back to slave state Missouri. Abolitionists pursued the dilemma by presenting a court case, stating that since Scott had lived in a free state and free territory, he was in actuality a free man. Two lower courts had ruled before the Supreme Court became involved, one ruling in favor and one against. The Supreme Court decided that residing in a free state and free territory did not make Scott a free man because Scott (and all other slaves) was not U.S. citizens or state citizens of Missouri. Therefore, he did not have the right to sue in state or federal courts. The Court went a step further and ruled that the old Missouri Compromise was now unconstitutional because Congress did not have the power to prohibit slavery in the Territories.

Anti-slavery supporters were stunned. They had just recently formed the new Republican Party and one of its platforms was keeping slavery out of the Territories. Now, according to the decision in the Dred Scott case, this basic party principle was unconstitutional. The only way to ban slavery in new areas was by a Constitutional amendment, requiring ratification by three-fourths of all states. At this time, this was out of the question because the supporters would be unable to get a majority due to Southern opposition.

In 1858, Abraham Lincoln and Stephen A. Douglas were running for the office of U.S. Senator from Illinois and participated in a series of debates, which directly affected the outcome of the 1860 Presidential election. Douglas, a Democrat, was up for re-election and knew that if he won this race, he had a good chance of becoming President in 1860. Lincoln, a Republican, was not an abolitionist but he believed that slavery was wrong morally and he firmly believed in and supported the Republican Party principle that slavery must not be allowed to extend any further.

Douglas, on the other hand, originated the doctrine of "popular sovereignty" and was responsible for supporting and getting through Congress the inflammatory Kansas-Nebraska Act. In the course of the debates, Lincoln challenged Douglas to show that popular sovereignty reconciled with the Dred Scott decision. Either way he answered Lincoln, Douglas would lose crucial support from one group or the other. If he supported the Dred Scott decision, Southerners would support him but he would lose Northern support. If he stayed with popular sovereignty, Northern support would be his but Southern support would be lost. His reply to Lincoln, stating that Territorial legislatures could exclude slavery by refusing to pass laws supporting it, gave him enough support and approval to be re-elected to the Senate. But it cost him the Democratic nomination for President in 1860.

Southerners came to the realization that Douglas supported and devoted to popular sovereignty but not necessarily to the expansion of slavery. On the other hand, two years later, Lincoln received the nomination of the Republican Party for President.

In 1859, abolitionist John Brown and his followers seized the federal arsenal at Harper's Ferry in what is now West Virginia. His purpose was to take the guns stored in the arsenal, give them to slaves nearby, and lead them in a widespread rebellion. He and his men were captured by Colonel Robert E. Lee of the United States Army and after a trial with a guilty verdict, he was hanged. Most Southerners felt that the majority of Northerners approved of Brown's actions but in actuality, most of them were stunned and shocked. Southern newspapers took great pains to quote a small but well-known minority of abolitionists who applauded and supported Brown's actions. This merely served to widen the gap between the two sections.

The final straw came with the election of Lincoln to the Presidency the next year. Due to a split in the Democratic Party, there were four candidates from four political parties. With Lincoln receiving a minority of the popular vote and a majority of electoral votes, the Southern states, one by one, voted to secede from the Union, as they had promised they would do if Lincoln and the Republicans were victorious. The die was cast.

It is ironic that South Carolina was the first state to secede from the Union and the first shots of the war were fired on Fort Sumter in Charleston Harbor. Both sides quickly prepared for war. The North had more in its favor: a larger population; superiority in finances and transportation facilities; manufacturing, agricultural, and natural resources. The North possessed most of the nation's gold, had about 92% of all industries, and almost all known supplies of copper, coal, iron, and various other minerals.

Most of the nation's railroads were in the North and mid-West, men and supplies could be moved wherever needed; food could be transported from the farms of the mid-West to workers in the East and to soldiers on the battlefields. Trade with nations overseas could go on as usual due to control of the navy and the merchant fleet. The Northern states numbered 24 and included western (California and Oregon) and border (Maryland, Delaware, Kentucky, Missouri, and West Virginia) states.

The Southern states numbered 11 and included South Carolina, Georgia, Florida, Alabama, Mississippi, Louisiana, Texas, Virginia, North Carolina, Tennessee, and Arkansas, making up the Confederacy. Although outnumbered in population, the South was completely confident of victory. They knew that all they had to do was fight a defensive war and protect their own territory. The North had to invade and defeat an area almost the size of Western Europe. They figured the North would tire of the struggle and gave up. Another advantage of the South was that a number of its best officers had graduated from the U.S. Military Academy at West Point and had had long years of army experience. Many had exercised varying degrees of command in the Indian wars and the war with Mexico. Men from the South were conditioned to living outdoors and were more familiar with horses and firearms than many men from northeastern cities. Since cotton was such an important crop, Southerners felt that British and French textile mills were so dependent on raw cotton that they would be forced to help the Confederacy in the war.

The South had specific reasons and goals for fighting the war, more so than the North. The major aim of the Confederacy never wavered: to win independence, the right to govern themselves as they wished, and to preserve slavery. The Northerners were not as clear in their reasons for conducting war. At the beginning, most believed, along with Lincoln, that preservation of the Union was paramount. Only a few extremely fanatical abolitionists looked on the war as a way to end slavery. However, by war's end, more and more northerners had come to believe that freeing the slaves was just as important as restoring the Union.

The war strategies for both sides were relatively clear and simple. The South planned a defensive war, wearing down the North until it agreed to peace on Southern terms. The only exception was to gain control of Washington, D.C., go North through the Shenandoah Valley into Maryland and Pennsylvania in order to drive a wedge between the Northeast and mid-West, interrupt the lines of communication, and end the war quickly. The North had three basic strategies:

1. blockade the Confederate coastline in order to cripple the South;
2. seize control of the Mississippi River and interior railroad lines to split the Confederacy in two;
3. seize the Confederate capital of Richmond, Virginia, driving southward joining up with Union forces coming east from the Mississippi Valley.

The South won decisively until the Battle of Gettysburg, July 1 - 3, 1863. Until Gettysburg, Lincoln's commanders, McDowell and McClellan, were less than desirable,. Lee, on the other hand, had many able officers, Jackson and Stuart depended on heavily by him. Jackson died at Chancellorsville and was replaced by Longstreet. Lee decided to invade the North and depended on J.E.B. Stuart and his cavalry to keep him informed of the location of Union troops and their strengths. Four things worked against Lee at Gettysburg:

- The Union troops gained the best positions and the best ground first, making it easier to make a stand there.

- Lee's move into Northern territory put him and his army a long way from food and supply lines. They were more or less on their own.

- Lee thought that his Army of Northern Virginia was invincible and could fight and win under any conditions or circumstances.

Stuart and his men did not arrive at Gettysburg until the end of the second day of fighting and by then, it was too little too late. He and the men had had to detour around Union soldiers and he was delayed getting the information Lee needed.

Consequently, he made the mistake of failing to listen to Longstreet and following the strategy of regrouping back into Southern territory to the supply lines. Lee felt that regrouping was retreating and almost an admission of defeat.

He was convinced the army would be victorious. Longstreet was concerned about the Union troops occupying the best positions and felt that regrouping to a better position would be an advantage. He was also very concerned about the distance from supply lines.

It was not the intention of either side to fight there but the fighting began when a Confederate brigade, who was looking for shoes, stumbled into a unit of Union cavalry. The third and last day Lee launched the final attempt to break Union lines. General George Pickett sent his division of three brigades under Generals Garnet, Kemper, and Armistead against Union troops on Cemetery Ridge under command of General Winfield Scott Hancock. Union lines held and Lee and the defeated Army of Northern Virginia made their way back to Virginia. Although Lincoln's commander George Meade successfully turned back a Confederate charge, he and the Union troops failed to pursue Lee and the Confederates. This battle was the turning point for the North. After this, Lee never again had the troop strength to launch a major offensive.

The day after Gettysburg, on July 4, Vicksburg, Mississippi surrendered to Union General Ulysses Grant, thus severing the western Confederacy from the eastern part. In September 1863, the Confederacy won its last important victory at Chickamauga. In November, the Union victory at Chattanooga made it possible for Union troops to go into Alabama and Georgia, splitting the eastern Confederacy in two. Lincoln gave Grant command of all Northern armies in March of 1864. Grant led his armies into battles in Virginia while Phil Sheridan and his cavalry did as much damage as possible. In a skirmish at a place called Yellow Tavern, Virginia, Sheridan's and Stuart's forces met, with Stuart being fatally wounded. The Union won the Battle of Mobile Bay and in May 1864, William Tecumseh Sherman began his march to successfully demolish Atlanta, then on to Savannah. He and his troops turned northward through the Carolinas to Grant in Virginia. On April 9, 1865, Lee formally surrendered to Grant at Appamattox Courthouse, Virginia.

The Civil War took more American lives than any other war in history, the South losing one-third of its soldiers in battle compared to about one-sixth for the North. More than half of the total deaths were caused by disease and the horrendous conditions of field hospitals. Both sides paid a tremendous economic price but the South suffered more severely from direct damages. Destruction was pervasive with towns, farms, trade, industry, lives and homes of men, women, children all destroyed and an entire Southern way of life was lost. The deep resentment, bitterness, and hatred that remained for generations gradually lessened as the years went by but legacies of it surface and remain to this day. The South had no voice in the political, social, and cultural affairs of the nation, lessening to a great degree the influence of the more traditional Southern ideals. The Northern Yankee Protestant ideals of hard work, education, and economic freedom became the standard of the United States and helped influence the development of the nation into a modem, industrial power.

The effects of the Civil War were tremendous. It changed the methods of waging war and has been called the first modern war. It introduced weapons and tactics that, when improved later, were used extensively in wars of the late 1800s and 1900s. Civil War soldiers were the first to fight in trenches, first to fight under a unified command, first to wage a defense called "major cordon defense", a strategy of advance on all fronts. They were also the first to use repeating and breech loading weapons. Observation balloons were first used during the war along with submarines, ironclad ships, and mines. Telegraphy and railroads were put to use first in the Civil War. It was considered a modern war because of the vast destruction and was "total war", involving the use of all resources of the opposing sides. There was probably no *way* it could have ended other than total defeat and unconditional surrender of one side or the other.

By executive proclamation and constitutional amendment, slavery was officially ended, although there remained deep prejudice and racism, still raising its ugly head today. Also, the Union was preserved and the states were finally truly united. Sectionalism, especially in the area of politics, remained strong for another 100 years but not to the degree and with the violence as existed before 1861. It has been noted that the Civil War may have been American democracy's greatest failure for, from 1861 to 1865, calm reason basic to democracy, fell to human passion. Yet, democracy did survive. The victory of the North established that no state has the right to end or leave the Union. Because of unity, the U.S. became a major global power. Lincoln never proposed to punish the South. He was most concerned with restoring the South to the Union in a program that was flexible and practical rather than rigid and unbending. In fact he never really felt that the states had succeeded in leaving the Union but that they had left the 'family circle" for a short time. His plans consisted of two major steps:

All Southerners taking an oath of allegiance to the Union promising to accept all federal laws and proclamations dealing with slavery would receive a full pardon. The only ones excluded from this were men who had resigned from civil and military positions in the federal government to serve in the Confederacy, those who were part of the Confederate government, those in the Confederate army above the rank of lieutenant, and Confederates who were guilty of mistreating prisoners of war and blacks.

A state would be able to write a new constitution, elect new officials, and return to the Union fully equal to all other states on certain conditions: a minimum number of persons (at least 10% of those who were qualified voters in their states before secession from the Union who had voted in the 1860 election) must take an oath of allegiance.

As the war dragged on to its bloody and destructive conclusion, Lincoln was very concerned and anxious to get the states restored to the Union. He showed flexibility in his thinking as he made changes to his Reconstruction program to make it as easy and painless as possible. Congress had final approval of many actions. It would be interesting to know how differently things might have turned out if Lincoln had lived to see some or all of his kind policies supported by fellow moderates, put into action. Unfortunately, it didn't turn out that way. After Andrew Johnson became President and the radical Republicans gained control of Congress, the harsh measures of radical Reconstruction were implemented.

Following the Civil War, the nation was faced with repairing the torn Union and readmitting the Confederate states. **Reconstruction** refers to this period between 1865 and 1877 when the federal and state governments debated and implemented plans to provide civil rights to freed slaves and to set the terms under which the former Confederate states might once again join the Union.

Planning for Reconstruction began early in the war, in 1861. Abraham Lincoln's Republican Party in Washington favored the extension of voting rights to black men, but was divided as to how far to extend the right. Moderates, such as Lincoln, wanted only literate blacks and those who had fought for the Union to be allowed to vote. Radical Republicans wanted to extend the vote to all black men. Conservative Democrats did not want to give black men the vote at all. In the case of former Confederate soldiers, moderates wanted to allow all but former leaders to vote, while the radicals wanted to require an oath from all eligible voters that they had never borne arms against the US, which would have excluded all former rebels. On the issue of readmission into the Union, moderates favored a much lower standard, with the radicals demanding nearly impossible conditions for rebel states to return.

Lincoln's moderate plan for Reconstruction was actually part of his effort to win the war. Lincoln and the moderates felt that if it remained easy for states to return to the Union, and if moderate proposals on black suffrage were made, that Confederate states involved in the hostilities might be swayed to re-join the Union rather than continue fighting. The radical plan was to ensure that Reconstruction did not actually start until after the war was over.

In 1863 Abraham Lincoln was assassinated leaving his Vice President Andrew Johnson to oversee the beginning of the actual implementation of Reconstruction. Johnson struck a moderate pose, and was willing to allow former confederates to keep control of their state governments. These governments quickly enacted Black Codes that denied the vote to blacks and granted them only limited civil rights.

The economic and social chaos in the South after the war was unbelievable with starvation and disease rampant, especially in the cities. The U.S. Army provided some relief of food and clothing for both white and blacks but the major responsibility fell to the Freedmen's Bureau. Though the bureau agents to a certain extent helped southern whites, their main responsibility was to the freed slaves. They were to assist the freedmen to become self-supporting and protect them from being taken advantage of by others. Northerners looked on it as a real, honest effort to help the South out of the chaos it was in. Most white Southerners charged the bureau with causing racial friction, deliberately encouraging the freedmen to consider former owners as enemies.

As a result, as southern leaders began to be able to restore life as it had once been, they adopted a set of laws known as "black codes", containing many of the provisions of the prewar "slave codes." There were certain improvements in the lives of freedmen, but the codes denied the freedmen their basic civil rights. In short, except for the condition of freedom and a few civil rights, white Southerners made every effort to keep the freedmen in a way of life subordinate to theirs.

Radicals in Congress pointed out these illegal actions by white Southerners as evidence that they were unwilling to recognize, accept, and support the complete freedom of black Americans and could not be trusted. Therefore, Congress drafted its own program of Reconstruction, including laws that would protect and further the rights of blacks. Three amendments were added to the Constitution: the 13th Amendment of 1865 outlawed slavery throughout the entire United States. The 14th Amendment of 1868 made blacks American citizens. The 15th Amendment of 1870 gave black Americans the right to vote and made it illegal to deny anyone the right to vote based on race.

Federal troops were stationed throughout the South and protected Republicans who took control of Southern governments. Bitterly resentful, white Southerners fought the new political system by joining a secret society called the Ku Klux Klan, using violence to keep black Americans from voting and getting equality. However, before being allowed to rejoin the Union, the Confederate states were required to agree to all federal laws. Between 1866 and 1870, all of them had returned to the Union, but Northern interest in Reconstruction was fading. Reconstruction officially ended when the last Federal troops left the South in 1877. It can be said that Reconstruction had a limited success as it set up public school systems and expanded legal rights of black Americans.

Lincoln and Johnson had considered the conflict of Civil War as a "rebellion of individuals". Congressional Radicals, such as Charles Sumner in the Senate, considered the Southern states as complete political organizations and were now in the same position as any unorganized Territory and should be treated as such. Radical House leader Thaddeus Stevens considered the Confederate States, not as Territories, but as conquered provinces and felt they should be treated that way. President Johnson refused to work with Congressional moderates, insisting on having his own way. As a result, the Radicals gained control of both houses of Congress and when Johnson opposed their harsh measures, they came within one vote of impeaching him. General Grant was elected President in 1868, serving two scandal-ridden terms. He was himself an honest, upright person but he greatly lacked political experience and his greatest weakness was a blind loyalty to his friends. He absolutely refused to believe that his friends were not honest and stubbornly would not admit to their using him to further their own interests. One of the sad results of the war was the rapid growth of business and industry with large corporations controlled by unscrupulous men. However, after 1877, some degree of normalcy returned and there was time for rebuilding, expansion, and growth.

Skill 1.2 **Demonstrate an understanding of the chronology, narratives, perspectives, and interpretations of major eras of U.S. history from Reconstruction to the present.**

The Development of the Industrial United States (1870-1900)

There was a marked degree of industrialization before and during the Civil War, but at war's end, industry in America was small. After the war, dramatic changes took place. Machines replaced hand labor, extensive nationwide railroad service made possible the wider distribution of goods, invention of new products made available in large quantities, and large amounts of money from bankers and investors for expansion of business operations. American life was definitely affected by this phenomenal industrial growth. Cities became the centers of this new business activity resulting in mass population movements there and tremendous growth. This new boom in business resulted in huge fortunes for some Americans and extreme poverty for many others. The discontent this caused resulted in a number of new reform movements from which came measures controlling the power and size of big business and helping the poor.

Of course, industry before, during, and after the Civil War was centered mainly in the North, especially the tremendous industrial growth after. The late 1800s and early 1900s saw the increasing buildup of military strength and the U.S. becoming a world power.

The use of machines in industry enabled workers to produce a large quantity of goods much faster than by hand. With the increase in business, hundreds of workers were hired, assigned to perform a certain job in the production process.

This was a method of organization called "division of labor" and by its increasing the rate of production, businesses lowered prices for their products making the products affordable for more people. As a result, sales and businesses were increasingly successful and profitable.

A great variety of new products or inventions became available such as: the typewriter, the telephone, barbed wire, the electric light, the phonograph, and the gasoline automobile. From this list, the one that had the greatest effect on America's economy was the automobile.

The increase in business and industry was greatly affected by the many rich natural resources that were found throughout the nation. The industrial machines were powered by the abundant water supply. The construction industry as well as products made from wood depended heavily on lumber from the forests. Coal and iron ore in abundance were needed for the steel industry, which profited and increased from the use of steel in such things as skyscrapers, automobiles, bridges, railroad tracks, and machines. Other minerals such as silver, copper, and petroleum played a large role in industrial growth, especially petroleum, from which gasoline was refined as fuel for the increasingly popular automobile.

Between 1870 and 1916, more than 25 million immigrants came into the United States adding to the phenomenal population growth taking place. This tremendous growth aided business and industry in two ways: (1) The number of consumers increased creating a greater demand for products thus enlarging the markets for the products. (2) with increased production and expanding business, more workers were available for newly created jobs. The completion of the nation's transcontinental railroad in 1869 contributed greatly to the nation's economic and industrial growth. Some examples of the benefits of using the railroads include raw materials were shipped quickly by the mining companies and finished products were sent to all parts of the country. Many wealthy industrialists and railroad owners saw tremendous profits steadily increasing due to this improved method of transportation.

As business grew, methods of sales and promotion were developed. Salespersons went to all parts of the country promoting the various products, opening large department stores in the growing cities, offering the varied products at reasonable affordable prices. People who lived too far from the cities, making it impossible to shop there, had the advantage of using a mail order service, buying what they needed from catalogs furnished by the companies. The developments in communication, such as the telephone and telegraph, increased the efficiency and prosperity of big business.

Investments in corporate stocks and bonds resulted from business prosperity. Individuals began investing heavily in an eager desire to share in the profits, their investments made available the needed capital for companies to expand their operations. From this, banks increased in number throughout the country, making loans to businesses and significant contributions to economic growth. At the same time, during the 1880s, government made little effort to regulate businesses. This gave rise to monopolies where larger businesses were rid of their smaller competitors and assumed complete control of their industries.

Some owners in the same business would join or merge to form one company. Others formed what were called "trusts," a type of monopoly in which rival businesses were controlled but not formally owned. Monopolies had some good effects on the economy. Out of them grew the large, efficient corporations, which made important contributions to the growth of the nation's economy. Also, the monopolies enabled businesses to keep their sales steady and avoid sharp fluctuations in price and production. At the same time, the downside of monopolies was the unfair business practices of the business leaders. Some acquired so much power that they took unfair advantage of others. Those who had little or no competition would require their suppliers to supply goods at a low cost, sell the finished products at high prices, and reduce the quality of the product to save money.

The late 1800s and early 1900s were a period of the efforts of many to make significant reforms and changes in the areas of politics, society, and the economy. There was a need to reduce the levels of poverty and to improve the living conditions of those affected by it. Regulations of big business, ridding governmental corruption and making it more responsive to the needs of the people were also on the list of reforms to be accomplished. Until 1890, there was very little success, but from 1890 on, the reformers gained increased public support and were able to achieve some influence in government. Since some of these individuals referred to themselves as "progressives," the period of 1890 to 1917 is referred to by historians as the Progressive Era.

Skilled laborers were organized into a labor union called the American Federation of Labor, in an effort to gain better working conditions and wages for its members. Farmers joined organizations such as the National Grange and Farmers Alliances. Farmers were producing more food than people could afford to buy. This was the result of (1) new farmlands rapidly sprouting on the plains and prairies, and (2) development and availability of new farm machinery and newer and better methods of farming. They tried selling their surplus abroad but faced stiff competition from other nations selling the same farm products.

Other problems contributed significantly to their situation. Items they needed for daily life were priced exorbitantly high. Having to borrow money to carry on farming activities kept them constantly in debt. Higher interest rates, shortage of money, falling farm prices, dealing with the so-called middlemen, and the increasingly high charges by the railroads to haul farm products to large markets all contributed to the desperate need for reform to relieve the plight of American farmers.

American women began actively campaigning for the right to vote. Elizabeth Cady Stanton and Susan B. Anthony in 1869 founded the organization called National Women Suffrage Association, the same year the Wyoming Territory gave women the right to vote. Soon after, a few states followed by giving women the right to vote, limited to local elections only.

Most students of American history are aware of the tremendous influx of immigrants to America during the 19th century. It is also a known fact that the majority settled in the ethnic neighborhoods and communities of the large cities, close to friends, relatives, and the work they were able to find. After the U.S. Congress passed the 1862 Homestead Act after the Civil War ended, the West began to open up for settlement. One interesting fact that some are not aware of is that more than half of the hardy pioneers who went to homestead and farm western lands were European immigrants: Swedes, Norwegians, Czechs, Germans, Danes, Finns, and Russians.

Governmental reform began with the passage of the Civil Service Act, also known as the Pendleton Act. It provided for the Civil Service Commission, a federal agency responsible for giving jobs based on merit rather than as political rewards or favors. Another successful reform was the adoption of the secret ballot in voting, as were such measures as the direct primary, referendum, recall, and direct election of U.S. Senators by the people rather than by their state legislatures. Following the success of reforms made at the national level, the progressives were successful in gaining reforms in government at state and local levels.

After 1890, more and more attention was called to needs and problems through the efforts of social workers and clergy and the writings of people such as Lincoln Steffans, Ida M. Tarbell, and Upton Sinclair.

By far, the nation's immigrants were an important reason for America's phenomenal industrial growth from 1865 to 1900. They came seeking work and better opportunities for themselves and their families than what life in their native country could give them. What they found in America was suspicion and distrust because they were competitors with Americans for jobs, housing, and decent wages. Their languages, customs, and ways of living were different, especially between the different national and ethnic groups. Until the early 1880s, most immigrants were from the parts of northwestern Europe such as Germany, Scandinavia, the Netherlands, Ireland, and Great Britain.

After 1890, the new arrivals increasingly came from eastern and southern Europe. Chinese immigrants on the Pacific coast, so crucial to the construction of the western part of the first transcontinental railroad, were the first to experience this increasing distrust which eventually erupted into violence and bloodshed. From about 1879 to the present time, the U.S. Congress made, repealed, and amended numerous pieces of legislation concerning quotas, restrictions, and other requirements pertaining to immigrants. The immigrant laborers, both skilled and unskilled, were the foundation of the modern labor union movement as a means of gaining recognition, support, respect, rights, fair wages, and better working conditions.

The historical record of African-Americans is known to all. Sold into slavery by rival tribes, they were brought against their will to the West Indies and southern America to slave on the plantations in a life-long condition of servitude and bondage. The 13th Constitutional Amendment abolished slavery; the 14th gave them U.S. citizenship; and the 15th gave them the right to vote. Efforts of well-known African-Americans resulted in some improvements although the struggle was continuous without let-up. Many were outspoken and urged and led protests against the continued onslaught of discrimination and inequality.

The leading black spokesman from 1890 to 1915 was educator Booker T. Washington. He recognized the need of vocational education for African-Americans, educating them for skills and training for such areas as domestic service, farming, the skilled trades, and small business enterprises. He founded and built in Alabama the famous Tuskegee Institute.

W.E.B. DuBois, another outstanding African-American leader and spokesman, believed that only continuous and vigorous protests against injustices and inequalities coupled with appeals to black pride would effect changes. The results of his efforts was the formation of the Urban League and the NAACP (the National Association for the Advancement of Colored People) which today continue to eliminate discriminations and secure equality and equal rights. Others who made significant contributions were Dr. George Washington Carver's work improving agricultural techniques for both black and white farmers; the writers William Wells Brown, Paul L. Dunbar, Langston Hughes, and Charles W. Chesnutt; the music of Duke Ellington, W.C. Handy, Marion Anderson, Louis Armstrong, Leontyne Price, Jessye Norman, Ella Fitzgerald, and many, many others.

Students of American history are greatly familiar with the accomplishments and contributions of American women. Previous mention has been made of the accomplishments of such 19th century women as: writer Louisa Mae Alcott; abolitionist Harriet Beecher Stowe; women's rights activists Elizabeth Cady Stanton and Lucretia Mott; physician Dr. Elizabeth Blackwell; women's education activists Mary Lyon, Catharine Esther Beecher, and Emma Hart Willard; prison and asylum reform activist Dorothea Dix; social reformer, humanitarian, pursuer of peace Jane Addams; aviatrix Amelia Earhart; women's suffrage activists Susan B. Anthony, Carrie Chapman Catt, and Anna Howard Shaw; Supreme Court Associate Justices Sandra Day O'Connor and Ruth Bader Ginsberg; and many, many more who have made tremendous contributions in science, politics and government, music and the arts (such as Jane Alexander who is National Chairperson of the National Endowment for the Arts), education, athletics, law, etc.

Presidents Theodore Roosevelt, William Howard Taft, and Woodrow Wilson supported many of the reform laws after 1890 and in 1884, President Grover Cleveland did much to see that the Civil Service Act was enforced. After 1880, a number of political or "third" parties were formed and although unsuccessful in getting their Presidential candidates elected, significant reform legislation, including Constitutional amendments, were passed by Congress and became law due to their efforts.

Such legislative acts included the Sherman Antitrust Act of 1890, the Clayton Antitrust Act of 1914, the Underwood Tariff of 1913, and the establishment of the Federal Trade Commission in 1914. By the 1890s and early 1900s, the United States had become a world power and began a leading role in international affairs. War loomed on the horizon again and the stage was set for increased activity in world affairs, which had been avoided since the end of the Civil War.

The Emergence of Modern America (1890-1930)

During the period of 1823 to the 1890s, the major interests and efforts of the American people were concentrated on expansion, settlement, and development of the continental United States. The Civil War 1861-1865, preserved the Union and eliminated the system of slavery. From 1865 onward, the focus was on taming the West and developing industry. During this period, travel and trade between the United States and Europe were continuous. By the 1890s, American interests turned to areas outside the boundaries of the United States. The West was developing into a major industrial area and people in the United States became very interested in selling their factory and farm surplus to overseas markets. In fact, some Americans desired getting and controlling land outside the U.S. boundaries.

Before the 1890s, the U.S. had little, if anything to do with foreign affairs, was not a strong nation militarily, and had inconsequential influence on international political affairs. In fact, the Europeans looked on the American diplomats as inept and bungling in their diplomatic efforts and activities. However, all of this changed and the Spanish-American War of 1898 saw the entry of the United States as a world power.

During the 1890s, Spain controlled such overseas possessions as Puerto Rico, the Philippines, and Cuba. Cubans rebelled against Spanish rule and the U.S. government found itself besieged by demands from Americans to assist the Cubans in their revolt. When the U.S. battleship Maine blew up off the coast of Havana, Cuba, Americans blamed the Spaniards for it and demanded American action against Spain. Two months later, Congress declared war on Spain and the U.S. quickly defeated them. The peace treaty gave the U.S. possession of Puerto Rico, the Philippines, Guam and Hawaii, which was annexed during the war.

This success enlarged and expanded the U.S. role in foreign affairs. Under the administration of Theodore Roosevelt, the U.S. armed forces were built up, greatly increasing its strength. Roosevelt's foreign policy was summed up in the slogan of "Speak softly and carry a big stick," backing up the efforts in diplomacy with a strong military. During the years before the outbreak of World War I, evidence of U.S. emergence as a world power could be seen in a number of actions. Using the Monroe Doctrine of non-involvement of Europe in the affairs of the Western Hemisphere, President Roosevelt forced Italy, Germany, and Great Britain to remove their blockade of Venezuela. He gained the rights to construct the Panama Canal by threatening force and assumed the finances of the Dominican Republic to stabilize it and prevent any intervention by Europeans. In 1916, under President Woodrow Wilson U.S. troops were sent to the Dominican Republic to keep order.

In Europe, war broke out in 1914, eventually involving nearly 30 nations, and ended in 1918. One of the major causes of the war was the tremendous surge of nationalism during the 1800s and early 1900s. People of the same nationality or ethnic group sharing a common history, language or culture began uniting or demanding the right of unification, especially in the empires of Eastern Europe, such as Russian Ottoman and Austrian-Hungarian Empires. Getting stronger and more intense were the beliefs of these peoples in loyalty to common political, social, and economic goals considered to be before any loyalty to the controlling nation or empire.

Emotions ran high and minor disputes magnified into major ones and sometimes quickly led to threats of war. Especially sensitive to these conditions was the area of the states on the Balkan Peninsula. Along with the imperialistic colonization for industrial raw materials, military build-up (especially by Germany), and diplomatic and military alliances, the conditions for one tiny spark to set off the explosion were in place. In July 1914, a Serbian national assassinated the Austrian heir to the throne and his wife and war began a few weeks later. There were a few attempts to keep war from starting, but these efforts were futile.

World War I saw the introduction of such warfare as use of tanks, airplanes, machine guns, submarines, poison gas, and flame throwers. Fighting on the Western front was characterized by a series of trenches that were used throughout the war until 1918. U.S. involvement in the war did not occur until 1916. When it began in 1914, President Woodrow Wilson declared that the U.S. was neutral and most Americans were opposed to any involvement anyway. In 1916, Wilson was reelected to a second term based on the slogan proclaiming his efforts at keeping America out of the war. For a few months after, he put forth most of his efforts to stopping the war but German submarines began unlimited warfare against American merchant shipping.

At the same time, Great Britain intercepted and decoded a secret message from Germany to Mexico urging Mexico to go to war against the U.S. The publishing of this information along with continued German destruction of American ships resulted in the eventual entry of the U.S. into the conflict, the first time the country prepared to fight in a conflict not on American soil. Though unprepared for war, governmental efforts and activities resulted in massive defense mobilization with America's economy directed to the war effort. Though America made important contributions of war materials, its greatest contribution to the war was manpower, soldiers desperately needed by the Allies.

Some ten months before the war ended, President Wilson had proposed a program called the Fourteen Points as a method of bringing the war to an end with an equitable peace settlement. In these Points he had five points setting out general ideals; there were eight pertaining to immediately working to resolve territorial and political problems; and the fourteenth point counseled establishing an organization of nations to help keep world peace.

When Germany agreed in 1918 to an armistice, it assumed that the peace settlement would be drawn up on the basis of these Fourteen Points. However, the peace conference in Paris ignored these points and Wilson had to be content with efforts at establishing the League of Nations. Italy, France, and Great Britain, having suffered and sacrificed far more in the war than America, wanted retribution. The treaties punished severely the Central Powers, taking away arms and territories and requiring payment of reparations. Germany was punished more than the others and, according to one clause in the treaty, was forced to assume the responsibility for causing the war.

Pre-war empires lost tremendous amounts of territories as well as the wealth of natural resources in them. New, independent nations were formed and some predominately ethnic areas came under control of nations of different cultural backgrounds. Some national boundary changes overlapped and created tensions and hard feelings as well as political and economic confusion. The wishes and desires of every national or cultural group could not possibly be realized and satisfied, resulting in disappointments for both; those who were victorious and those who were defeated. Germany received harsher terms than expected from the treaty which weakened its post-war government. Along with the worldwide depression of the 1930s, the stage was set for the rise of Adolf Hitler and his Nationalist Socialist Party and World War II.

President Wilson lost in his efforts to get the U.S. Senate to approve the peace treaty. The Senate at the time was a reflection of American public opinion and its rejection of the treaty was a rejection of Wilson. The approval of the treaty would have made the U.S. a member of the League of Nations but Americans had just come off a bloody war to ensure that democracy would exist throughout the world. Americans just did not want to accept any responsibility that resulted from its new position of power and were afraid that membership in the League of Nations would embroil the U.S. in future disputes in Europe.

The end of World War I and the decade of the 1920s saw tremendous changes in the United States, signifying the beginning of its development into its modern society today. The shift from farm to city life was occurring in tremendous numbers. Social changes and problems were occurring at such a fast pace that it was extremely difficult and perplexing for many Americans to adjust to them. Politically the 18th Amendment to the Constitution, the so-called Prohibition Amendment, prohibited selling alcoholic beverages throughout the U.S. resulting in problems affecting all aspects of society. The passage of the 19th Amendment gave to women the right to vote in all elections. The decade of the 1920s also showed a marked change in roles and opportunities for women with more and more of them seeking and finding careers outside the home. They began to think of themselves as the equal of men and not as much as housewives and mothers.

The influence of the automobile, the entertainment industry, and the rejection of the morals and values of pre-World War I life, resulted in the fast-paced "Roaring Twenties". There were significant effects on events leading to the depression-era 1930s and another world war. Many Americans greatly desired the pre-war life and supported political policies and candidates in favor of the return to what was considered normal. It was desired to end government's strong role and adopt a policy of isolating the country from world affairs, a result of the war.

Prohibition of the sale of alcohol had caused the increased activities of bootlegging and the rise of underworld gangs and the illegal speakeasies, the jazz music and dances they promoted. The customers of these clubs were considered "modern," reflected by extremes in clothing, hairstyles, and attitudes towards authority and life. Movies and, to a certain degree, other types of entertainment, along with increased interest in sports figures and the accomplishments of national heroes, such as Lindbergh, influenced Americans to admire, emulate, and support individual accomplishments.

As wild and uninhibited modern behavior became, this decade witnessed an increase in a religious tradition known as "revivalism," emotional preaching. Although law and order were demanded by many Americans, the administration of President Warren G. Harding was marked by widespread corruption and scandal, not unlike the administration of Ulysses S. Grant, except Grant was honest and innocent. The decade of the 20s also saw the resurgence of such racist organizations as the Ku Klux Klan.

The U.S. economy experienced a tremendous period of boom. Restrictions on business because of war no longer existed and the conservatives in control adopted policies that helped and encouraged big business. To keep foreign goods from competing with American goods, tariffs were raised to the highest level. New products were developed by American manufacturers and many different items became readily available to the people. These included refrigerators, radios, washing machines, and, most importantly, the automobile.

Americans in the 1920s heavily invested in corporation stocks, providing companies a large amount of capital for expanding their businesses. The more money investors put into the stock market, the more the value of the stocks increased. This, in turn, led to widespread speculation that increased stock value to a point beyond the level that was justified by earnings and dividends.

Much of the stock speculation involved paying a small part of the cost and borrowing the rest. This led eventually to the stock market crash of 1929, financial ruin for many investors, a weakening of the nation's economy, and the Great Depression of the 1930s. The depression hit the United States tremendously hard resulting in bank failures, loss of jobs due to cutbacks in production and a lack of money leading to a sharp decline in spending. This in turn affected businesses, factories, and stores and higher unemployment. Farm products were not affordable so the farmers suffered even more. Foreign trade sharply decreased and in the early 1930s, the U.S. economy was effectively paralyzed. Europe was affected even more so.

The war had seriously damaged the economies of the European countries, both the victors and the defeated, leaving them deeply in debt. There was difficulty on both sides paying off war debts and loans. It was difficult to find jobs and some countries like Japan and Italy found themselves without enough resources and more than enough people. Solving these problems by expanding the territory merely set up conditions for war later. Germany suffered horribly with runaway inflation ruining the value of its money and wiping out the savings of millions. Despite the U.S. loans to Germany which helped the government to restore some order and which provided a short existence of some economic stability in Europe, the Great Depression only served to undo any good that had been done. Mass unemployment, poverty, and despair greatly weakened the democratic governments that had been formed and greatly strengthened the increasing power and influence of extreme political movements such as communism, fascism, and national socialism. These movements promised to put an end to the economic problems.

The extreme form of patriotism called nationalism that had been the chief cause of World War I grew even stronger after the war ended in 1918. The political, social, and economic unrest fueled nationalism and it became an effective tool enabling dictators to gain and maintain power from the 1930s to the end of World War II in 1945. In the Soviet Union, Joseph Stalin succeeded in gaining political control and establishing a strong harsh dictatorship. Benito Mussolini and the Fascist party, promising prosperity and order in Italy, gained national support, and set up a strong government. In Japan, although the ruler was considered Emperor Hirohito, actual control and administration of government came under military officers. In Germany, the results of war, harsh treaty terms, loss of territory, great economic chaos and collapse all enabled Adolf Hitler and his Nazi party to gain complete power and control.

Germany, Italy, and Japan initiated a policy of aggressive territorial expansion with Japan being the first to conquer. In 1931, the Japanese forces seized control of Manchuria, a part of China containing rich natural resources, and in 1937 began an attack on China, occupying most of its eastern part by 1938. Italy invaded Ethiopia in Africa in 1935, having it totally under its control by 1936. The Soviet Union did not invade or take over any territory. Like Italy and Germany, the Soviet Union actively participated in the Spanish Civil War, using it as a proving ground to test tactics and weapons setting the stage for World War II.

In Germany, almost immediately after taking power, in direct violation of the World War I peace treaty, Hitler began the buildup of the armed forces. He sent troops into the Rhineland in 1936, invaded Austria in 1938 and united it with Germany, seized control of the Sudetenland in 1938 (part of western Czechoslovakia and containing mostly Germans) and the rest of Czechoslovakia in March 1939. On September 1, 1939, World War II began in Europe by invading Poland. In 1940, Germany invaded and controlled Norway, Denmark, Belgium, Luxembourg, the Netherlands, and France.

After the war began in Europe, U.S. President Franklin D. Roosevelt announced that the United States was neutral. Most Americans, although hoping for an Allied victory, wanted the U.S. to stay out of the war. President Roosevelt and his supporters, called "interventionists," favored all aid except war to the Allied nations fighting Axis aggression. They were fearful that an Axis victory would seriously threaten and endanger all democracies. On the other hand, the "isolationists" were against any U.S. aid being given to the warring nations, accusing President Roosevelt of leading the U.S. into a war very much unprepared to fight. Roosevelt's plan was to defeat the Axis nations by sending the Allied nations the equipment needed to fight; ships, aircraft, tanks, and other war materials.

In Asia, the U.S. had opposed Japan's invasion of Southeast Asia, an effort to gain Japanese control of that region's rich resources. Consequently, the U.S. stopped all important exports to Japan, whose industries depended heavily on petroleum, scrap metal, and other raw materials. Later Roosevelt refused the Japanese withdrawal of its funds from American banks. General Tojo became the Japanese premier in October 1941 and quickly realized that the U.S. Navy was powerful enough to block Japanese expansion into Asia. Deciding to cripple the Pacific Fleet, the Japanese aircraft, without warning, bombed the Fleet December 7, 1941, while at anchor in Pearl Harbor in Hawaii. Temporarily it was a success. It destroyed many aircraft and disabled much of the U.S. Pacific Fleet. In the end, it was a costly mistake as it quickly motivated the Americans to prepare for and wage war.

Military strategy in the European theater of war as developed by Roosevelt, Churchill, and Stalin was to concentrate on Germany's defeat first, then Japan's. The start was made in North Africa, pushing Germans and Italians off the continent, beginning in the summer of 1942 and ending successfully in May, 1943. Before the war, Hitler and Stalin had signed a non-aggression pact in 1939, which Hitler violated in 1941 by invading the Soviet Union. The German defeat at Stalingrad, marked a turning point in the war, was brought about by a combination of entrapment by Soviet troops and death of German troops by starvation and freezing due to the horrendous winter conditions. All this occurred at the same time the Allies were driving them out of North Africa.

The liberation of Italy began in July 1943 and ended May 2, 1945. The third part of the strategy was D-Day, June 6, 1944, with the Allied invasion of France at Normandy. At the same time, starting in January 1943, the Soviets began pushing the German troops back into Europe and they were greatly assisted by supplies from Britain and the United States. By April 1945, Allies occupied positions beyond the Rhine and the Soviets moved on to Berlin, surrounding it by April 25. Germany surrendered May 7 and the war in Europe was finally over.

Meanwhile, in the Pacific, in the six months after the attack on Pearl Harbor, Japanese forces moved across Southeast Asia and the western Pacific Ocean. By August 1942, the Japanese Empire was at its largest size and stretched northeast to Alaska's Aleutian Islands, west to Burma, south to what is now Indonesia. Invaded and controlled areas included Hong Kong, Guam, Wake Island, Thailand, part of Malaysia, Singapore, the Philippines, and bombed Darwin on the north coast of Australia.

The raid of General Doolittle's bombers on Japanese cities and the American naval victory at Midway along with the fighting in the Battle of the Coral Sea helped turn the tide against Japan. Island-hopping by U.S. Seabees and Marines and the grueling bloody battles fought resulted in gradually pushing the Japanese back towards Japan.

After victory was attained in Europe, concentrated efforts were made to secure Japan's surrender, but it took dropping two atomic bombs on the cities of Hiroshima and Nagasaki to finally end the war in the Pacific. Japan formally surrendered on September 2, 1945, aboard the U.S. battleship Missouri, anchored in Tokyo Bay. The war was finally ended.

Before war in Europe had ended, the Allies had agreed on a military occupation of Germany. It was divided into four zones each one occupied by Great Britain, France, the Soviet Union, and the United States with the four powers jointly administering Berlin. After the war, the Allies agreed that Germany's armed forces would be abolished, the Nazi Party outlawed, and the territory east of the Oder and Neisse Rivers taken away. Nazi leaders were accused of war crimes and brought to trial. After Japan's defeat, the Allies began a military occupation directed by American General Douglas MacArthur, who introduced a number of reforms eventually ridding Japan of its military institutions transforming it into a democracy. A constitution was drawn up in 1947 transferring all political rights from the emperor to the people, granting women the right to vote, and denying Japan the right to declare war. War crimes trials of 25 war leaders and government officials were also conducted. The U.S. did not sign a peace treaty until 1951. The treaty permitted Japan to rearm but took away its overseas empire.

Again, after a major world war came efforts to prevent war from occurring again throughout the world. Preliminary work began in 1943 when the U.S., Great Britain, the Soviet Union, and China sent representatives to Moscow where they agreed to set up an international organization that would work to promote peace around the earth. In 1944, the four Allied powers met again and made the decision to name the organization the United Nations. In 1945, a charter for the U. N. was drawn up and signed, taking effect in October of that year.

Major consequences of the war included horrendous death and destruction, millions of displaced persons, the gaining of strength and spread of Communism and Cold War tensions as a result of the beginning of the nuclear age. World War II ended more lives and caused more devastation than any other war.

Besides the losses of millions of military personnel, the devastation and destruction directly affected civilians, reducing cities, houses, and factories to ruin and rubble and totally wrecking communication and transportation systems. Millions of civilian deaths, especially in China and the Soviet Union, were the results of famine.

More than 12 million people were uprooted by war's end having no place to live. Those included were prisoners of war, those that survived Nazi concentration camps and slave labor camps, orphans, and people who escaped war-torn areas and invading armies. Changing national boundary lines also caused the mass movement of displaced persons.

Germany and Japan were completely defeated; Great Britain and France were seriously weakened; and the Soviet Union and the United States became the world's leading powers. Although allied during the war, the alliance fell apart as the Soviets pushed Communism in Europe and Asia. In spite of the tremendous destruction it suffered, the Soviet Union was stronger than ever. During the war, it took control of Lithuania, Estonia, and Latvia and by mid-1945 parts of Poland, Czechoslovakia, Finland, and Romania. It helped Communist governments gain power in Bulgaria, Romania, Hungary, Czechoslovakia, Poland, and North Korea. China fell to Mao Zedong's Communist forces in 1949. Until the fall of the Berlin Wall in 1989 and the dissolution of Communist governments in Eastern Europe and the Soviet Union, the United States and the Soviet Union faced off in what was called a Cold War. The possibility of the terrifying destruction by nuclear weapons loomed over both nations.

Postwar United States (1945-1970)

The major thrust of U.S. foreign policy from the end of World War II to 1990 was the post-war struggle between non-Communist nations, led by the United States, and the Soviet Union and the Communist nations who were its allies. It was referred to as a "Cold War" because its conflicts did not lead to a major war of fighting, or a "hot war." Both the Soviet Union and the United States embarked on an arsenal buildup of atomic and hydrogen bombs as well as other nuclear weapons. Both nations had the capability of destroying each other but because of the continuous threat of nuclear war and accidents, extreme caution was practiced on both sides. The efforts of both sides to serve and protect their political philosophies and to support and assist their allies resulted in a number of events during this 45-year period.

In 1946, Josef Stalin stated publicly that the presence of capitalism and its development of the world's economy made international peace impossible. This resulted in an American diplomat in Moscow named George F. Kennan to propose in response to Stalin, a statement of U.S. foreign policy. The idea and goal of the U.S. was to contain or limit the extension or expansion of Soviet Communist policies and activities. After Soviet efforts to make trouble in Iran, Greece, and Turkey, U.S. President Harry Truman stated what is known as the Truman Doctrine which committed the U.S. to a policy of intervention in order to contain or stop the spread of communism throughout the world.

After 1945, social and economic chaos continued in Western Europe, especially in Germany. Secretary of State George C. Marshall came to realize that the U.S. had greatly serious problems and to assist in the recovery, he proposed a program known as the European Recovery Program or the Marshall Plan. Although the Soviet Union withdrew from any participation, the U.S. continued the work of assisting Europe in regaining economic stability. In Germany, the situation was critical with the American Army shouldering the staggering burden of relieving the serious problems of the German economy. In February 1948, Britain and the U.S. combined their two zones, with France joining in June.

The Soviets were opposed to German unification and in April 1948 took serious action to either stop it or to force the Allies to give up control of West Berlin to the Soviets. The Soviets blocked all road traffic access to West Berlin from West Germany. To avoid any armed conflict, it was decided to airlift into West Berlin the needed food and supplies. From June 1948 to mid-May 1949 Allied air forces flew in all that was needed for the West Berliners, forcing the Soviets to lift the blockade and permit vehicular traffic access to the city.

The first "hot war" in the post-World War II era was the Korean War, begun June 25, 1950 and ending July 27, 1953. Troops from Communist North Korea invaded democratic South Korea in an effort to unite both sections under Communist control. The United Nations organization asked its member nations to furnish troops to help restore peace. Many nations responded and President Truman sent American troops to help the South Koreans. The war dragged on for three years and ended with a truce, not a peace treaty. Like Germany then, Korea remained divided and does so to this day.

In 1954, the French were forced to give up their colonial claims in Indochina, the present-day countries of Vietnam, Laos, and Cambodia. Afterwards, the Communist northern part of Vietnam began battling with the democratic southern part over control of the entire country. In the late 1950s and early 1960s, U.S. Presidents Eisenhower and Kennedy sent to Vietnam a number of military advisers and military aid to assist and support South Vietnam's non-Communist government. During Lyndon Johnson's presidency, the war escalated with thousands of American troops being sent to participate in combat with the South Vietnamese. The war was extremely unpopular in America and caused such serious divisiveness among its citizens that Johnson decided not to seek reelection in 1968. It was in President Richard Nixon's second term in office that the U.S. signed an agreement ending war in Vietnam and restoring peace. This was done January 27, 1973, and by March 29, the last American combat troops and American prisoners of war left Vietnam for home. It was the longest war in U.S. history and to this day carries the perception that it was a "lost war."

In 1962, during the administration of President John F. Kennedy, Premier Khrushchev and the Soviets decided, as a protective measure for Cuba against an American invasion, to install nuclear missiles on the island. In October, American U-2 spy planes photographed over Cuba what were identified as missile bases under construction. The decision in the White House was how to handle the situation without starting a war. The only recourse was removal of the missile sites and preventing more being set up. Kennedy announced that the U.S. had set up a "quarantine" of Soviet ships heading to Cuba. It was in reality a blockade but the word itself could not be used publicly as a blockade was actually considered an act of war.

A week of incredible tension and anxiety gripped the entire world until Khrushchev capitulated. Soviet ships carrying missiles for the Cuban bases turned back and the crisis eased. What precipitated the crisis was Khrushchev's underestimation of Kennedy. The President made no effort to prevent the erection of the Berlin Wall and was reluctant to commit American troops to invade Cuba and overthrow Fidel Castro. The Soviets assumed this was a weakness and decided they could install the missiles without any interference.

The Soviets were concerned about American missiles installed in Turkey aimed at the Soviet Union and about a possible invasion of Cuba. If successful, Khrushchev would demonstrate to the Russian and Chinese critics of his policy of peaceful coexistence that he was tough and not to be intimidated. At the same time, the Americans feared that if Russian missiles were put in place and launched from Cuba to the U.S., the short distance of 90 miles would not allow enough time for adequate warning. Furthermore, it would originate from a direction that radar systems could not detect. It was felt that if America gave in and allowed a Soviet presence practically at the back door that the effect on American security and morale would be devastating.

As tensions eased in the aftermath of the crisis, several agreements were made. The missiles in Turkey were removed, as they were obsolete. A telephone "hot line" was set up between Moscow and Washington to make it possible for the two heads of government to have instant contact with each other. The U.S. agreed to sell its surplus wheat to the Soviets.

During the late 1800s and early 1900s, many Americans were concerned about and began actively campaigning for significant changes and reforms in the social, economic, and political systems in the country. Among their goals was ridding government corruption, regulating big businesses, reducing poverty, improving the lives of the poor and their living conditions, and ensuring more government response to the needs of the people.

Early efforts at reform began with movements to organize farmers and laborers, the push to give women the right to vote, and the successful passage of Congressional legislation establishing merit as the basis for federal jobs rather than political favoritism. Other efforts were directed towards improvements in education, living conditions in city slums, breaking up trusts, and monopolies in big businesses.

After World War I ended, the 18th Amendment to the U.S. Constitution was passed, forbidding the sale of alcoholic beverages. The wild financial speculations came to an abrupt end with the stock market crash of October 1929, plunging the U.S. into the Great Depression. The election of Franklin Roosevelt to the office of President in 1932 was the start of the social and economic recovery and reform legislative acts designed to gradually ease the country back to more prosperity. These acts included relief for the nation's farmers, regulation of banks, public works providing jobs for the unemployed, and giving aid to manufacturers. Some of the agencies set up to implement these measures included the Works Progress Administration (WPA), Civilian Conservation Camps (CCC), the Farm Credit Administration (FCA), and the Social Security Board. These last two agencies gave credit to farmers and set up the nation's social security system.

After World War II and the Korean War, efforts began to relieve the problems of millions of African-Americans, including ending discrimination in education, housing, and jobs and the grinding widespread poverty. The efforts of civil rights leaders found success in a number of Supreme Court decisions, the best-known case, "Brown vs Board of Education of Topeka (1954)" ending compulsory segregation in public schools. In the 1960s, the civil rights movement under the leadership of Dr. Martin Luther King, Jr. really gained momentum. Under President Lyndon B. Johnson the Civil Rights Acts of 1964 and 1968 prohibited discrimination in housing sales and rentals, employment, public accommodations, and voter registration.

Poverty remained a serious problem in the central sections of large cities resulting in riots and soaring crime rates, which ultimately found its way to the suburbs. The escalation of the war in Vietnam and the social conflict and upheaval of support versus opposition to U.S. involvement, led to antiwar demonstrations. The escalation of drug abuse, weakening of the family unit, homelessness, poverty, mental illness, along with increasing social, mental, and physical problems experienced by the Vietnam veterans returning to families, marriages, contributed to a country divided and torn apart.

Contemporary United States (1968 – present)

Probably the highlight of the foreign policy of President Richard Nixon, after the end of the Vietnam War and withdrawal of troops, was his 1972 trip to China. When the Communists gained control of China in 1949, the policy of the U.S. government was refusal to recognize the Communist government. It regarded as the legitimate government of China to be that of Chiang Kai-shek, exiled on the island of Taiwan. In 1971, Nixon sent Henry Kissinger on a secret trip to Peking to investigate whether or not it would be possible for America to give recognition to China. In February 1972, President and Mrs. Nixon spent a number of days in the country visiting well-known Chinese landmarks, dining with the two leaders, Mao Tse-tung and Chou En-lai. Agreements were made for cultural and scientific exchanges, eventual resumption of trade, and future unification of the mainland with Taiwan. In 1979, formal diplomatic recognition was achieved. With this one visit, the pattern of the Cold War was essentially shifted.

Under the administration of President Jimmy Carter, Egyptian President Anwar el-Sadat and Israeli Prime Minister Menachem Begin met at presidential retreat Camp David and agreed, after a series of meetings, to sign a formal treaty of peace between the two countries. In 1979, the Soviet invasion of Afghanistan was perceived by Carter and his advisers as a threat to the rich oil fields in the Persian Gulf but at the time U.S. military capability to prevent further Soviet aggression in the Middle East was weak. The last year of Carter's presidential term was taken up with the 53 American hostages held in Iran. The shah had been deposed and control of the government and the country was in the hands of Muslim leader, Ayatollah Ruhollah Khomeini.

Khomeini's extreme hatred for the U.S. was the result of the 1953 overthrow of Iran's Mossadegh government, sponsored by the CIA. To make matters worse, the CIA proceeded to train the shah's ruthless secret police force. So when the terminally ill exiled shah was allowed into the U.S. for medical treatment, a fanatical mob stormed into the American embassy taking the 53 Americans as prisoners, supported and encouraged by Khomeini.

President Carter froze all Iranian assets in the U.S., set up trade restrictions, and approved a risky rescue attempt, which failed. He had appealed to the UN for aid in gaining release for the hostages and to European allies to join the trade embargo on Iran. Khomeini ignored UN requests for releasing the Americans and Europeans refused to support the embargo so as not to risk losing access to Iran's oil. American prestige was damaged and Carter's chances for reelection were doomed. The hostages were released on the day of Ronald Reagan's inauguration as President when Carter released Iranian assets as ransom.

The foreign policy of President Ronald Reagan was, in his first term, focused primarily on the Western Hemisphere, particularly in Central America and the West Indies. U.S. involvement in the domestic revolutions of El Salvador and Nicaragua continued into Reagan's second term when Congress held televised hearings on what came to be known as the Iran-Contra Affair. A cover-up was exposed showing that profits from secretly selling military hardware to Iran had been used to give support to rebels, called Contras, who were fighting in Nicaragua. In 1983 in Lebanon, 241 American Marines were killed when an Islamic suicide bomber drove an explosive-laden truck into U.S. Marines headquarters located at the airport in Beirut. This tragic event came as part of the unrest and violence between the Israelis and the Palestinian Liberation Organization (PLO) forces in southern Lebanon.

In the same month, 1,900 U.S. Marines landed on the island of Grenada to rescue a small group of American medical students at the medical school and depose the leftist government. Perhaps the most intriguing and far-reaching event towards the end of Reagan's second term was the arms-reduction agreement Reagan reached with Soviet General Secretary Mikhail Gorbachev. Gorbachev began easing East-West tensions by stressing the importance of cooperation with the West and easing the harsh and restrictive life of the people in the Soviet Union. In retrospect, it was clearly a prelude to the events occurring during the administration of President George Bush.

After Bush took office, it appeared for a brief period that democracy would gain a hold and influence in China but the brief movement was quickly and decisively crushed. The biggest surprise was the fall of the Berlin Wall resulting in the unification of all of Germany. The loss of the Communists' power in other Eastern European countries, and the fall of Communism in the Soviet Union and the breakup of its republics into independent nations were no less surprising. The countries of Poland, Hungary, Romania, Czechoslovakia, Albania, and Bulgaria replaced Communist rule for a democratic one.

The former Yugoslavia broke apart into individual ethnic enclaves with the republics of Serbia, Croatia, and Bosnia-Herzegovina embarking on wars of ethnic cleansing between Catholics, Orthodox, and Muslims. In Russia, as in the other former republics and satellites, democratic governments were put into operation and the difficult task of changing communist economies into ones of capitalistic free enterprise began. For all practical purposes, it appeared that the tensions and dangers of the post-World War II "Cold War" between the U.S. and Soviet-led Communism were over.

President Bush, in December of 1989, sent U.S. troops to invade Panama and arrest the Panamanian dictator Manuel Noriega. Although he had periodically assisted CIA operations with intelligence information, at the same time, Noriega laundered money from drug smuggling and gunrunning through Panama's banks. Though ignored for a short time, it became too embarrassing for the American intelligence community. When a political associate tried unsuccessfully to depose him and an off-duty U.S. Marine was shot and killed at a roadblock, Bush acted. Noriega was brought to the U.S. where he stood trial on charges of drug distribution and racketeering.

During the time of the American hostage crisis, Iraq and Iran fought a war in which the U.S. and most of Iraq's neighbors supported Iraq. In a five-year period, Saddam Hussein received from the U.S. $500 million worth of American technology, including lasers, advanced computers, and special machine tools used in missile development. The Iraq-Iran war was a bloody one resulting in a stalemate with a UN truce. Neighboring Kuwait, in direct opposition to OPEC agreements, increased oil production.

This caused oil prices to drop, which upset Hussein, who was deeply in debt from the war and totally dependent on oil revenues. After a short period, Saddam invaded and occupied Kuwait. The U.S. made extensive plans to put into operation strategy to successfully carry out Operation Desert Storm, the liberation of Kuwait. In four days, February 24-28, 1991, the war was over and Iraq had been defeated, its troops driven back into their country. Saddam remained in power although Iraq's economy was seriously damaged.

President Bill Clinton sent U.S. troops to Haiti to protect the efforts of Jean-Bertrand Aristide to gain democratic power and to Bosnia to assist UN peacekeeping forces. He also inherited from the Bush administration the problem of Somalia in East Africa, where U.S. troops had been sent in December 1992 to support UN efforts to end the starvation of the Somalis and restore peace. The efforts were successful at first, but eventually failed due to the severity of the intricate political problems within the country. After U.S. soldiers were killed in an ambush along with 300 Somalis, American troops were withdrawn and returned home.

The Watergate scandal resulting in the first-ever resignation of a sitting American president was the most crucial domestic crisis of the 1970s. The population of the U.S. had greatly increased and along with it the nation's industries and the resulting harmful pollution of the environment. Factory smoke, automobile exhaust, waste from factories and other sources all combined to create hazardous air, water, and ground pollution which, if not brought under control and significantly diminished, would severely endanger all life on earth. The 1980s was the decade of the horrible Exxon Valdez oil spill off the Alaskan coast and the nuclear accident and melt-down at the Ukrainian nuclear power plant at Chernobyl. The U.S. had a narrow escape with the near disaster at Three Mile Island Nuclear Plant in Pennsylvania.

Inflation increased in the late 1960s, and the 1970s witnessed a period of high unemployment, the result of a severe recession. The decision of the OPEC (Organization of Petroleum Exporting Countries) ministers to cut back on oil production thus raising the price of a barrel of oil created a fuel shortage. This made it clear that energy and fuel conservation was necessary in the American economy, especially since fuel shortages created two energy crises during the decade of the 1970s. Americans experienced shortages of fuel oil for heating and gasoline for cars and other vehicles.

The 1980s saw the difficulties of rising inflation, recession, recovery, and the insecurity of long-term employment. Foreign competition and imports, the use of robots and other advanced technology in industries, the opening and operation of American companies and factories in other countries to lower labor costs all contributed to the economic and employment problems.

The nation's farmers experienced economic hardships and October 1987 saw another one-day significant drop in the Dow Jones on the New York Stock Exchange. January 28, 1986 was the day of the loss of the seven crew members of the NASA space shuttle "Challenger". The reliability and soundness of numerous savings and loans institutions were in serious jeopardy when hundreds of these failed and others went into bankruptcy due to customer default on loans and mismanagement. Congressional legislation helped rebuild the industry.

Skill 1.3   Demonstrate an understanding of the chronology, narratives, perspectives, and interpretations of major eras in world history up to 1500.

The Beginnings of Human Society, Early Civilizations and the Emergence of Pastoral Peoples (4000-1000 BCE)

Prehistory is defined as the period of man's achievements before the development of writing.   In the Stone Age cultures, there were three different periods. They are the Lower Paleolithic Period with the use of crude tools. The Upper Paleolithic Period exhibiting a greater variety of better-made tools and implements, the wearing of clothing, highly organized group life, and skills in art. And finally the Neolithic Period which showed domesticated animals, food production, the arts of knitting, spinning and weaving cloth, starting fires through friction, building houses rather than living in caves, the development of institutions including the family, religion, and a form of government or the origin of the state.

Ancient civilizations were those cultures which developed to a greater degree and were considered advanced. These included the following eleven with their major accomplishments.

Egypt made numerous significant contributions including construction of the great pyramids; development of hieroglyphic writing; preservation of bodies after death; making paper from papyrus; contributing to developments in arithmetic and geometry; the invention of the method of counting in groups of 1-10 (the decimal system); completion of a solar calendar; and laying the foundation for science and astronomy.

The ancient civilization of the Sumerians invented the wheel; developed irrigation through use of canals, dikes, and devices for raising water; devised the system of cuneiform writing; learned to divide time; and built large boats for trade. The Babylonians devised the famous Code of Hammurabi, a code of laws.

The ancient Assyrians were warlike and aggressive due to a highly organized military and used horse drawn chariots.

The Hebrews, also known as the ancient Israelites instituted "monotheism," which is the worship of one God, Yahweh, and combined the 66 books of the Hebrew and Christian Greek scriptures into the Bible we have today.

The Minoans had a system of writing using symbols to represent syllables in words. They built palaces with multiple levels containing many rooms, water and sewage systems with flush toilets, bathtubs, hot and cold running water, and bright paintings on the walls.

The Mycenaeans changed the Minoan writing system to aid their own language and used symbols to represent syllables.

The Phoenicians were sea traders well known for their manufacturing skills in glass and metals and the development of their famous purple dye. They became so very proficient in the skill of navigation that they were able to sail by the stars at night. Further, they devised an alphabet using symbols to represent single sounds, which was an improved extension of the Egyptian principle and writing system.

In India, the caste system was developed, the principle of zero in mathematics was discovered, and the major religion of Hinduism was begun.

China began building the Great Wall; practiced crop rotation and terrace farming; increased the importance of the silk industry, and developed caravan routes across Central Asia for extensive trade. Also, they increased proficiency in rice cultivation and developed a written language based on drawings or pictographs (no alphabet symbolizing sounds as each word or character had a form different from all others).

The ancient Persians developed an alphabet; contributed the religions/philosophies of Zoroastrianism, Mithraism, and Gnosticism; and allowed conquered peoples to retain their own customs, laws, and religions

Classical Traditions, Major Religions, and Giant Empires (1000 BCE – 300 CE)

The classical civilization of Greece reached the highest levels in human achievements based on the foundations already laid by such ancient groups as the Egyptians, Phoenicians, Minoans, and Mycenaeans.

Among the more important contributions of Greece were the Greek alphabet derived from the Phoenician letters which formed the basis for the Roman alphabet and our present-day alphabet. Extensive trading and colonization resulted in the spread of the Greek civilization. The love of sports, with emphasis on a sound body, led to the tradition of the Olympic games. Greece was responsible for the rise of independent, strong city-states. Note the complete contrast between independent, freedom-loving Athens with its practice of pure democracy i.e. direct, personal, active participation in government by qualified citizens and the rigid, totalitarian, militaristic Sparta. Other important areas that the Greeks are credited with influencing include drama, epic and lyric poetry, fables, myths centered on the many gods and goddesses, science, astronomy, medicine, mathematics, philosophy, art, architecture, and recording historical events. The conquests of Alexander the Great spread Greek ideas to the areas he conquered and brought to the Greek world many ideas from Asia.

SCHOOL OF EDUCATION
CURRICULUM LABORATORY
UM-DEARBORN

Above all, the value of ideas, wisdom, curiosity, and the desire to learn as much about the world as possible.

The ancient civilization of Rome lasted approximately 1,000 years including the periods of republic and empire, although its lasting influence on Europe and its history was for a much longer period. There was a very sharp contrast between the curious, imaginative, inquisitive Greeks and the practical, simple, down-to-earth, no-nonsense Romans, who spread and preserved the ideas of ancient Greece and other culture groups. The contributions and accomplishments of the Romans are numerous but their greatest included language, engineering, building, law, government, roads, trade, and the "Pax Romana". Pax Romana was the long period of peace enabling free travel and trade, spreading people, cultures, goods, and ideas all over a vast area of the known world.

A most interesting and significant characteristic of the Greek, Hellenic, and Roman civilizations was "secularism" where emphasis shifted away from religion to the state. Men were not absorbed in or dominated by religion as had been the case in Egypt and the nations located in Mesopotamia. Religion and its leaders did not dominate the state and its authority was greatly diminished.

In India, Hinduism was a continuing influence along with the rise of Buddhism. Industry and commerce developed along with extensive trading with the Near East. Outstanding advances in the fields of science and medicine were made along with being one of the first to be active in navigation and maritime enterprises during this time.

China is considered by some historians to be the oldest, uninterrupted civilization in the world and was in existence around the same time as the ancient civilizations founded in Egypt, Mesopotamia, and the Indus Valley. The Chinese studied nature and weather; stressed the importance of education, family, and a strong central government; followed the religions of Buddhism, Confucianism, and Taoism; and invented such things as gunpowder, paper, printing, and the magnetic compass.

The civilization in Japan appeared during this time having borrowed much of their culture from China. It was the last of these classical civilizations to develop. Although they used, accepted, and copied Chinese art, law, architecture, dress, and writing, the Japanese refined these into their own unique way of life, including incorporating the religion of Buddhism into their culture.

The civilizations in Africa south of the Sahara were developing the refining and use of iron, especially for farm implements and later for weapons. Trading was overland using camels and at important seaports. The Arab influence was extremely important, as was their later contact with Indians, Christian Nubians, and Persians. In fact, their trading activities were probably the most important factor in the spread of and assimilation of different ideas and stimulation of cultural growth.

Expanding Zones of Exchange and Encounter (300 – 1000 CE)

The official end of the Roman Empire came when Germanic tribes took over and controlled most of Europe. The five major tribes were the Visigoths, Ostrogoths, Vandals, Saxons, and the Franks. In later years, the Franks successfully stopped the invasion of southern Europe by Muslims by defeating them under the leadership of Charles Martel at the Battle of Tours in 732 AD. Thirty-six years later in 768 AD, the grandson of Charles Martel became King of the Franks and is known throughout history as Charlemagne. Charlemagne was a man of war but was unique in his respect for and encouragement of learning. He made great efforts to rule fairly and ensure just treatment for his people.

The Vikings had a lot of influence at this time with spreading their ideas and knowledge of trade routes and sailing, accomplished first through their conquests and later through trade.

Intensified Hemispheric Interactions (1000 – 1500 CE)

The purpose of the Crusades was to rid Jerusalem of Muslim control and these series of violent, bloody conflicts did affect trade and stimulated later explorations seeking the new, exotic products such as silks and spices. The Crusaders came into contact with other religions and cultures and learned and spread many new ideas.

During this time, the system of feudalism became the dominant feature. It was a system of loyalty and protection. The strong protected the weak that returned the service with farm labor, military service, and loyalty. Life was lived out on a vast estate, owned by a nobleman and his family, called a "manor." It was a complete village supporting a few hundred people, mostly peasants. Improved tools and farming methods made life more bearable although most never left the manor or traveled from their village during their lifetime.

Also coming into importance at this time was the era of knighthood and its code of chivalry as well as the tremendous influence of the Church (Roman Catholic). Until the period of the Renaissance, the Church was the only place where people could be educated. The Bible and other books were hand-copied by monks in the monasteries. Cathedrals were built and were decorated with art depicting religious subjects.

With the increase in trade and travel, cities sprang up and began to grow. Craft workers in the cities developed their skills to a high degree, eventually organizing guilds to protect the quality of the work and to regulate the buying and selling of their products. City government developed and flourished centered on strong town councils. Active in city government and the town councils were the wealthy businessmen who made up the rising middle class.

The end of the feudal manorial system was sealed by the outbreak and spread of the infamous Black Death, which killed over one-third of the total population of Europe. Those who survived and were skilled in any job or occupation were in demand and many serfs or peasants found freedom and, for that time, a decidedly improved standard of living. Strong nation-states became powerful and people developed a renewed interest in life and learning.

In other parts of the world were the Byzantine and Saracenic (or Islamic) civilizations, both dominated by religion. The major contributions of the Saracens were in the areas of science and philosophy. Included were accomplishments in astronomy, mathematics, physics, chemistry, medicine, literature, art, trade and manufacturing, agriculture, and a marked influence on the Renaissance period of history.

The Byzantines (Christians) made important contributions in art and the preservation of Greek and Roman achievements including architecture (especially in Eastern Europe and Russia), the Code of Justinian and Roman law.

Skill 1.4   Demonstrate an understanding of the chronology, narratives, perspectives, and interpretations of major eras in world history from 1500 to the present.

The Emergence of the First Global Age (1450 – 1770)

The word "Renaissance" literally means "rebirth", and signaled the rekindling of interest in the glory of ancient classical Greek and Roman civilizations. It was the period in human history marking the start of many ideas and innovations leading to our modern age.

The Renaissance began in Italy with many of its ideas starting in Florence, controlled by the infamous Medici family. Education, especially for some of the merchants, required reading, writing, math, the study of law, and the writings of classical Greek and Roman writers. Contributions of the Italian Renaissance period were in:

art - the more important artists were Giotto and his development of perspective in paintings; Leonardo da Vinci was not only an artist but also a scientist and inventor; Michelangelo was a sculptor, painter, and architect; and others including Raphael, Donatello, Titian, and Tintoretto

political philosophy - the writings of Machiavelli

literature - the writings of Petrarch and Boccaccio

science - Galileo

medicine - the work of Brussels-born Andrea Vesalius earned him the title of "father of anatomy" and had a profound influence on the Spaniard Michael Servetus and the Englishman William Harvey

In Germany, Gutenberg's invention of the printing press with movable type facilitated the rapid spread of Renaissance ideas, writings and innovations, thus ensuring the enlightenment of most of Western Europe. Contributions were also made by Durer and Holbein in art and by Paracelsus in science and medicine. The effects of the Renaissance in the Low Countries can be seen in the literature and philosophy of Erasmus and the art of van Eyck and Breughel the Elder. Rabelais and de Montaigne in France also contributed to literature and philosophy. In Spain, the art of El Greco and de Morales flourished, as did the writings of Cervantes and De Vega. In England, Sir Thomas More and Sir Francis Bacon wrote and taught philosophy and inspired by Vesalius. William Harvey made important contributions in medicine. The greatest talent was found in literature and drama and given to mankind by Chaucer, Spenser, Marlowe, Jonson, and the incomparable Shakespeare.

The Reformation period consisted of two phases: the Protestant Revolution and the Catholic Reformation. The Protestant Revolution came about because of religious, political, and economic reasons. The religious reasons stemmed from abuses in the Catholic Church including fraudulent clergy with their scandalous immoral lifestyles; the sale of religious offices, indulgences, and dispensations; different theologies within the Church; and frauds involving sacred relics.

The political reasons for the Protestant Revolution involved the increase in the power of rulers who were considered "absolute monarchs", who desired all power and control, especially over the Church. The growth of "nationalism" or patriotic pride in one's own country was another contributing factor.

Economic reasons included the greed of ruling monarchs to possess and control all lands and wealth of the Church, the deep animosity against the burdensome papal taxation, the rise of the affluent middle class and its clash with medieval Church ideals, and the increase of an active system of "intense" capitalism.

The Protestant Revolution began in Germany with the revolt of Martin Luther against Church abuses. It spread to Switzerland where it was led by Calvin. It began in England with the efforts of King Henry VIII to have his marriage to Catherine of Aragon annulled so he could wed another and have a male heir. The results were the increasing support given not only by the people but also by nobles and some rulers, and of course, the attempts of the Church to stop it.

The Catholic Reformation was undertaken by the Church to "clean up its act" and to slow or stop the Protestant Revolution. The major efforts to this end were supplied by the Council of Trent and the Jesuits. Six major results of the Reformation included:
• Religious freedom,
• Religious tolerance,
• More opportunities for education,
• Power and control of rulers limited,
• Increase in religious wars, and
• An increase in fanaticism and persecution

A number of individuals and events led to the time of exploration and discoveries. The Vivaldo brothers and Marco Polo wrote of their travels and experiences, which signaled the early beginnings. From the Crusades, the survivors made their way home to different places in Europe bringing with them fascinating, new information about exotic lands, people, customs, and desired foods and goods such as spices and silks.

The Renaissance ushered in a time of curiosity, learning, and incredible energy sparking the desire for trade to procure these new, exotic products and to find better, faster, cheaper trade routes to get to them. The work of geographers, astronomers and mapmakers made important contributions and many studied and applied the work of such men as Hipparchus of Greece, Ptolemy of Egypt, Tycho Brahe of Denmark, and Fra Mauro of Italy.

Portugal made the start under the encouragement, support, and financing of Prince Henry the Navigator. The better known explorers who sailed under the flag of Portugal included Cabral, Diaz, and Vasco da Gama, who successfully sailed all the way from Portugal, around the southern tip of Africa, to Calcutta, India.

Christopher Columbus, sailing for Spain, is credited with the discovery of America although he never set foot on its soil. Magellan is credited with the first circumnavigation of the earth. Other Spanish explorers made their marks in parts of what are now the United States, Mexico, and South America.

For France, claims to various parts of North America were the result of the efforts of such men as Verrazano, Champlain, Cartier, LaSalle, Father Marquette and Joliet. Dutch claims were based on the work of one Henry Hudson. John Cabot gave England its stake in North America along with John Hawkins, Sir Francis Drake, and the half-brothers Sir Walter Raleigh and Sir Humphrey Gilbert.

Actually the first Europeans in the New World were Norsemen led by Eric the Red and later, his son Leif the Lucky. However, before any of these, the ancestors of today's Native Americans and Latin American Indians crossed the Bering Strait from Asia to Alaska, eventually settling in all parts of the Americas

An Age of Revolutions (1750 – 1914)

The period from the 1700s to the 1800s was characterized in Western countries by opposing political ideas of democracy and nationalism. This resulted in strong nationalistic feelings and people of common cultures asserting their belief in the right to have a part in their government.

The American Revolution resulted in the successful efforts of the English colonists in America to win their freedom from Great Britain. After more than one hundred years of mostly self-government, the colonists resented the increased British meddling and control, they declared their freedom, won the Revolutionary War with aid from France, and formed a new independent nation.

The French Revolution was the revolt of the middle and lower classes against the gross political and economic excesses of the rulers and the supporting nobility. It ended with the establishment of the First in a series of French Republics. Conditions leading to revolt included extreme taxation, inflation, lack of food, and the total disregard for the impossible, degrading, and unacceptable condition of the people on the part of the rulers, nobility, and the Church.

The Industrial Revolution, which began in Great Britain and spread elsewhere, was the development of power-driven machinery (fueled by coal and steam) leading to the accelerated growth of industry with large factories replacing homes and small workshops as work centers. The lives of people changed drastically and a largely agricultural society changed to an industrial one. In Western Europe, the period of empire and colonialism began. The industrialized nations seized and claimed parts of Africa and Asia in an effort to control and provide the raw materials needed to feed the industries and machines in the "mother country". Later developments included power based on electricity and internal combustion, replacing coal and steam.

The Russian Revolution occurred first in March (or February on the old calendar) 1917 with the abdication of Tsar Nicholas II and the establishment of a democratic government. Those who were the extreme Marxists and had a majority in Russia's Socialist Party, the Bolsheviks, overcame opposition, and in November (October on the old calendar), did away with the provisional democratic government and set up the world's first Marxist state.

The conditions in Russia in previous centuries led up to this. Russia's harsh climate, tremendous size, and physical isolation from the rest of Europe, along with the brutal despotic rule and control of the tsars over enslaved peasants, contributed to the final conditions leading to revolution. Despite the tremendous efforts of Peter the Great to bring his country up to the social, cultural, and economic standards of the rest of Europe, Russia always remained a hundred years or more behind. Autocratic rule, the existence of the system of serfdom or slavery of the peasants, lack of money, defeats in wars, lack of enough food and food production, little, if any, industrialization--all of these contributed to conditions ripe for revolt.

By 1914, Russia's industrial growth was even faster than Germany's and agricultural production was improving, along with better transportation. However, the conditions of poverty were horrendous. The Orthodox Church was steeped in political activities and the absolute rule of the tsar was the order of the day. By the time the nation entered World War I, conditions were just right for revolution. Marxist socialism seemed to be the solution or answer to all the problems. Russia had to stop participation in the war, although winning a big battle. Industry could not meet the military's needs.

Transportation by rail was severely disrupted and it was most difficult to procure supplies from the Allies. The people had had enough of war, injustice, starvation, poverty, slavery, and cruelty. The support for and strength of the Bolsheviks were mainly in the cities. After two or three years of civil war, fighting foreign invasions, and opposing other revolutionary groups, the Bolsheviks were finally successful in making possible a type of "pre-Utopia" for the workers and the people.

As succeeding Marxist or Communist leaders came to power, the effects of this violent revolution were felt all around the earth. From 1989 until 1991, Communism eventually gave way to various forms of democracies and free enterprise societies in Eastern Europe and the former Soviet Union. The foreign policies of all free Western nations were directly and immensely affected by the Marxist-Communist ideology. Its effect on Eastern Europe and the former Soviet Union was felt politically, economically, socially, culturally, and geographically. The people of ancient Russia simply exchanged one autocratic dictatorial system for another and its impact on all of the people on the earth is still being felt to this day.

The time from 1830 to 1914 is characterized by the extraordinary growth and spread of patriotic pride in a nation along with intense, widespread imperialism. Loyalty to one's nation included national pride, extending and maintaining sovereign political boundaries, and unification of smaller states with common language, history, and culture into a more powerful nation. As part of a larger multicultural empire, there were smaller groups who wished to separate into smaller, political, cultural nations. Examples of major events of this time resulting from the insurgence of nationalism include:

In the United States, territorial expansion occurred in the expansion westward under the banner of "Manifest Destiny." In addition, the U.S. was involved in the War with Mexico, the Spanish-American War, and support of the Latin American colonies of Spain in their revolt for independence. In Latin America, the Spanish colonies were successful in their fight for independence and self-government.

In Europe, Italy and Germany were each totally united into one nation from many smaller states. There were revolutions in Austria and Hungary, the Franco-Prussian War, the dividing of Africa among the strong European nations, interference and intervention of Western nations in Asia, and the breakup of Turkish dominance in the Balkans.

In Africa, France, Great Britain, Italy, Portugal, Spain, Germany, and Belgium controlled the entire continent except Liberia and Ethiopia. In Asia and the Pacific Islands, only China, Japan, and present-day Thailand (Siam) kept their independence. The others were controlled by the strong European nations.

An additional reason for European imperialism was the harsh, urgent demand for the raw materials needed to fuel and feed the great Industrial Revolution. These resources were not available in the huge quantity so desperately needed which necessitated (and rationalized) the partitioning of the continent of Africa and parts of Asia. In turn, these colonial areas would purchase the finished manufactured goods.

The Twentieth Century

World War I ■ 1914 to 1918

Causes were: the surge of nationalism, the increasing strength of military capabilities, massive colonization for raw materials needed for industrialization and manufacturing, and military and diplomatic alliances. The initial spark, which started the conflagration, was the assassination of Austrian Archduke Francis Ferdinand and his wife in Sarajevo.

There were 28 nations involved in the war, not including colonies and territories. It began July 28, 1914 and ended November 11, 1918 with the signing of the Treaty of Versailles. Economically, the war cost a total of $337 billion; increased inflation and huge war debts; and caused a loss of markets, goods, jobs, and factories. Politically, old empires collapsed; many monarchies disappeared; smaller countries gained temporary independence; Communists seized power in Russia; and, in some cases, nationalism increased. Socially, total populations decreased because of war casualties and low birth rates. There were millions of displaced persons and villages and farms were destroyed. Cities grew while women made significant gains in the work force and the ballot box. There was less social distinction and classes. Attitudes completely changed and old beliefs and values were questioned. The peace settlement established the League of Nations to ensure peace, but it failed to do so.

World War II ■ 1939 to 1945

Causes were:

Ironically, the Treaty of Paris, the peace treaty ending World War I, ultimately led to the Second World War. Countries that fought in the first war were either dissatisfied over the "spoils" of war, or were punished so harshly that resentment continued building to an eruption twenty years later.

The economic problems of both winners and losers of the first war were never resolved and the worldwide Great Depression of the 1930s dealt the final blow to any immediate rapid recovery. Democratic governments in Europe were severely strained and weakened which in turn gave strength and encouragement to those political movements that were extreme and made promises to end the economic chaos in their countries.

Nationalism, which was a major cause of World War I, grew even stronger and seemed to feed the feelings of discontent, which became increasingly rampant.

Because of unstable economic conditions and political unrest, harsh dictatorships arose in several of the countries, especially where there was no history of experience in democratic government.

Countries such as Germany, Japan, and Italy began to aggressively expand their borders and acquire additional territory.

In all, 59 nations became embroiled in World War II, which began September 1, 1939 and ended September 2, 1945. These dates include both the European and Pacific Theaters of war. The horrible tragic results of this second global confrontation were more deaths and more destruction than in any other armed conflict. It completely uprooted and displaced millions of people. The end of the war brought renewed power struggles, especially in Europe and China, with many Eastern European nations as well as China coming under complete control and domination of the Communists, supported and backed by the Soviet Union. With the development of and two-time deployment of an atomic bomb against two Japanese cities, the world found itself in the nuclear age. The peace settlement established the United Nations Organization, still existing and operating today.

Korean War ■ 1950 to 1953

Causes: Korea was under control of Japan from 1895 to the end of the Second World War in 1945. At war's end, the Soviet and U.S. military troops moved into Korea with the U.S. troops in the southern half and the Soviet troops in the northern half with the 38 degree North Latitude line as the boundary.

The General Assembly of the UN in 1947 ordered elections throughout all of Korea to select one government for the entire country. The Soviet Union would not allow the North Koreans to vote, so they set up a Communist government there. The South Koreans set up a democratic government but both claimed the entire country. At times, there were clashes between the troops from 1948 to 1950. After the U.S. removed its remaining troops in 1949 and announced in early 1950 that Korea was not part of its defense line in Asia, the Communists decided to act and invaded the south.

Participants were: North and South Korea, United States of America, Australia, New Zealand, China, Canada. France, Great Britain, Turkey, Belgium, Ethiopia, Colombia, Greece, South Africa, Luxembourg, Thailand, the Netherlands, and the Philippines. It was the first war in which a world organization played a major military role and it presented quite a challenge to the UN, which had only been in existence five years.

The war began June 25, 1950 and ended July 27, 1953. A truce was drawn up and an armistice agreement was signed ending the fighting. A permanent treaty of peace has never been signed and the country remains divided between the Communist North and the Democratic South. It was a very costly and bloody war destroying villages and homes, displacing and killing millions of people.

The Vietnam War
U.S. Involvement ■ 1957 to 1973

Causes: U.S. involvement was the second phase of three in Vietnam's history. The first phase began in 1946 when the Vietnamese fought French troops for control of the country. Vietnam prior to 1946 had been part of the French colony of Indochina (since 1861 along with Laos and Kampuchea or Cambodia). In 1954, the defeated French left and the country became divided into Communist North and Democratic South. United States' aid and influence continued as part of the U.S. "Cold War" foreign policy to help any nation threatened by Communism.

The second phase involved the U.S. commitment. The Communist Vietnamese considered the war one of national liberation, a struggle to avoid continual dominance and influence of a foreign power. A cease-fire was arranged in January 1973 and a few months later U.S. troops left for good. The third and final phase consisted of fighting between the Vietnamese but ended April 30, 1975, with the surrender of South Vietnam, the entire country being united under Communist ruler.

Participants were the United States of America, Australia, New Zealand, South and North Vietnam, South Korea, Thailand, and the Philippines. With active U.S. involvement from 1957 to 1973, it was the longest war participated in by the U.S.; was tremendously destructive and completely divided the American public in their opinions and feelings about the war. Many were frustrated and angered by the fact that it was the first war fought on foreign soil in which U.S. combat forces were totally unable to achieve their goals and objectives.

Returning veterans faced not only readjustment to normal civilian life but also faced bitterness, anger, rejection, and no heroes' welcomes. Many suffered severe physical and deep psychological problems. The war set a precedent with Congress and the American people actively challenging U.S. military and foreign policy. The conflict, though tempered markedly by time, still exists and still has a definite effect on people.

The struggle between the Communist world under Soviet Union leadership and the non-Communist world under Anglo-American leadership resulted in what became known as the Cold War. Communism crept into the Western Hemisphere with Cuban leader Fidel Castro and his regime. Most colonies in Africa, Asia, and the Middle East gained independence from European and Western influence and control. In South Africa in the early 1990s, the system of racial segregation, called "apartheid," was abolished.

The Soviet Union was the first industrialized nation to successfully begin a program of space flight and exploration, launching Sputnik and putting the first man in space. The United States also experienced success in its space program successfully landing space crews on the moon. In the late 1980s and early 1990s, the Berlin Wall was torn down and Communism fell in the Soviet Union and Eastern Europe. The 15 republics of the former USSR became independent nations with varying degrees of freedom and democracy in government and together formed the Commonwealth of Independent States (CIS). The former Communist nations of Eastern Europe also emphasized their independence with democratic forms of government.

Tremendous progress in communication and transportation has tied all parts of the earth and drawn them closer. There are still vast areas of the former Soviet Union that have unproductive land, extreme poverty, food shortages, rampant diseases, violent friction between cultures, the ever-present nuclear threat, environmental pollution, rapid reduction of natural resources, urban over-crowding, acceleration in global terrorism and violent crimes, and a diminishing middle class.

Skill 1.5 Demonstrate an understanding of the chronology, narratives, perspectives, and interpretations of major eras in Michigan history.

Skill 1.5 a Describe major eras in the history of Michigan.

Michigan was, first and foremost, a Native American homeland. Various tribes inhabited what we now call Michigan early on in the area's habitation, including Chippewa, Miami, Kickapoo, and Ottawa.

Among the first Europeans to explore the Michigan territory were the famous French pair Marquette and Joliet. The famous Jesuit missionary and fur trader were seeking the Northwest Passage. Another famous Frenchman, Robert Cavelier Sieur de la Salle, explored the area, including the adjoining Great Lake, quite a bit. Detroit was the result of the efforts of yet another Frenchman, Antoine de la Mothe Cadillac, angling to protect French efforts against both Native Americans and British.

The British victory in 1763 eliminated the French presence in Michigan and brought to the Native Americans living there a new level of irritation. A series of battles, led mainly by Pontiac, resulted in a reduction in British forces in the area. However, it took the end of the War of 1812 to eliminate the British presence.

The American settlers weren't much more sympathetic to Native American requests of co-existence. Pressing their land claims thanks to the Northwest Ordinance, Americans moved in increasing numbers westward, including to Michigan. British soldiers, still stationed in Canada, aided Native Americans in resisting American settlements. A major engagement was the Battle of Fallen Timbers (1794), in which Americans under General "Mad" Anthony Wayne scored a decisive victory over a determined Native American force. A short 11 years later, Michigan became a territory of the U.S.

The new state was definitely a battleground during the War of 1812. Detroit, specifically, was surrendered to the British without any kind of spirited defense. The Battle of the River Raisin was also a serious blow to American prestige and morale. The ultimate victory in 1814, however, stopped British incursions for good.

The opening of the Erie Canal, in 1825, really sent the Michigan economy skyrocketing. The rich agricultural and other products from Michigan farms and storehouses could be sent to New York and then elsewhere in the world. In a sort of reverse development, many immigrants traveled to Michigan at this time as well, seeking new opportunities in a suddenly growing state. This influx pushed the territory's population into state status. Michigan officially became a state in 1837.

Michigan led the nation in copper production and was also a major supplier of iron, salt, lumber, and natural gas. All of these things—and especially men and weapons—were supplied to the Union war effort during the Civil War. A full 90,000 Michigan soldiers fought in the war. Of those, 15,000 died.

The coming of the railroads again made Michigan a prime destination for goods and people. Near the end of the nineteenth century and into the beginning of the twentieth century, Henry Ford revolutionized the country with his automobile and his assembly line. General Motors followed suit soon after and Detroit soon became the auto capital of the world.

Michigan men and women served in both World War I and World War II. During the latter war, Michigan also produced a large number of war equipment, including tanks and bombers. This wartime production was the high point of heavy machinery operations in the state in the twentieth century, however. Advances in automaking, especially, in Japan, South Korea, and Germany cut deeply into Detroit's share of the global auto market. That trend continues to this day. The economic downturns of the second half of the twentieth century hurt Michigan especially hard.

Michigan was also the focus of concerted efforts for equality during the Civil Rights Movement. In many ways, this struggle for equality continues to this day.

Skill 1.5 b   Examine relationships including cause and effect among important events.

Detroit was, at one point, the automaking capital of the world. Early in the twentieth century, automakers in and around Detroit accounted for the vast majority of cars and trucks sold to people all around the world. Following the lead of Henry Ford, the other large automakers increased production and personnel to meet a growing demand for vehicles. For decades, Detroit was synonymous with success. American cars were the best-known, best-made, and most preferred in the world. All that began to change after the end of World War II.

In Japan especially but also in South Korea and Germany, automakers began to produce cars that were smaller and more fuel-efficient than their American counterparts. These postwar countries, devastated as a result of the war, underwent massive rebuilding efforts. In Japan especially, factories were built from scratch. As such, they were built using the most modern of technologies and allowing for the most modern work techniques. They were, from the beginning, more efficient than those in America. Following on the lead of Henry Ford more than 50 years earlier, automotive factories in Japan instituted more robotic "workers" and used their human workers efficiently.

The combination of a more efficient production process and an emphasis on fuel efficiency produced a dizzying array of successful cars, from automakers such as Honda, Toyota, and Datsun. Slowly but surely, Japanese cars began to appear in America.

Japanese cars were smaller and more fuel-efficient than cars made in America. And, they cost less. Americans at first were loyal to the vehicles still coming out of Detroit. American pride in American engineering and American tradition still won out. Little by little, however, Japanese cars began to find homes in America. Especially in the economic downturns in the 1970s and 1980s, Americans were pinching their pennies and looking for ways to cut costs. One prime expense for most Americans is the vehicle that they drive every day. Especially since gasoline prices rose precipitously during the second half of the twentieth century, Americans began to move in droves toward more fuel-efficient vehicles. American automakers were slow to respond to this trend, and Japanese cars gained a strong foothold in the U.S.

The Big Three have changed their strategies in the past 30 years, moving toward more fuel-efficient vehicles and more cost-effective strategies. At the same time, more and more Japanese automakers have opened up factories in America. More and more, a car that is "Made in America" could very well be a Honda Civic or a Toyota Corolla.

American automakers responded to this trend also by making larger and larger vehicles. The SUV craze was huge in the 1990s, as Americans by the thousands bought "family cars"—vans, minivans, and SUVs. That trend has waned of late, as concerns over fuel efficiency have gotten back in the driver's seat. In the present day, price and fuel efficiency are the prime concerns for Americans buying cars. Detroit is still the automaking capital of America, but it is no longer the automaking capital of the world. One of the Big Three, Chrysler, is now owned by a German company. German and South Korean cars, too, are popular in America, sometimes much more popular than those made by GM or Ford.

Increasingly in the twenty-first century, American automakers found themselves hamstrung by costs associated with current and previous worker compensation packages. Such costs make up more and more of the budgets of the Big Three, which are continually struggling to cut expenses while increasing revenues. In the face of continuing fierce competition from Japan, South Korea, and Germany, American automakers still fight for market share and struggle for recognition.

Skill 1.5 c   **Use narratives and graphic data about significant eras in the history of Michigan and their connections to the United States and the world, identify people involved, describe the setting, and sequence events.**

"Brothers, when the white men first set foot on our grounds, they were hungry; they had no place on which to spread their blankets, or to kindle their fires. They were feeble; they could do nothing for themselves. Our father commiserated their distress, and shared freely with them whatever the Great Spirit had given his red children. They gave them food when hungry, medicine when sick, spread skins for them to sleep on, and gave them grounds, that they might hunt and raise corn.
"Brothers, the white people came among us feeble, and now we have made them strong, they wish to kill us, or drive us back, as they would wolves and panthers."
—Tecumseh, 1811

The struggle for Detroit was a gruesome affair. The settlement and its uniquely promising geographical location proved an irresistible target for Native Americans, like Tecumseh, who saw in the establishment of the French settlement and subsequent occupation by British and American settlers a path toward destruction. Tecumseh, the great Shawnee leader, sought to end the encroachment of the white man, through violence, because he saw that as the only way to stop it.

Brothers, the white men are not friends to the Indians: at first, they only asked for land sufficient for a wigwam; now, nothing will satisfy them but the whole of our hunting grounds, from the rising to the setting sun.

Tecumseh aimed to build a First Nations Confederacy, and he was marginally successful. He did convince members of his own and other tribes to band with him. He did solidify an alliance with British soldiers, particularly General Isaac Brock, who was looking for allies in the years before the War of 1812. This alliance came to fruition in the Battle of Detroit, which actually wasn't much of a battle.

Brothers, - We must be united; we must smoke the same pipe; we must fight each other' battles; and more than all, we must love the Great Spirit; he is for us; he will destroy our enemies, and make all his red children happy."

Tecumseh had 500 Native Americans on his side in mid-August of 1812. That was more than enough to scare the life out of American General William Hull, who, seeing the advancing British soldiers as well and thinking that he was sorely outnumbered, surrendered the entire Fort Detroit and all of his men. A few shots might have been fired, but no battle took place.

It was a temporary victory for Tecumseh, who chose the British side and eventually died in the Battle of the Thames, his dream for stopping American settlement on his people's homelands drowned in defeat and death. It was a significant era in Michigan history, however, for it marked the permanent changing of the guard. No longer would Native Americans roam freely about the Michigan Territory. No longer would British soldiers build forts in the region. The Americans had come to stay. The dreams of the Shawnee, Kickapoo, and other Michigan Native Americans died with Tecumseh, in spite of his best efforts.

Brothers, the white men despise and cheat the Indians; they abuse and insult them; they do not think the red men sufficiently good to live.

Skill 1.5 d   Analyze and compare interpretations of events by people from a variety of perspectives and use evidence to recreate the past.

The best we can do is size up the chances, calculate the risks involved, estimate our ability to deal with them, and then make our plans with confidence.
— Henry Ford

Henry Ford, inventor and automaker extraordinaire, certainly lived by those words. He was not afraid to take chances, he was not afraid to be unpopular, and he was not shy about expressing his opinion. He was also an expert businessman.

He did not invent the automobile or the assembly line. He put them together to create one of the most innovative revolutions in the world's history. With his **Model A** and **Model T** Fords popping up in more and more places around the United States, he gained a reputation for being a businessman who was willing to take risks yet treat his employees fairly. Indeed, his workers were some of the highest-paid in the country at that time. (They earned $5 a day, which doesn't sound like anything now but was a good deal in 1914, more than double what other workers were making.)

Ford saw the possibilities in the **automobile**. He invested heavily in a factory that could be set up to produce many cars at a time. He went out on a financial limb, believing that he would be able to make cars and money in a way that hadn't been done before. Yes, the automobile was a relatively new invention, but the assembly line process that Ford perfected had been used for guns and small machinery but not for larger machines, like cars. Ford was such a perfectionist that he enjoyed initial success with the Detroit Automobile Company but soon spent all the money on research. The result was a bankruptcy for the company but progress on the path to success by Henry Ford.

He continued to tinker, perfecting his beloved Quadrimobile concept until it was ready to be built right. He left another company, the Henry Ford Company, for the same reason that he left the Detroit Automobile Company—he had nothing to show for his efforts. The third time was the charm, however, as he convinced another group of investors to help him start the Ford Motor Company. By that time, Ford was in the final stages of tinkering and had the basic workings of what would become the first reliable gas-powered car, the Model T. His persistence paid off. So did the patience of his fellow investors. The Model T was a huge hit, partly because it was priced so low and partly because it was a dynamic new invention that transformed the way people got from place to place.

The risks involved for Henry Ford weren't all that much to begin with. He lost investors, yes, but he had money of his own and he had the tenacity and belief in himself that characterized his business acumen throughout his life. He was certainly able to overcome those initial obstacles while staying true to his vision, and the results speak for themselves. His idea of "welfare capitalism" was a winner as well, as his workers were consistently the highest-paid and the happiest workers in the country. Ford wanted his workers to come to work happy and go home satisfied, and he believed that a higher than normal wage and more than adequate working conditions could help create the workplace ideal that would create more products of a higher quality than could his competitors.

Skill 1.5 e   Analyze the implications and long term consequences of key decision in the history of Michigan.

In 1701, a Frenchman named Antoine de la Mothe Cadillac decided to found a settlement at what is now Detroit. The name of the settlement came from geography. *Le detroit* was the straits between Lake St. Clair and Lake Erie. Cadillac thought that this was an ideal place for a French settlement, a base of operations for France's growing fur trade and a potential watch site against British operations in the area. Cadillac was right: It was a great spot for a settlement.

The British at the beginning of the eighteenth century were looking to expand their empire beyond Canada and the western reaches of the American settlements. Always looking for an angle, British settlers were beginning to encroach on French trade routes in and around the Great Lakes. The Native American tribes who had been living in the area were also increasingly unhappy with the number of Europeans pursuing economic treasures. Cadillac, and other Frenchmen like him, found the need to put down roots overwhelming. The result was Fort Pontchartrain, and its surrounding settlement, Detroit.

It was just a 200-square-foot structure, and it was manned by just a handful of soldiers; but it was a presence all the same. It told the British, the Native Americans, and anybody else who wanted to listen or was paying attention that the French aimed to maintain their control over the territory that they were mining for furs, metals, and other precious commodities.

Detroit was certainly attractive to Native Americans and to British soldiers and settlers. The settlement and the fort were the target of a large handful of attacks during the eighteenth century. The British inherited both the settlement and the fort at the end of the French and Indian War, lost both to the Americans after the Revolutionary War, regained both briefly during the War of 1812, and then lost it all for good at the end of that war. Through it all, Detroit continued to grow.

The town had been incorporated in 1802. A fire three years later destroyed all but one of the 300 buildings in town. Detroit rebounded quickly, however. The development of the canals network—especially the Erie Canal, which opened in 1825—brought much growth in population and industry to Detroit. The arrival of the railroad increased that growth several-fold, with Detroit making railroad cars and ships to fill a growing need for transportation vehicles in America. The real growth, though, came about as a result of one man: Henry Ford.

The famed automaker set up shop in Detroit, beginning the Ford Motor Company and launching the automaking business that would forever change the landscape and reputation of the city of Detroit. Other automakers followed suit, creating the world capital of auto production. For the next several decades, Detroit enjoyed wild success. The city's geographical location, on one of the Great Lakes and so near to waterways that lead to the rest of the world, has served the automotive industry well. Cadillac would be proud (especially of the car that bears his name).

Skill 2.1   Describe, compare, and explain the locations and characteristics of places, cultures, and settlements.

Physical locations of the earth's surface features include the four major hemispheres and the parts of the earth's continents in them. Political locations are the political divisions, if any, within each continent. Both physical and political locations are precisely determined in two *ways:* (1) Surveying is done to determine boundary lines and distance from other features. (2) Exact locations are precisely determined by imaginary lines of latitude (parallels) and longitude (meridians). The intersection of these lines at right angles forms a grid, making it impossible to pinpoint an exact location of any place using any two grip coordinates.

The Eastern Hemisphere, located between the North and South Poles and between the Prime Meridian (0 degrees longitude) east to the International Date Line at 180 degrees longitude, consists of most of Europe, all of Australia, most of Africa, and all of Asia, except for a tiny piece of the easternmost part of Russia that extends east of 180 degrees longitude.

The Western Hemisphere, located between the North and South Poles and between the Prime Meridian (0 degrees longitude) west to the International Date Line at 180 degrees longitude, consists of all of North and South America, a tiny part of the easternmost part of Russia that extends east of 180 degrees longitude, and a part of Europe that extends west of the Prime Meridian (0 degrees longitude).

The Northern Hemisphere, located between the North Pole and the Equator, contains all of the continents of Europe and North America and parts of South America, Africa, and most of Asia.

The Southern Hemisphere, located between the South Pole and the Equator, contains all of Australia, a small part of Asia, about one-third of Africa, most of South America, and all of Antarctica.

Of the seven continents, only one contains just one entire country and is the only island continent, Australia. Its political divisions consist of six states and one territory: Western Australia, South Australia, Tasmania, Victoria, New South Wales, Queensland, and Northern Territory.

Africa is made up of 54 separate countries, the major ones being Egypt, Nigeria, South Africa, Zaire, Kenya, Algeria, Morocco, and the large island of Madagascar.

Asia consists of 49 separate countries, some of which include China, Japan, India, Turkey, Israel, Iraq, Iran, Indonesia, Jordan, Vietnam, Thailand, and the Philippines.

Europe's 43 separate nations include France, Russia, Malta, Denmark, Hungary, Greece, Bosnia and Herzegovina.

North America consists of Canada and the United States of America and the island nations of the West Indies and the "land bridge" of Middle America, including Cuba, Jamaica, Mexico, Panama, and others.

Thirteen separate nations together occupy the continent of South America, among them such nations as Brazil, Paraguay, Ecuador, and Suriname.

The continent of Antarctica has no political boundaries or divisions but is the location of a number of science and research stations managed by nations such as Russia, Japan, France, Australia, and India.

Social scientists use the term culture to describe the way of life of a group of people. This would include not only art, music, and literature but also beliefs, customs, languages, traditions, inventions--in short, any way of life whether complex or simple. The term geography is defined as the study of earth's features and living things as to their location, relationship with each other, how they came to be there, and why so important.

Physical geography is concerned with the locations of such earth features as climate, water, and land; how these relate to and affect each other and human activities; and what forces shaped and changed them. All three of these earth features affect the lives of all humans having a direct influence on what is made and produced, where it occurs, how it occurs, and what makes it possible. The combination of the different climate conditions and types of landforms and other surface features work together all around the earth to give the many varied cultures their unique characteristics and distinctions.

Cultural geography studies the location, characteristics, and influence of the physical environment on different cultures around the earth. Also included in these studies are comparisons and influences of the many varied cultures. Ease of travel and up-to-the-minute, state-of-the-art communication techniques ease the difficulties of understanding cultural differences making it easier to come in contact with them.

Skill 2.2   Describe, compare, and explain the locations and characteristics of ecosystems, resources, human adaptation, environmental impact, and the interrelationships among them.

The earth's surface is made up of 70% water and 30% land. Physical features of the land surface include mountains, hills, plateaus, valleys, and plains. Other minor landforms include deserts, deltas, canyons, mesas, basins, foothills, marshes and swamps. Earth's water features include oceans, seas, lakes, rivers, and canals.

Mountains are landforms with rather steep slopes at least 2,000 feet or more above sea level. Mountains are found in groups called mountain chains or mountain ranges. At least one range can be found on six of the earth's seven continents. North America has the Appalachian and Rocky Mountains; South America the Andes; Asia the Himalayas; Australia the Great Dividing Range; Europe the Alps; and Africa the Atlas, Ahaggar, and Drakensburg Mountains.

Hills are elevated landforms rising to an elevation of about 500 to 2000 feet. They are found everywhere on earth including Antarctica where they are covered by ice.

Plateaus are elevated landforms usually level on top. Depending on location, they range from being an area that is very cold to one that is cool and healthful. Some plateaus are dry because they are surrounded by mountains that keep out any moisture. Some examples include the Kenya Plateau in East Africa, which is very cool. The plateau extending north from the Himalayas is extremely dry while those in Antarctica and Greenland are covered with ice and snow.

Plains are described as areas of flat or slightly rolling land, usually lower than the landforms next to them. Sometimes called lowlands (and sometimes located along seacoasts) they support the majority of the world's people. Some are found inland and many have been formed by large rivers. This resulted in extremely fertile soil for successful cultivation of crops and numerous large settlements of people. In North America, the vast plains areas extend from the Gulf of Mexico north to the Arctic Ocean and between the Appalachian and Rocky Mountains. In Europe, rich plains extend east from Great Britain into central Europe on into the Siberian region of Russia. Plains in river valleys are found in China (the Yangtze River valley), India (the Ganges River valley), and Southeast Asia (the Mekong River valley).

Valleys are land areas that are found between hills and mountains. Some have gentle slopes containing trees and plants; others have very steep walls and are referred to as canyons. One famous example is Arizona's Grand Canyon of the Colorado River.

Deserts are large dry areas of land receiving ten inches or less of rainfall each year. Among the better known deserts are Africa's large Sahara Desert, the Arabian Desert on the Arabian Peninsula, and the desert Outback covering roughly one third of Australia.

Deltas are areas of lowlands formed by soil and sediment deposited at the mouths of rivers. The soil is generally very fertile and most fertile river deltas are important crop-growing areas. One well-known example is the delta of Egypt's Nile River, known for its production of cotton.

Mesas are the flat tops of hills or mountains usually with steep sides. Sometimes plateaus are also called mesas. Basins are considered to be low areas drained by rivers or low spots in mountains. Foothills are generally considered a low series of hills found between a plain and a mountain range. Marshes and swamps are wet lowlands providing growth of such plants as rushes and reeds.

Oceans are the largest bodies of water on the planet. The four oceans of the earth are the Atlantic Ocean, one-half the size of the Pacific and separating North and South America from Africa and Europe; the Pacific Ocean, covering almost one-third of the entire surface of the earth and separating North and South America from Asia and Australia; the Indian Ocean, touching Africa, Asia, and Australia; and the ice-filled Arctic Ocean, extending from North America and Europe to the North Pole. The waters of the Atlantic, Pacific, and Indian Oceans also touch the shores of Antarctica.

Seas are smaller than oceans and are surrounded by land. Some examples include the Mediterranean Sea found between Europe, Asia, and Africa; and the Caribbean Sea, touching the West Indies, South and Central America. A lake is a body of water surrounded by land. The Great Lakes in North America are a good example.

Rivers, considered a nation's lifeblood, usually begin as very small streams, formed by melting snow and rainfall, flowing from higher to lower land, emptying into a larger body of water, usually a sea or an ocean. Examples of important rivers for the people and countries affected by and/or dependent on them include the Nile, Niger, and Zaire Rivers of Africa; the Rhine, Danube, and Thames Rivers of Europe; the Yangtze, Ganges, Mekong, Hwang He, and Irrawaddy Rivers of Asia; the Murray-Darling in Australia; and the Orinoco in South America. River systems are made up of large rivers and numerous smaller rivers or tributaries flowing into them. Examples include the vast Amazon Rivers system in South America and the Mississippi River system in the United States. Canals are man-made water passages constructed to connect two larger bodies of water. Famous examples include the Panama Canal across Panama's isthmus connecting the Atlantic and Pacific Oceans and the Suez Canal in the Middle East between Africa and the Arabian peninsula connecting the Red and Mediterranean Seas.

Weather is the condition of the air which surrounds the day-to-day atmospheric conditions including temperature, air pressure, wind and moisture or precipitation which includes rain, snow, hail, or sleet.

Climate is average weather or daily weather conditions for a specific region or location over a long or extended period of time. Studying the climate of an area includes information gathered on the area's monthly and yearly temperatures and its monthly and yearly amounts of precipitation. In addition, a characteristic of an area's climate is the length of its growing season. Four reasons for the different climate regions on the earth are differences in:

Latitude,
The amount of moisture,
Temperatures in land and water, and
The earth's land surface.

There are many different climates throughout the earth. It is most unusual if a country contains just one kind of climate. Regions of climates are divided according to latitudes:

0 - 23 1 /2 degrees are the "low latitudes"
23 1/2 - 66 1/2 degrees are the "middle latitudes"
66 1/2 degrees to the Poles are the " "

The low latitudes are comprised of the rainforest, savanna, and desert climates. The tropical rainforest climate is found in equatorial lowlands and is hot and wet. There is sun, extreme heat and rain--everyday. Although daily temperatures rarely rise above 90 degrees F, the daily humidity is always high, leaving everything sticky and damp. North and south of the tropical rainforests are the tropical grasslands called "savannas," the "lands of two seasons"--a winter dry season and a summer wet season. Further north and south of the tropical grasslands or savannas are the deserts. These areas are the hottest and driest parts of the earth receiving less than 10 inches of rain a year. These areas have extreme temperatures between night and day. After the sun sets, the land cools quickly dropping the temperature as much as 50 degrees F.

The middle latitudes contain the Mediterranean, humid-subtropical, humid-continental, marine, steppe, and desert climates. Lands containing the Mediterranean climate are considered "sunny" lands found in six areas of the world: lands bordering the Mediterranean Sea, a small portion of southwestern Africa, areas in southern and southwestern Australia, a small part of the Ukraine near the Black Sea, central Chile, and Southern California. Summers are hot and dry with mild winters. The growing season usually lasts all year and what little rain falls are during the winter months. What is rather unusual is that the Mediterranean climate is located between 30 and 40 degrees north and south latitude on the western coasts of countries.

The humid subtropical climate is found north and south of the tropics and is moist indeed. The areas having this type of climate are found on the eastern side of their continents and include Japan, mainland China, Australia, Africa, South America, and the United States--the southeastern coasts of these areas. An interesting feature of their locations is that warm ocean currents are found there. The winds that blow across these currents bring in warm moist air all year round. Long, warm summers; short, mild winters; a long growing season allow for different crops to be grown several times a year. All contribute to the productivity of this climate type which supports more people than any of the other climates.

The marine climate is found in Western Europe, the British Isles, the U.S. Pacific Northwest, the western coast of Canada and southern Chile, along with southern New Zealand and southeastern Australia. A common characteristic of these lands is that they are either near water or surrounded by it. The ocean winds are wet and warm bringing a mild, rainy climate to these areas. In the summer, the daily temperatures average at or below 70 degrees F. During the winter, because of the warming effect of the ocean waters, the temperatures rarely fall below freezing.

In northern and central United States, northern China, south central and southeastern Canada, and the western and southeastern parts of the former Soviet Union is found the "climate of four seasons," the humid continental climate--spring, summer, fall, and winter. Cold winters, hot summers, and enough rainfall to grow a variety of crops are the major characteristics of this climate. In areas where the humid continental climate is found are some of the world's best farmlands as well as important activities such as trading and mining. Differences in temperatures throughout the year are determined by the distance a place is inland, away from the coasts.

The steppe or prairie climate is located in the interiors of the large continents like Asia and North America. These dry flatlands are far from ocean breezes and are called prairies or the Great Plains in Canada and the United States and steppes in Asia. Although the summers are hot and the winters are cold as in the humid continental climate, the big difference is rainfall. In the steppe climate, rainfall is light and uncertain, 10 to 20 inches a year mainly in spring and summer and is considered normal. Where rain is more plentiful, grass grows; in areas of less, the steppes or prairies gradually become deserts. These are found in the Gobi Desert of Asia, central and Western Australia, southwestern United States, and in the smaller deserts found in Pakistan, Argentina, and Africa south of the Equator.

The two major climates found in the high latitudes are "tundra" and "taiga." The word "tundra" meaning "marshy plain" is a Russian word and aptly describes the climatic conditions in the northern areas of Russia, Europe, and Canada. Winters are extremely cold and very long. Surprisingly less snow falls in the area of the tundra than in the eastern part of the United States. However, due to the harshness of the extreme cold, very few people live there and no crops can be raised. Despite having a small human population, many plants and animals are found there.

The "taiga" is the northern forest region and is located south of the tundra. In fact, the Russian word "taiga" means 'forest." The world's largest forestlands are found here along with vast mineral wealth and forbearing animals. The climate is extreme that very few people live here, unable to raise crops due to the extremely short growing season. The winter temperatures are colder and the summer temperatures are hotter than those in the tundra are because the taiga climate region is farther from the waters of the Arctic Ocean. The taiga is found in the northern parts of Russia, Sweden, Norway, Finland, Canada, and Alaska with most of their lands covered with marshes and swamps.

In certain areas of the earth there exists a type of climate unique to areas with high mountains, usually different from their surroundings. This type of climate is called a "vertical climate" because the temperatures, crops, vegetation, and human activities change and become different as one ascends the different levels of elevation. At the foot of the mountain, a hot and rainy climate is found with the cultivation of many lowland crops. As one climbs higher, the air becomes cooler, the climate changes sharply and different economic activities change, such as grazing sheep and growing corn. At the top of many mountains, snow is found year round.

Skill 2.3 **Describe, compare, and explain the locations and characteristics of economic activities, trade, political activities, migration, information flow, and the interrelationships among them.**

Free enterprise, individual entrepreneurship, competitive markets and consumer sovereignty are all parts of a **market economy**. Individuals have the right to make their own decisions as to what they want to do as a career. The financial incentives are there for individuals who are willing to take the risk. A successful venture earns profit. It is these financial incentives that serve to motivate inventors and small businesses. The same is true for businesses. They are free to determine what production technique they want to use and what output they want to produce within the confines of the legal system. They can make investments based on their own decisions. Nobody is telling them what to do. Competitive markets, relatively free from government interference are also a manifestation of the freedom that the U.S. economic system is based on.

These markets function on the basis of supply and demand to determine output mix and resource allocation. There is no commissar dictating what is produced and how. Since consumers buy the goods and services that give them satisfaction, this means that, for the most part, they don't buy the goods and services that they don't want that don't give them satisfaction.

Consumers are, in effect, voting for the goods and services that they want with the dollars or what is called dollar voting. Consumers are basically signaling firms as to how they want society's scarce resources used with their dollar votes. A good that society wants acquires enough dollar votes for the producer to experience profits – a situation where the firm's revenues exceed the firm's costs. The existence of profits indicate to the firm that it is producing the goods and services that consumers want and that society's scarce resources are being used in accordance with consumer preferences. When a firm does not have a profitable product, it is because that product is not tabulating enough dollar votes of consumers. Consumers don't want the good or service and they don't want society's scarce resources being used in its production.

This process where consumers vote with their dollars is called **consumer sovereignty**. Consumers are basically directing the allocation of scarce resources in the economy with the dollar spending. Firms, who are in business to earn profit, then hire resources, or inputs, in accordance with consumer preferences. This is the way in which resources are allocated in a market economy. This is the manner in which society achieves the output mix that it desires.

Profit, capital and competition all go together in the U.S. economic system. Competition is determined by market structure. Since the cost curves are the same for all the firms, the only difference comes from the revenue side. The most competitive of all market structures is perfect competition, characterized by numerous buyers and sellers, all with perfect knowledge. No one seller is big enough to influence price so the firm is a price taker. Products are homogenous so buyers are indifferent as to whom they buy from. The absence of barriers to entry makes it easy for firms to enter and leave the industry. At the other end of the spectrum is monopoly, the only seller of a unique product. Barriers to entry are significant enough to keep firms from entering or leaving the industry. In monopolistic competition firms sell similar products in an industry with low barriers to entry, making it easy for firms to enter and leave the industry. Oligopoly is a market structure with a few large firms selling heterogeneous or homogeneous product in a market structure with the strength of barriers to entry varying. Each firm maximizes profit by producing at the point where marginal cost equals marginal revenue. The existence of economic profits, an above normal rate of return, attracts capital to an industry and results in expansion.

Whether or not new firms can enter depends on barriers to entry. Firms can enter easily in perfect competition and the expansion will continue until economic profits are eliminated and firms earn a normal rate of return. The significant barriers to entry in monopoly serve to keep firms out so the monopolist continues to earn an above normal rate of return. Some firms will be able to enter in monopolistic competition but won't have a monopoly over the existing firm's brand name. The competitiveness of the market structure determines whether new firms or capital can enter in response to profits.

There are two markets. The **input market** is where factor owners sell their factors and employers hire their inputs. The **output market** is where firms sell the output they produce with their inputs. It's where factors owners spend their incomes on goods and services. There are two sectors, households and businesses. **Households** sell their factors in the input market and use their income to purchase goods and services in the output market. So wages, interest, rent and profit flow from the business sectors to the household sector. Households that earn their factor incomes in the factor market, spend their incomes on goods and services produced by businesses and sold in the output market. Receipts for goods and services flow from households to businesses.

Government receives tax payments from households and businesses and provides services to businesses and households. Each of the three is a component of the aggregate sectors of the economy and as such makes a contribution to the GDP.

Labor unions in America arose in response to deplorable working conditions. Employees had to no say in their working conditions and began to join forces to try to obtain some input. Viewed in this perspective, the history of the labor movement can be traced back to the colonial period as workers banded together amongst themselves and with other organizations in support of different goals. The workers that engaged in these activities were subject to actions from dismissal to blacklisting. It wasn't until 1881 that the first permanent union structure was founded on the principles of Samuel Gompers. This became known as the **American Federation of Labor** and was based on three principles. The first principle is practical business unionism, which is the belief that unions should only concern themselves with the problems of their members: working conditions, hours, wages, job security, etc. The second principle is political neutrality. Unions should stay out of politics, and the government should stay out of the union movement and the collective bargaining process.

The third principle is trade autonomy, the belief that unions should be organized on the basis of trade. There should be one union for each craft or trade; there should not be unions consisting of members from all trades. The AFL organized only craft or trade workers, and not industrial workers. The large pool of industrial workers was eventually organized by the Congress of Industrial Organization, and in 1955 the two merged to become the AFL-CIO.

The unions have various methods they can use to obtain benefits for their members. They have supported the enactment of various kinds of labor law legislation that eventually regulated both sides of the labor market, union and employer from various unfair labor and union practices, like yellow-dog contracts, boycotts, featherbedding, and hot cargo clauses. They have also supported legislation that resulted in minimum wage and unemployment insurance. Supporting and opposing legislation isn't the only way of obtaining benefits for members. The most direct way of obtaining benefits is through the collective bargaining process. **Collective bargaining** refers to the negotiating of a labor agreement or the settling of a grievance under an existing contract. When the union and the employee can't come to terms, there is always the weapon of the **strike**. During a strike, the union members withhold their labor services. The purpose is to put financial pressure on the employer. The employer can respond with a **lockout**, which puts pressure on the union and the workers. Eventually an agreement is reached, with or without a strike or lockout.

Unions have benefited their members tremendously over the years in terms of gaining wage and benefit concessions from employers. The existence of organized labor has benefited non-union labor by raising the level of wages and benefits since non-union firms had to raise wages to keep their employees.

U.S. economic policy is based on promoting full employment and stable prices in the economy. The economy needs a stable environment in which to function. With this end in mind, monetary policy and/or fiscal policy is used to fine-tune the economy and to steer it toward its goals. Contractionary monetary and/or fiscal policies are used to slow an economy that is expanding too quickly. Expansionary monetary and/or fiscal policies are used to stimulate a sluggish economy to eliminate unemployment.

Economic mobility and inequality exist within the U.S. economic system. **Economic mobility** refers to the ability of factors, particularly labor to move around the country in response to employment opportunities. The U.S. economy is so big that there can be unemployment in one part of the country while there are labor shortages in other parts of the country. In many cases there are institutional rigidities, like lack of information, that prevent workers from migrating in response to employment opportunities. State job services exist to provide information about available job opportunities, even though many workers are reluctant to migrate due to family situations.

Inequality exists within the U.S. economic system. An unequal distribution of income is a part of market economies. Wages are based on contributions which are partly dependent on education and training. The more highly specialized the labor skill provided, the higher the income. So no matter what kind of policies there are, there will also be an unequal distribution of income.

Skill 2.4   Describe and compare characteristics of ecosystems, states, regions, countries, major world regions, and patterns, and explain the processes that created them.

Economic systems refer to the arrangements a society has devised to answer what are known as the Three Questions: What goods to produce, How to produce the goods, and For Whom are the goods being produced, or how is the allocation of the output determined. Different economic systems answer these questions in different ways. These are the different "isms" that exist that define the method of resource and output allocation.

A market economy answers these questions in terms of demand and supply and the use of markets. Consumers vote for the products they want with their dollar spending. Goods acquiring enough dollar votes are profitable, signaling to the producers that society wants their scarce resources used in this way. This is how the "What" question is answered. The producer then hires inputs in accordance with the goods consumers want, looking for the most efficient or lowest cost method of production. The lower the firm's costs for any given level of revenue, the higher the firm's profits. This is the way in which the "How" question is answered in a market economy. The "For Whom" question is answered in the marketplace by the determination of the equilibrium price. Price serves to ration the good to those that can and will transact at the market price of better. Those who can't or won't are excluded from the market. The United States has a market economy.

The opposite of the market economy is called the centrally planned economy. This used to be called Communism, even though the term in not correct in a strict Marxian sense. In a planned economy, the means of production are publicly owned with little, if any public ownership. Instead of the Three Questions being solved by markets, they have a planning authority that makes the decisions in place of markets. The planning authority decides what will be produced and how. Since most planned economies directed resources into the production of capital and military goods, there was little remaining for consumer goods and the result was chronic shortages. Price functioned as an accounting measure and did not reflect scarcity. The former Soviet Union and most of the Eastern Bloc countries were planned economies of this sort.

In between the two extremes is market socialism. This is a mixed economic system that uses both markets and planning. Planning is usually used to direct resources at the upper levels of the economy, with markets being used to determine prices of consumer goods and wages. This kind of economic system answers the three questions with planning and markets. The former Yugoslavia was a market socialist economy.

The social structure of a society is definitely affected by the type of economic system. A traditional economy where they do things the way they always have, based on tradition is not receptive to change. The social structure is the same as it was generations ago. Incentives are there to improve or get ahead because of tradition. They don't have much of a tax base to raise revenues and implement social welfare programs. A planned economy with government ownership of the means of production was supposed to be a classless society, but the upper levels of government and the military were a notch above the population. Individual and entrepreneurial incentives were lacking since there was no private ownership of business or possibility of profit. In a mixed economy and in a market economy, the individual is allowed the financial rewards for his entrepreneurial ventures. More people are willing to take the risk for the chance of succeeding. Therefore, the resulting social structure is a spectrum from very poor to very rich.

You can put each nation of the world on a continuum in terms of these characteristics and rank them from most capitalistic to the most planned. The United States would probably rank as the most capitalistic and North Korea would probably rank as the most planned, but this doesn't mean that the United States doesn't engage in planning or that economies like mainland China don't use markets.

Skill 2.5   Describe and explain the causes, consequences, and geographic contexts of major global issues and events.

The Agricultural Revolution, initiated by the invention of the plow, led to a thoroughgoing transformation of human society by making large-scale agricultural production possible and facilitating the development of agrarian societies. During the period during which the plow was invented, the wheel, numbers, and writing were also invented. Coinciding with the shift from hunting wild game to the domestication of animals, this period was one of dramatic social and economic change.

Numerous changes in lifestyle and thinking accompanied the development of stable agricultural communities. Rather than gathering a wide variety of plants as hunter-gatherers, agricultural communities become dependent of a limited number of plants or crops that are harvested. Subsistence becomes vulnerable to the weather and dependent upon planting and harvesting times. Agriculture also required a great deal of physical labor and the development of a sense of discipline. Agricultural communities become sedentary or stable in terms of location. This makes the construction of dwellings appropriate. These tend to be built relatively close together, creating villages or towns. Stable communities also free people from the need to carry everything with them and the move from hunting ground to hunting ground. This facilitates the invention of larger, more complex tools. As new tools are envisioned and developed it begins to make sense to have some specialization within the society.

Skills begin to have greater value, and people begin to do work on behalf of the community that utilizes their particular skills and abilities. Settled community life also gives rise to the notion of wealth. It is now possible to keep possessions.

In the beginning of the transition to agriculture, the tools that were used for hunting and gathering were adequate to the tasks of agriculture. The initial challenge was in adapting to a new way of life. Once that challenge was met, attention turned to the development of more advanced tools and sources of energy. Six thousand years ago the first plow was invented in Mesopotamia. This plow was pulled by animals. Agriculture was now possible on a much larger scale. Soon tools were developed that make such basic tasks as gathering seeds, planting, and cutting grain faster and easier.

It also becomes necessary to maintain social and political stability to ensure that planting and harvesting times are not interrupted by internal discord or a war with a neighboring community. It also becomes necessary to develop ways to store the crop and prevent its destruction by the elements and animals. And then it must be protected from thieves.

Settled communities that produce the necessities of life are self-supporting. Advances in agricultural technology and the ability to produce a surplus of produce create two opportunities: first, the opportunity to trade the surplus goods for other desired goods, and second, the vulnerability to others who steal to take those goods. Protecting domesticated livestock and surplus, as well as stored, crops become an issue for the community. This, in turn, leads to the construction of walls and other fortifications around the community.

The ability to produce surplus crops creates the opportunity to trade or barter with other communities in exchange for desired goods. Traders and trade routes begin to develop between villages and cities. The domestication of animals expands the range of trade and facilitates an exchange of ideas and knowledge.

The Industrial Revolution of the eighteenth and nineteenth centuries resulted in even greater changes in human civilization and even greater opportunities for trade, increased production, and the exchange of ideas and knowledge.

The first phase of the Industrial Revolution (1750-1830) saw the mechanization of the textile industry, vast improvements in mining, with the invention of the steam engine, and numerous improvements in transportation, with the development and improvement of turnpikes, canals, and the invention of the railroad.

The second phase (1830-1910) resulted in vast improvements in a number of industries that had already been mechanized through such inventions as the Bessemer steel process and the invention of steam ships. New industries arose as a result of the new technological advances, such as photography, electricity, and chemical processes. New sources of power were harnessed and applied, including petroleum and hydroelectric power. Precision instruments were developed and engineering was launched. It was during this second phase that the industrial revolution spread to other European countries, to Japan, and to the United States.

The direct results of the industrial revolution, particularly as they affected industry, commerce, and agriculture, included:
- Enormous increase in productivity
- Huge increase in world trade
- Specialization and division of labor
- Standardization of parts and mass production
- Growth of giant business conglomerates and monopolies
- A new revolution in agriculture facilitated by the steam engine, machinery, chemical fertilizers, processing, canning, and refrigeration

The political results included:
- Growth of complex government by technical experts
- Centralization of government, including regulatory administrative agencies
- Advantages to democratic development, including extension of franchise to the middle class, and later to all elements of the population, mass education to meet the needs of an industrial society, the development of media of public communication, including radio, television, and cheap newspapers
- Dangers to democracy included the risk of manipulation of the media of mass communication, facilitation of dictatorial centralization and totalitarian control, subordination of the legislative function to administrative directives, efforts to achieve uniformity and conformity, and social impersonalization.

The economic results were numerous:
- The conflict between free trade and low tariffs and protectionism
- The issue of free enterprise against government regulation
- Struggles between labor and capital, including the trade-union movement
- The rise of socialism
- The rise of the utopian socialists
- The rise of Marxian or scientific socialism

The social results of the Industrial Revolution include:
- Increase of population, especially in industrial centers
- Advances in science applied to agriculture, sanitation and medicine
- Growth of great cities
- Disappearance of the difference between city dwellers and farmers
- Faster tempo of life and increased stress from the monotony of the work routine
- The emancipation of women
- The decline of religion
- Rise of scientific materialism
- Darwin's theory of evolution

Increased mobility produced a rapid diffusion of knowledge and ideas. Increased mobility also resulted in wide-scale immigration to industrialized countries. Cultures clashed and cultures melded.

GATT, NAFTA, WTO and EU are all forms of trade liberalization. The GATT was founded in 1947 and today, as the WTO, has 147 member nations. It was based on three principles. The first was Most Favored National status for all members. This means trade based on comparative advantage without tariffs or trade barriers. The second principle was elimination of quotas and third, reduction of trade barriers through multi-lateral trade negotiations. The WTO is the successor to the GATT and came into being in 1995. Its object is to promote free trade. As such it administers trade agreements, settles disputes, and provides a forum for trade discussions and negotiations.

NAFTA and the EU are both forms of regional economic integration. Economic integration is a method of trade liberalization on a regional basis. NAFTA represents the lowest form or first step in the regional trade integration process. A free trade area consists for two or more countries that abolish tariffs and other trade barriers among themselves but maintain their own trade barriers against the rest of the world. A free trade area allows for specialization and trade on the basis of comparative advantage within the area. The next stage in the integration process is a customs union, which is a free trade area that has common external tariffs against non-members. The third stage is a common market which is a customs union with free factor mobility within the area. Factors migrate where they find the best payment within the area. The fourth state is economic union where the common market members have common or coordinated economic and social policies. The final stage is monetary union where the area has a common currency. This is what Europe is working toward. They have a common market with elements of the fourth and fifth stages of integration.

The WTO does not change or blur the significance of political borders and territorial sovereignty in the same way that economic integration does, although the WTO is a way of settling trade disputes that arise from the different integration agreements. In the advanced stages of economic integration the political borders remain, but economic and social policies are common or coordinated and in monetary union, there is one common currency. Each nation is its own independent entity but they give up some sovereignty in the interest of having a successful union.

Trade agreements proliferate in the world today. The Smoot Hawley Tariffs and the rounds of retaliation in the 1930s are what laid the basis for what today are the WTO and the EU. The GATT and the beginnings of what is now the EU came into being as organizations trying to undo the effects of the Great Depression and the world war. Free trade without trade barriers results in the most efficient use of resources, with higher consumption, employment and income levels for all participants. This is why there are so many free trade agreements being negotiated in today's world.

Skill 3.1   Identify the purposes of national, state, and local governments in the United States, describe how citizens organize government to accomplish their purpose, and assess the governments' effectiveness.

The terms "civil liberties" and "civil rights" are often used interchangeably, but there are some fine distinctions between the two terms. The term civil liberties is often used to imply that the state has a positive role to play in assuring that all its' citizens will have equal protection and justice under the law. The term implies equal opportunities to exercise their privileges of citizenship and to participate fully in the life of the nation, regardless of race, religion, sex, color or creed. The term civil rights is used more often to refer to rights that may be described as guarantees that are specified as against the state authority implying limitations on the actions of the state to interfere with citizens' liberties. Although the term "civil rights" has thus been identified with the ideal of equality and the term "civil liberties" with the idea of freedom, the two concepts are really inseparable and interacting. Equality implies the proper ordering of liberty in a society so that one individual's freedom does not infringe on the rights of others.

The beginnings of civil liberties and the idea of civil rights in the United States go back to the ideas of the Greeks. The early British struggle for civil rights and to the very philosophies that led people to come to the New World in the first place. Religious freedom, political freedom, and the right to live one's life as one sees fit are basic to the American ideal. These were embodied in the ideas expressed in the Declaration of Independence and the Constitution.

All these ideas found their final expression in the United States Constitution's first ten amendments, known as the Bill of Rights. In 1789, the first Congress passed these first amendments and by December 1791, three-fourths of the states at that time had ratified them. The Bill of Rights protects certain liberties and basic rights. James Madison who wrote the amendments said that the Bill of Rights does not give Americans these rights. People, Madison said, already have these rights. They are natural rights that belong to all human beings. The Bill of Rights simply prevents the governments from taking away these rights.

To summarize:

The first amendment guarantees the basic rights of freedom of religion, freedom of speech, freedom of the press, and freedom of assembly.

The next three amendments came out of the colonists' struggle with Great Britain. For example, the third amendment prevents Congress from forcing citizens to keep troops in their homes. Before the Revolution, Great Britain tried to coerce the colonists to house soldiers.

Amendments five through eight protect citizens who are accused of crimes and are brought to trial. Every citizen has the right to due process of law (due process as defined earlier, being that the government must follow the same fair rules for everyone brought to trial.) These rules include the right to a trial by an impartial jury, the right to be defended by a lawyer, and the right to a speedy trial.

The last two amendments limit the powers of the federal government to those that are expressly granted in the Constitution, any rights not expressly mentioned in the Constitution, thus, belong to the states or to the people.

In regards to specific guarantees:

Freedom of Religion: Religious freedom has not been seriously threatened in the United States historically. The policy of the government has been guided by the premise that church and state should be separate. When religious practices have been at cross purposes with attitudes prevailing in the nation at particular times, there has been restrictions placed on these practices. Some of these have been restrictions against the practice of polygamy that is supported by certain religious groups. The idea of animal sacrifice that is promoted by some religious beliefs is generally prohibited. The use of mind altering illegal substances that some use in religious rituals has been restricted. In the United States, all recognized religious institutions are tax-exempt in following the idea of separation of church and state, and therefore, there have been many quasi-religious groups that have in the past tried to take advantage of this fact. All of these issues continue, and most likely will continue to occupy both political and legal considerations for some time to come.

Freedom of Speech, Press, and Assembly: These rights historically have been given wide latitude in their practices, though there has been instances when one or the other have been limited for various reasons. The classic limitation, for instance, in regards to freedom of speech, has been the famous precept that an individual is prohibited from yelling fire! in a crowded theatre. This prohibition is an example of the state saying that freedom of speech does not extend to speech that might endanger other people. There is also a prohibition against slander, or the knowingly stating of a deliberately falsehood against one party by another. Also there are many regulations regarding freedom of the press, the most common example are the various laws against libel, (or the printing of a known falsehood). In times of national emergency, various restrictions have been placed on the rights of press, speech and sometimes assembly.

The legal system in recent years has also undergone a number of serious changes some would say challenges, with the interpretation of some constitutional guarantees.

America also has a number of organizations that put themselves out as champions of the fight for civil liberties and civil rights in this country. Much criticism, however, has been raised at times against these groups as to whether or not they are really protecting rights, or by following a specific ideology, perhaps are attempting to create "new" rights. Or are simply in many cases, looking at the strict letter of the law, as opposed to what the law actually intends.

"Rights" come with a measure of responsibility and respect for the public order, all of which must be taken into consideration.

Overall, the American experience has been one of exemplary conduct regarding the protection of individual rights. Overall, there has been a lag in its practice. Notably the refusal to grant full and equal rights to blacks, the fact of their enslavement, and the second class status of women for much of American history, negates the good that the country has done in other areas. Other than the American Civil War, the country has proved itself to be more or less resilient in being able for the most part, to change peacefully when it has not lived up to its' stated ideals in practice. What has been called "the virtual bloodless civil rights revolution" is a case in point.

Though much effort and suffering accompanied the struggle, in the end it did succeed in spite of all. In changing the basic foundation of society in such a profound way that would have been unheard of in many other countries, without the strong tradition of freedom and liberty that was, and is, the underlying feature of American society.

How best to move forward with ensuring civil liberties and civil rights for all continues to dominate the national debate. In recent times, issues seem to revolve not around individual rights, but what has been called "group rights" has been raised. At the forefront of the debate is whether some specific remedies like affirmative action, quotas, gerrymandering and various other forms of preferential treatment are actually fair or just as bad as the ills they are supposed to cure. At the present, no easy answers seem to be forthcoming. It is a testament to the American system that it has shown itself able to enter into these debates, to find solutions and tended to come out stronger.

The fact that the United States has the longest single constitutional history in the modern era is just one reason to be optimistic about the future of American liberty.

Skill 3.2 **Explain the meaning and origin of the ideas, including the core democratic values, expressed in the Declaration of Independence, the Constitution, and other foundational documents of the United States.**

Declaration of Independence - The Declaration of Independence was the founding document of the United States of America. The Articles of Confederation were the first attempt of the newly independent states to reach a new understanding amongst themselves. The Declaration was intended to demonstrate the reasons that the colonies were seeking separation from Great Britain. Conceived by and written for the most part by Thomas Jefferson, it is not only important for what it says, but also for how it says it. The Declaration is in many respects a poetic document. Instead of a simple recitation of the colonists' grievances, it set out clearly the reasons why the colonists were seeking their freedom from Great Britain. They had tried all means to resolve the dispute peacefully. It was the right of a people, when all other methods of addressing their grievances have been tried and failed, to separate themselves from that power that was keeping them from fully expressing their rights to "**life, liberty, and the pursuit of happiness**".

The Declaration of independence is an outgrowth of both ancient Greek ideas of democracy and individual rights and the ideas of the European Enlightenment and the Renaissance, especially the ideology of the political thinker *John Locke*. Thomas Jefferson (1743-1826) the principle author of the Declaration borrowed much from Locke's theories and writings.

Essentially, Jefferson applied Locke's principles to the contemporary American situation. Jefferson argued that the currently reigning King George III had repeatedly violated the rights of the colonists as subjects of the British Crown. Disdaining the colonial petition for redress of grievances (a right guaranteed by the Declaration of Rights of 1689), the King seemed bent upon establishing an "absolute tyranny" over the colonies. Such disgraceful behavior itself violated the reasons for which government had been instituted. The American colonists were left with no choice, *"it is their right, it is their duty, to throw off such a government, and to provide new guards for their future security"* so wrote Thomas Jefferson.

Yet, though his fundamental principles were derived from Locke's, Jefferson was bolder than his intellectual mentor was. He went farther in that his view of natural rights was much broader than Locke's and less tied to the idea of property rights.

See also Section 1.1

Magna Carta - The document that guaranteed rights to English nobles, forced on the British King John in 1215. It is considered an important forerunner to the idea of government having a written limitation of its power.

Articles of Confederation - The first American document that attempted to unite the newly independent colonies after the Revolution. It proved to be unworkable. It was superseded by the Constitution in 1787.

Constitutional Convention - Meeting of delegates from 12 states who wrote a new constitution for the United States in 1787.

Constitution - The written document that describes and defines the system and structure of the United States government. Ratification of the Constitution by the required number of states, (nine of the original thirteen), was completed on June 21, *1788,* and thus the Constitution officially became the law of the land.

Declaration Of Independence - The document that stated that the British colonies in America had become a free and independent nation, adopted July 4, 1776.

Bill Of Rights - The first ten amendments to the United States Constitution dealing with civil liberties and civil rights. They were written mostly by James Madison. They are in brief:

1.   **Freedom of Religion.**
2.   **Right To Bear Arms.**
3.   **Security from the quartering of troops in homes.**
4.   **Right against unreasonable search and seizures.**
5.   **Right against self-incrimination.**
6.   **Right to trial by jury, right to legal council.**
7.   **Right to jury trial for civil actions.**
8.   **No cruel or unusual punishment allowed.**
9.   **These rights shall not deny other rights the people enjoy.**
10.   **Powers not mentioned in the Constitution shall be retained by the states or the people.**

Amendment - An amendment is a change or addition to the United States Constitution. Two-thirds of both houses of Congress must propose and then pass one. Or two-thirds of the state legislatures must call a convention to propose one and then it must be ratified by three-fourths of the state legislatures. To date there are only 26 amendments to the Constitution that have passed.

Skill 3.3   Describe the political and legal processes created to make decisions, seek consensus, and resolve conflicts in a free society.

The term suffrage means voting or the right to vote. Historically the right to vote has always been very limited. Although elections have always been associated with democratic practices, various limitations have been placed on the right to vote throughout history. These have included property qualifications, poll taxes, residency requirements, and restrictions against the right of women to vote.

In 1787, the Constitution of the United States provided for the election of the chief executive in Article II, Section I, and members of the national legislature in Article I, Section II. A number of election abuses, however, led to the adoption of what was known as the Australian, or secret, ballot and the practice of registering voters prior to Election Day. Voting machines were first used in the United States in 1892. During the 19th century, the electorate in the United States grew considerably most of the states franchised all white male adults, although the so-called poll tax was retained. It was abolished by the 24th Amendment to the Constitution, ratified in 1964. The 15th Amendment to the United States Constitution ratified in 1870 extended the vote to the former black slaves. In the period after the Civil War, known as Reconstruction, many blacks were elected to high office for the first time in American history.

It was during the post-Civil War period that the primary system of selecting candidates for public office became widely used. By 1900, the system of primaries was regulated by law in most states. Women in the United States were granted the right to vote by the 19th Amendment to the Constitution, which was ratified in 1920. The right to vote was extended to those eighteen years of age by the 26th Amendment to the Constitution in 1971.

The struggle over what is to be the fair method to ensure equal political representation for all different groups in the United States continues to dominate the national debate. This has revolved around the problems of trying to ensure proper racial and minority representation. Various civil rights acts, notable the Voting Rights Act of 1965, sought to eliminate the remaining features of unequal suffrage in the United States.

Most recently, the question has revolved around the issue of what is called "Gerrymandering", which involves the adjustment of various electoral districts in order to achieve a predetermined goal. Usually this is used in regards to the problem of minority political representation. The fact that gerrymandering sometimes creates odd and unusual looking districts (this is where the practice gets its name) and most often the sole basis of the adjustments is racial. This has led to the questioning of this practice being a fair, let alone constitutional, way for society to achieve its desired goals. This subject promises to be the major issue in national electoral politics for some time to come.

The debate has centered on those of the "left" (Liberals), who favor such methods, and the "right" (Conservatives), who oppose them. Overall, most Americans would consider themselves in the "middle" (Moderates).

Political parties are not mentioned in the United States Constitution. In fact, George Washington himself warned against the creation of "factions" in American politics that cause "jealousies and false alarms" and the damage they could cause to the body politic. Thomas Jefferson echoed this warning, yet he would come to lead a party himself.

Americans had good reason to fear the emergence of political parties. They had witnessed how parties worked in Great Britain. Parties, called "factions" in Britain, thus Washington's warning, were made up of a few people who schemed to win favors from the government. They were more interested in their own personal profit and advantage than in the public good. Thus, the new American leaders were very interested in keeping factions from forming. It was, ironically, disagreements between two of Washington's chief advisors, Thomas Jefferson and Alexander Hamilton that spurred the formation of the first political parties in the newly formed United States of America.

The two parties that developed through the early 1790s were led by Jefferson as the Secretary of State and Alexander Hamilton as the Secretary of the Treasury. Jefferson and Hamilton were different in many ways. Not the least was their views on what should be the proper form of government of the United States. This difference helped to shape the parties that formed around them.

Hamilton wanted the federal government to be stronger than the state governments. Jefferson believed that the state governments should be stronger. Hamilton supported the creation of the first Bank of the United States, Jefferson opposed it because he felt that it gave too much power to wealthy investors who would help run it. Jefferson interpreted the Constitution strictly; he argued that nowhere did the Constitution give the federal government the power to create a national bank. Hamilton interpreted the Constitution much more loosely. He pointed out that the Constitution gave Congress the power to make all laws "necessary and proper" to carry out its duties. He reasoned that since Congress had the right to collect taxes, then Congress had the right to create the bank. Hamilton wanted the government to encourage economic growth. He favored the growth of trade, manufacturing, and the rise of cities as the necessary parts of economic growth. He favored the business leaders and mistrusted the common people. Jefferson believed that the common people, especially the farmers, were the backbone of the nation. He thought that the rise of big cities and manufacturing would corrupt American life.

Finally, Hamilton and Jefferson had their disagreements only in private. But when Congress began to pass many of Hamilton's ideas and programs, Jefferson and his friend, James Madison, decided to organize support for their own views. They moved quietly and very cautiously in the beginning. In 1791, they went to New York telling people that they were going to just study its wildlife. Actually, Jefferson was more interested in meeting with several important New York politicians such as its governor George Clinton and Aaron Burr, a strong critic of Hamilton. Jefferson asked Clinton and Burr to help defeat Hamilton's program by getting New Yorkers to vote for Jefferson's supporters in the next election. Before long, leaders in other states began to organize support for either Jefferson or Hamilton. Jefferson's supporters called themselves Democratic-Republicans (often this was shortened just to Republicans, though in actuality it was the forerunner of today's Democratic Party, not the Republican). Hamilton and his supporters were known as Federalists, because they favored a strong federal government. The Federalists had the support of the merchants and ship owners in the Northeast and some planters in the South. Small farmers, craft workers, and some of the wealthier landowners supported Jefferson and the Democratic-Republicans.

Newspapers, then as now, influenced the growth of political parties. Newspaper publishers and editors took sides on the issues. Thus, from the very beginning, American newspapers and each new branch of the media have played an important role in helping to shape public opinion.

By the time Washington retired from office in 1796, the new political parties would come to play an important role in choosing his successor. Each party would put up its own candidates for office. The election of 1796 was the first one in which political parties played a role. By the beginning of the 1800s, the Federalist Party, torn by internal divisions, began suffering a decline. The election in 1800 of Thomas Jefferson as President, Hamilton's bitter rival, and after its leader Alexander Hamilton was killed in 1804 in a duel with Aaron Burr, the Federalist Party began to collapse. By 1816, after losing a string of important elections, (Jefferson was reelected in 1804, and James Madison, a Democratic-Republican was elected in 1808), the Federalist Party ceased to be an effective political force, and soon passed off the national stage.

By the late 1820s, new political parties had grown up. The Democratic-Republican Party, or simply the Republican Party, had been the major party for many years, but differences within it about the direction the country was headed in caused a split after 1824. Those who favored strong national growth took the name Whigs after a similar party in Great Britain and united around then President John Quincy Adams. Many business people in the Northeast as well as some wealthy planters in the South supported it.

Those who favored slower growth and were more worker and small farmer oriented went on to form the new Democratic Party, with Andrew Jackson being its first leader as well as becoming the first President from it. It is the forerunner of today's present party of the same name.

In the mid-1850s, the slavery issue was beginning to heat up and in 1854, those opposed to slavery, the Whigs, and some Northern Democrats opposed to slavery, united to form the Republican Party. Before the Civil War, the Democratic Party was more heavily represented in the South and was thus pro-slavery for the most part.

Thus, by the time of the Civil War, the present form of the major political parties had been formed. Though there would sometimes be drastic changes in ideology and platforms over the years, no other political parties would manage to gain enough strength to seriously challenge the "Big Two" parties.

In fact, they have shown themselves adaptable to changing times. In many instances, they have managed to shut out other parties by simply adapting their platforms, such as in the 1930s during the Great Depression and in the years immediately proceeding. The Democratic Party adapted much of the Socialist Party platform and, under Franklin Roosevelt, put much of it into effect thus managing to eliminate it as any serious threat. Since the Civil War, no other political party has managed to gain enough support to either elect substantial members to Congress or elect a President. Some have come closer than others, but barring any unforeseen circumstances, the absolute monopoly on national political debate seems very secure in the hands of the Republican and Democratic parties.

Skill 3.4   Explain how American governmental institutions at the local, state, and federal levels provide for the limitation and sharing of power and how the nation's political system provides for the exercise of power.

In the United States, the three branches of the federal government, the Executive, the Legislative, and the Judicial, divide up their powers thus:

Legislative – Article 1 of the Constitution established the legislative, or law-making branch of the government called the Congress. It is made up of two houses, the House of Representatives and the Senate. Voters in all states elect the members who serve in each respective House of Congress. The legislative branch is responsible for making laws, raising and printing money, regulating trade, establishing the postal service and federal courts, approving the President's appointments, declaring war and supporting the armed forces. The Congress also has the power to change the Constitution itself, and to *impeach* (bring charges against) the President. Charges for impeachment are brought by the House of Representatives, and are then tried in the Senate.

Executive – Article 2 of the Constitution created the Executive branch of the government, headed by the President, who leads the country, recommends new laws, and can veto bills passed by the legislative branch. As the chief of state, the President is responsible for carrying out the laws of the country and the treaties and declarations of war passed by the legislative branch. The President also appoints federal judges and is commander-in-chief of the military when it is called into service. Other members of the Executive branch include the Vice-President, also elected, and various cabinet members as he might appoint: ambassadors, presidential advisors, members of the armed forces, and other appointed and civil servants of government agencies, departments and bureaus. Though the President appoints them, they must be approved by the legislative branch.

Judicial – Article 3 of the Constitution established the judicial branch of government headed by the Supreme Court. The Supreme Court has the power to rule that a law passed by the legislature, or an act of the Executive branch is illegal and unconstitutional. Citizens, businesses, and government officials can in an appeal capacity, ask the Supreme Court to review a decision made in a lower court if someone believes that the ruling by a judge is unconstitutional. The Judicial branch also includes lower federal courts known as federal district courts that have been established by the Congress. These courts try lawbreakers and review cases referred from other courts.

Powers delegated to the federal government: Powers reserved to the states:

1. To tax.	1. To regulate intrastate trade.
2. To borrow and coin money	2. To establish local governments.
3. To establish postal service.	3. To protect general welfare.
4. To grant patents and copyrights.	4. To protect life and property.
5. To regulate interstate and foreign commerce.	5. To ratify amendments.
6. To establish courts.	6. To conduct elections.
7. To declare war.	7. To make state and local laws.
8. To raise and support the armed forces.	
9. To govern territories.	
10. To define and punish felonies and piracy on the high seas.	
11. To fix standards of weights and measures.	
12. To conduct foreign affairs.	

Concurrent powers of the federal government and states:

1. Both Congress and the states may tax.
2. Both may borrow money.
3. Both may charter banks and corporations.
4. Both may establish courts.
5. Both may make and enforce laws.
6. Both may take property for public purposes.
7. Both may spend money to provide for the public welfare.

Implied powers of the federal government.

1. To establish banks or other corporations, implied from delegated powers to tax, borrow, and to regulate commerce.
2. To spend money for roads, schools, health, insurance, etc. implied from powers to establish post roads, to tax to provide for general welfare and defense, and to regulate commerce.
3. To create military academies, implied from powers to raise and support an armed force.
4. To locate and generate sources of power and sell surplus, implied from powers to dispose of government property, commerce, and war powers.
5. To assist and regulate agriculture, implied from power to tax and spend for general welfare and regulate commerce.

Skill 3.5 **Understand how the world is organized politically, the formation of American foreign policy, and the roles the United States plays in the international arena.**

Government ultimately began as a form of protection. A strong person, usually one of the best warriors or someone who had the support of many strong men, assumed command of a people or a city or a land. The power to rule those people rested in his hands. (The vast majority of rulers throughout history have been male.) Laws existed insofar as the pronouncements and decision of the ruler and were not, in practice, written down, leading to inconsistency. Religious leaders had a strong hand in governing the lives of people, and in many instances the political leader was also the primary religious figure.

First in Greece and then in Rome and then in other places throughout the world, the idea of government by more than one person or more than just a handful came to the fore. Even though more people were involved, the purpose of government hadn't changed. These governments still existed to keep the peace and protect their people from encroachments by both inside and outside forces.

Through the Middle Ages and on into even the 20th century, many countries still had **monarchs** as their heads of state. These monarchs made laws (or, later, upheld laws), but the laws were still designed to protect the welfare of the people—and the state.

In the modern day, people are subject to **laws** made by many levels of government. Local governments such as city and county bodies are allowed to pass ordinances covering certain local matters, such as property taxation, school districting, civil infractions and business licensing. These local bodies have perhaps the least political power in the governmental hierarchy, but being small and relatively accessible, they are often the level at which many citizens become directly involved with government. Funding for local governments often comes from property and sales taxes.

State governments in the United States are mainly patterned after the federal government, with an elected legislative body, a judicial system, and a governor who oversees the executive branch. Like the federal government, state governments derive their authority from **constitutions**. State legislation applies to all residents of that state, and local laws must conform. State government funding is frequently from state income tax and sales taxes.

The national, or federal government of the United States derives its power from the US Constitution and has three branches, the legislative, executive and judicial. The federal government exists to make national policy and to legislate matters that affect the residents of all states, and to settle matters between states. National income tax is the primary source for federal funding.

The US Constitution also provides the federal government with the authority to make treaties and enter agreements with foreign countries, creating a body of international law. While there is no authoritative international government, organizations such as the United Nations, the European Union and other smaller groups exist to promote economic and political cooperation between nations.

The elements of the U.S. Government that pursue and conduct foreign policy are large and varied. Some are in the Legislative Branch; others are in the Executive Branch.

The most well known foreign policy advocate is the **Secretary of State**, who resides in the Executive Branch and is appointed by the President and confirmed by Congress. The Secretary of State is the country's primary ambassador to other countries, having prime responsibilities in this regard for attending international meetings, brokering peace deals, and negotiating treaties. The Secretary of State often acts as the "voice of the country," speaking for the interests of the United States to the rest of the world.: Since the Secretary of State is appointed by the President, he or she is expected to follow the policy directives of the President. It is usually the case that the two people are of the same political party and share political views on important issues.

The Executive Branch also has a **National Security Council**, which advises the President on matters of foreign policy. Members of this group are not nearly as visible or well traveled as the Secretary of State, but they do provide the President and other members of the Government with valuable information and perspectives.

The most numerous of the Executive Branch members involved in foreign policy are the **ambassadors**. Most countries throughout the world have ambassadors, people who reside in other countries in order to represent their home countries' interests. The United States has ambassadors to most countries in the world; by the same token, most countries in the world have embassies, buildings and organizations that contain offices for these ambassadors. These ambassadors attend official functions in their "adopted" countries and speak for their countries in international meetings.

The Legislative Branch plays an important role in U.S. foreign policy as well. The Senate in particular is responsible for approving treaties and ambassadorial appointments. Both houses of Congress have committees of lawmakers who specialize in foreign policy. These lawmakers make a habit of keeping abreast of happenings elsewhere in the world and advising their fellow lawmakers on foreign businesses, issues, and conflicts. These foreign policy-focused lawmakers often tour other countries and attend state functions, but they don't have the voice or responsibility of ambassadors.

Increasingly, state and local governments practice foreign policy as well. Governors and lawmakers of many states have trade agreements with other countries; these agreements are not on the order of national agreements, but they do deal with foreign relations all the same, mainly with economics. Local governments, too, get involved with things overseas. A good example of this is the growing practice of implementing a "sister city," whereby a city in the U.S. "adopts" a city in another country and exchanges ideas, goods, services, and technology and other resources with its new "companion."

Skill 4.1   **Describe and demonstrate how the economic forces of scarcity and choice affect the management of personal financial resources; shape consumer decisions regarding the purchase, use, and disposal of goods and services; and affect the economic well-being of individuals and society.**

Free enterprise, individual entrepreneurship, competitive markets and consumer sovereignty are all parts of a **market economy**. Individuals have the right to make their own decisions as to what they want to do as a career. The financial incentives are there for individuals who are willing to take the risk. A successful venture earns profit. It is these financial incentives that serve to motivate inventors and small businesses. The same is true for businesses. They are free to determine what production technique they want to use and what output they want to produce within the confines of the legal system. They can make investments based on their own decisions. Nobody is telling them what to do. Competitive markets, relatively free from government interference are also a manifestation of the freedom that the U.S. economic system is based on. These markets function on the basis of supply and demand to determine output mix and resource allocation. There is no commissar dictating what is produced and how. Since consumers buy the goods and services that give them satisfaction, this means that, for the most part, they don't buy the goods and services that they don't want that don't give them satisfaction.

Consumers are, in effect, voting for the goods and services that they want with the dollars or what is called dollar voting. Consumers are basically signaling firms as to how they want society's scarce resources used with their dollar votes. A good that society wants acquires enough dollar votes for the producer to experience profits – a situation where the firm's revenues exceed the firm's costs. The existence of profits indicate to the firm that it is producing the goods and services that consumers want and that society's scarce resources are being used in accordance with consumer preferences. When a firm does not have a profitable product, it is because that product is not tabulating enough dollar votes of consumers. Consumers don't want the good or service and they don't want society's scarce resources being used in its production.

This process where consumers vote with their dollars is called **consumer sovereignty**. Consumers are basically directing the allocation of scarce resources in the economy with the dollar spending. Firms, who are in business to earn profit, then hire resources, or inputs, in accordance with consumer preferences. This is the way in which resources are allocated in a market economy. This is the manner in which society achieves the output mix that it desires.

The fact that resources are scarce is the basis for the existence of economics. Economics is defined as a study of how scarce resources are allocated to satisfy unlimited wants. Resources refer to the four factors of production: **labor, capital, land and entrepreneurship**. The fact that the supply of these resources is finite means that society cannot have as much of everything that it wants. There is a constraint on production and consumption and on the kinds of goods and services that can be produced and consumed. **Scarcity** means that choices have to be made. If society decides to produce more of one good, this means that there are fewer resources available for the production of other goods. Assume a society can produce two goods, good A and good B. The society uses resources in the production of each good. If producing one unit of good A results in an amount of resources used to produce three units of good B then producing one more unit of good A results in a decrease in 3 units of good B. In effect, one unit of good A "costs" three units of good B. This cost is referred to as opportunity cost. **Opportunity cost** is the value of the sacrificed alternative, the value of what had to be given up in order to have the output of good A. Opportunity cost does not just refer to production. Your opportunity cost of studying with this guide is the value of what you are not doing because you are studying, whether it is watching TV, spending time with family, working, or whatever. Every choice has an opportunity cost.

Marginal analysis is used greatly in the study of economics. The term marginal always means "the change in". There are benefits and costs associated with every decision. The benefits are the gains or the advantages of a decision or action. If we are talking about production, the gains are the increases in output. If we are talking about an additional hour of study with this guide, the gains are the amount of material covered. There are also costs associated with each. The production costs involve the cost of the resources involved and the cost of their alternative uses. The costs of studying are the opportunity costs of what you have to give up, whether it is sleep, socializing, working, etc. In terms of marginal analysis, what are the marginal benefits and marginal costs of an additional unit of output or amount of a change is there in benefits and costs from producing the additional unit? The marginal benefits of the additional unit is the change in total benefits from a one unit change in output, or mathematically, the change in total benefits divided by the change in the quantity of output. The same is true for marginal cost.

Marginal cost is the increase in costs from producing one more unit of output, or the change in total cost divided by the change in quantity of output. Looking at costs and benefits in this way is referred to as making decisions at the margin and this is the methodology used in the study of economics.

Skill 4.2   Explain and demonstrate how businesses confront scarcity and choice when organizing, producing, and using resources, and when supplying the marketplace.

Economic systems refer to the arrangements a society has devised to answer what are known as the Three Questions: What goods to produce, How to produce the goods, and For Whom are the goods being produced, or how is the allocation of the output determined. Different economic systems answer these questions in different ways.

A market economy answers these questions in terms of demand and supply and the use of markets. Consumers vote for the products they want with their dollar spending. Goods acquiring enough dollar votes are profitable, signaling to the producers that society wants their scarce resources used in this way. This is how the "What" question is answered. The producer then hires inputs in accordance with the goods consumers want, looking for the most efficient or lowest cost method of production. The lower the firm's costs for any given level of revenue, the higher the firm's profits. This is the way in which the "How" question is answered in a market economy. The "For Whom" question is answered in the marketplace by the determination of the equilibrium price. Price serves to ration the good to those that can and will transact at the market price of better. Those who can't or won't are excluded from the market. The United States has a market economy.

The opposite of the market economy is called the centrally planned economy. This used to be called Communism, even though the term in not correct in a strict Marxian sense. In a planned economy, the means of production are publicly owned with little, if any private ownership. Instead of the Three Questions being solved by markets, they have a planning authority that makes the decisions in place of markets. The planning authority decides what will be produced and how. Since most planned economies directed resources into the production of capital and military goods, there was little remaining for consumer goods and the result was chronic shortages. Price functioned as an accounting measure and did not reflect scarcity. The former Soviet Union and most of the Eastern Bloc countries were planned economies of this sort.

In between the two extremes is market socialism. This is a mixed economic system that uses both markets and planning. Planning is usually used to direct resources at the upper levels of the economy, with markets being used to determine prices of consumer goods and wages. This kind of economic system answers the three questions with planning and markets. The former Yugoslavia was a market socialist economy. You can put each nation of the world on a continuum in terms of these characteristics and rank them from most capitalistic to the most planned.

The United States would probably rank as the most capitalistic and North Korea would probably rank as the most planned, but this doesn't mean that the United States doesn't engage in planning or that economies like mainland China don't use markets.

Skill 4.3   Describe how government decisions on taxation, spending, public goods, and regulation impact what is produced, how it is produced, and who receives the benefits of production.

Government policies, whether they are federal, state or local, affect economic decision-making and in many cases, the distribution of resources. This is the purpose of most economic policies imposed at the federal level. Governments don't implement monetary and fiscal policy at the state or local level, only at the national level. Most state and local laws that affect economic decision-making and the distribution of resources have to do with taxation. If taxes are imposed or raised at the state or local level, the effect is less spending. The purpose of these taxes is to raise revenues for the state and local government, not to affect the level of aggregate demand and inflation. At the federal level, the major purpose of these policies is to affect the level of aggregate demand and the inflation rate or the unemployment rate.

Government at all three levels affect the distribution of resources and economic decision-making through transfer payments. This is an attempt to bring about a redistribution of income and to correct the problem of income inequality. Programs like Food Stamps, AFDC (welfare), unemployment compensation, Medicaid all fall into this category. Technically, these government transfer programs result in a rearrangement of private consumption, not a real reallocation of resources. Price support programs in agriculture also result in a redistribution of income and a misallocation of resources. The imposition of artificially high prices results in too many resources going into agriculture and leads to product surpluses.

Laws can be enacted at all three levels to correct for the problem of externalities. An externality occurs when uninvolved third parties are affected by some market activity, like pollution. Dumping obnoxious and sometimes poisonous wastes into the air and water means that the air and water are being treated as a free input by the firm. The market does not register all of the costs of production because the firm does not have to pay to use the air or water. The result of the free inputs is lower production costs for the firm and an over allocation of resources into the production of the good the firm is producing. The role for government here is to cause a redistribution of resources by somehow shifting all or part of the cost on to the offending firm. They can impose fines, taxes, require pollution abatement equipment, sell pollution permits, etc. Whatever method they choose, this raises the costs of production for the firms and forces them to bear some of the cost.

Policies can be enacted in order to encourage labor to migrate from one sector of the economy to another. This is primarily done at the national level. The United States economy is so large that it is possible to have unemployment in different areas while the economy is at full employment. The purpose here is to cause unemployed labor in one area to migrate to another area where there are open jobs. State unemployment and labor agencies provide the information for these people.

Fiscal policy refers to changes in the levels of government spending and taxation. All three levels of government engage in fiscal policy that has economic and social effects. At the state and local levels, the purpose of government spending and taxes is to run the state and local governments. When taxes are raised at the state or local level, the purpose is to provide revenues for the government to function, not to affect the level of aggregate spending in the economy. Even though, these taxes still have economic and social effects on the local population who has less money to spend. Local merchants may see a decrease in their revenues from less spending, in addition to having to pay taxes themselves. When state and local governments spend money through local programs, like repairing or building roads, the effect is to inject money into the local economy even though the purpose is to promote transportation. The purpose isn't to stimulate spending in the area.

Fiscal policy at the national level differs from that at the state and local levels because the purpose of the fiscal policy is to affect the level of aggregate spending in the economy. One of the functions of the federal government is to promote economic stabilization. This means to correct for inflation and unemployment. The way they do this is through changing the level of government spending and/or the level of taxation. Inflation occurs when there is too high a level of aggregate spending. There is too much spending in the economy. Producers can't keep up with the demand and the result in rising prices. In this situation the government implements contractionary fiscal policy which consists of a decrease in government spending and/ or an increase in taxes. The purpose is to slow down an economy that is expanding too quickly by enacting policies that result in people having less money to spend. These policies, depending on how they are implemented, will affect the components of aggregate demand – consumption, investment and government spending. Spending on imports will also decrease. The result of the contractionary fiscal policy will be, hopefully, to end the inflation.

Unemployment is another macro economic problem that requires expansionary fiscal policy. Unemployment occurs due to a lack of spending in the economy. There is not enough aggregate demand in the economy to fully employ the labor force. Here the role for government is to stimulate spending. If they can increase spending, producers will increase their output and hire more resources, including labor, thus eliminating the problem of unemployment. Expansionary fiscal policy consists of increasing government spending and/or lowering taxes. The increase in government spending injects money into the economy. Government programs to build roads mean more jobs. More jobs mean more spending and a higher level of aggregate demand. As producers see an increase in the demand for their product, they increase their output levels. As they expand, they require more resources, including labor. As more of the labor force works, the level of spending increases still further, and so on. Lowering taxes affects the consumption and possibly the investment components of aggregate demand leaving consumers and businesses with more money to spend, thus leading to a higher level of spending and eliminating unemployment.

Nations need a smoothly functioning banking system in order to experience economic growth. The Federal Reserve implements monetary policy through the banking system and it is a tool used to promote economic stability at the macro level of the economy. There are three components of monetary policy: the **reserve ratio**, the **discount rate** and **open market operations**. Changes in any of these three components affect the amount of money in the banking system and thus, the level of spending in the economy.

The reserve ratio refers to the portion of deposits that banks are required to hold as vault cash or on deposit with the Fed. The purpose of this reserve ratio is to give the Fed a way to control the money supply. These funds can't be used for any other purpose. When the Fed changes the reserve ratio, it changes the money creation and lending ability of the banking system. When the Fed wants to expand the money supply it lowers the reserve ratio, leaving banks with more money to loan. This is one aspect of expansionary monetary policy. When the reserve ratio is increased, this results in banks having less money to make loans with, which is a form of contractionary monetary policy, which leads to a lower level of spending in the economy.

Another way in which monetary policy is implemented is by changing the discount rate. When banks have temporary cash shortages, they can borrow from the Fed. The interest rate on the funds they borrow is called the discount rate. Raising and lowering the discount rate is a way of controlling the money supply. Lowering the discount rate encourages banks to borrow from the Fed, instead of restricting their lending to deal with the temporary cash shortage.

By encouraging banks to borrow, their lending ability is increased and this results in a higher level of spending in the economy. Lowering the discount rate is a form of expansionary monetary policy. Discouraging bank lending by raising the discount rate, then is a form of contractionary monetary policy.

The final tool of monetary policy is called open market operations. This consists of the Fed buying or selling government securities with the public or with the banking system. When the Fed sells bonds, it is taking money out of the banking system. The public and the banks pay for the bonds, thus resulting in fewer dollars in the economy and a lower level of spending. The Fed selling bonds is a form of contractionary monetary policy that leads to a lower level of spending in the economy. The Fed is expanding the money supply when it buys bonds from the public or the banking system because it is paying for those bonds with dollars that enter the income-expenditures stream. The result of the Fed buying bonds is to increase the level of spending in the economy.

Modern mixed economies do not result in an equal distribution of income for all of their members. Some people are very rich and some people are very poor. The remainder of the population is somewhere in-between. The reason is that not everyone has the same resource skills to supply in the input market from which they derive their income. The fact that they don't supply the same skills means that they don't all receive the same factor income. Resource owners supplying highly demanded rare skills receive more compensation than those supplying little or no skills: the more abundant the factor skill or lack of skills, the lower the factor compensation. An efficient economy does not result in an equal or equitable distribution of income. This is a fact of capitalism. A role for government then is to implement certain kinds of social policies to try to correct for the income inequality resulting from a market economy. These policies basically effect a redistribution of income from those in the higher income brackets to those in the lower income brackets. There are different ways of accomplishing this income redistribution.

One way of redistributing income is through the federal income tax system. Taxes can be progressive, regressive or proportional. A **progressive tax** is when the tax rate increases as income increases. Those in higher income brackets pay a larger percentage of their income in taxes than those in lower income brackets do. The federal income tax is a progressive tax. A **regressive tax** is the opposite, where the tax rate decreases as the level of income increases. Here, the tax rate is higher on lower income brackets than on higher income brackets. The social security tax is in this category. A **proportional tax** is where the tax rate is the same for all income levels. The progressive tax is based on the idea of equity, that the tax burden should be heavier on people with higher income than on people with lower incomes.

There are many social programs that distribute transfer payments. This is another way of bringing about a redistribution of income and trying to correct for the inequities of a mixed economy. Transfers payment programs are programs like food stamps, Aid to Families with Dependent Children (AFDC) which people refer to as welfare, Medicaid, etc. All of these programs are redistributing tax dollars from the upper income levels to the lower income levels. Most of these programs provide aid to the lower income levels for a specific purpose, whether its food, medical care, support of children or whatever. With the exception of AFDC, they are know as in-kind programs because the aid is geared to a specific area and supplies the good or service instead of just supplying dollars for them to spend in whatever way they want.

Agricultural price support programs also bring about a redistribution of income from the population to the agricultural sector by legally mandating prices higher than the market. The farmers could not survive without this program and they produce the food for the nation. All of these programs are implemented to try to correct for some of the inequities that result from a market economy.

See also 4.2

Skill 4.4   Explain how a free market economic system works, as well as other economic systems, to coordinate and facilitate the exchange, production, distribution, and consumption of goods and services.

A consumer is a person who uses goods and services and, in a capitalist or free enterprise economy, decides with other consumers what is produced by what they choose to buy. The terms "supply and demand" are used to explain the influence of consumers on production. This law or principle of supply and demand means that prices of goods rise due to an increased demand and fall when there is an increase in the supply of goods.

Due to unstable economies, inflation, job insecurity due to downsizing, bankruptcy and other factors, having cash on hand while buying is less prevalent than having credit cards. These cards are frequently referred to as "plastic money" but in reality are not money. They are a convenient tool for receiving a short-term loan from the financial institutions issuing the cards. These popular pieces of plastic aid consumers in such economic activities as purchasing items on "installment plans." Financial institutions are not the only ones issuing credit cards. Oil companies, airlines, national automobile manufacturers, and large corporations are just some of the backers of credit cards. Department store charge cards do not enable the holder to obtain money from an Automated Teller Machine (ATM) but do enable one to buy on credit or on the installment plan. Automobile dealerships, banks, credit unions, loan companies all, in similar ways, make it possible for just about anyone to purchase on installment and drive a car. Mortgages allow people to pay for their own homes or condominiums.

Those other important modern economic and ideological systems that have had the greatest effect in modern era are *Socialism, Communism,* and *Fascism.*

Each will be examined in its turn.

Socialism – This is a fairly recent political phenomenon though its roots can be traced pretty far back in time in many respects. At the core, both socialism and communism are fundamentally economic philosophies that advocate public rather than private ownership, especially over means of production, yet even here, there are many distinctions. Karl Marx basically concentrated his attention on the industrial worker and on state domination over the means of production.

In practice, this Marxian dogma has largely been followed the most in those countries that profess to be Communist. In conjunction with massive programs for the development of heavy industry, this emphasis on production regardless of the wants or comforts of the individual in the given society. Socialism by contrast, usually occurring where industry has already been developed, has concerned itself more with the welfare of the individual and the fair distribution of whatever wealth is available.

Communism has a rigid theology, and a bible (*Das Capital*), that sees Communism emerging as a result of almost cosmic laws. Modern socialism sees change in human society and hopes for improvement, but there is no unchanging millennium at the end of the road. Communism is sure that it will achieve the perfect state and in this certainty it is willing to use any and all means, however ruthless, to bring it about.

Socialism on the other hand, confident only that the human condition is always changing, makes no easy approximation between ends and means and so cannot justify brutalities. This distinction in philosophy, of course, makes for an immense conflict in methods. Communism, believing that revolution is inevitable, works toward it by emphasizing class antagonisms. Socialism, while seeking change, insists on the use of democratic procedures within the existing social order of a given society. In it, the upper classes and capitalists are not to be violently overthrown but instead to be won over by logical persuasion.

It is interesting to note that in every perfect, idealized community or society that people have dreamed about throughout history, where human beings are pictured living in a special harmony that transcends their natural instincts, there has been a touch of socialism. This tendency was especially found in the *Utopian-Socialists* of the early 19th century, whose basic aim was the repudiation of the private-property system with its economic inefficiency and social injustice. Their criticisms rather than any actual achievements would linger after them. Like Marx, they envisioned industrial capitalism as becoming more and more inhumane and oppressive. They could not imagine the mass of workers prospering in such a system. Yet the workers soon developed their own powerful organizations and institutions. They began to bend the economic system to their own benefit. Thus a split did occur.

First, between those who after the growing success of the labor movement rejected the earlier utopian ideas as being impractical. Second, those who saw in this newfound political awareness of the working class the key to organizing a realistic ability of revolution, who saw this as inevitable based on their previous observations and study of history. Having reached a point where it has managed to jeopardize its very own survival, the inevitable revolution of those opposed to the present capitalist system had to occur, history has proven this so, and history is always right and irrefutable.

These believers in the absolute correctness of this doctrine gathered around Marx in what he called *Scientific Socialism*. In contempt to all other kinds which he considered not to be scientific, and therefore, useless as a realistic political philosophy.

The next split would occur between those who believed in the absolute inevitability of the coming revolution (the *Revolutionary Socialists* or as they came to be known, the *Communists*), and those while accepting the basic idea that the current capitalist system could not last, saw in the growing political awareness of the working class the beginnings of an ability to effect peaceful and gradual change in the social order. They believed this is better in the long run for everyone concerned as opposed to a cataclysmic, apocalyptic uprising (the *Democratic-Socialists*).

Major strides for the *Democratic-Socialists* were made before the First World War. A war that the Socialists, by philosophy pacifists, initially resisted, giving only reluctant support only once the struggle had begun. During the conflict, public sentiment against pacifism tended generally to weaken the movement, but with peace, reaction set in. The cause of world socialism leaped forward, often overcompensating by adhering to revolutionary communism which in the Revolution of 1917, had taken hold of in Russia. The between wars period saw the sudden spurt of socialism, whether their leanings were democratic or not, all socialists were bound together for a time in their resistance to fascism.

The decade following World War II saw tremendous growth in socialism. Economic planning and the nationalization of industry was undertaken in many countries and to this day have not been repudiated, though a subsequent return to self-confidence in the private business community and among voters, in general, has frequently weakened the socialist majority or reduced it to the status of an opposition party. This political balance leaves most industrialized countries with a mixed socialist-capitalist economy. So long as there is no major world-wide depression, this situation may remain relatively stable. The consequences of World War II, particularly the independence of former European colonies, has opened vast new areas for the attempted development of socialist forms. Most have tried to aspire to the democratic type but very few have succeeded except where democratic traditions were strong.

Socialism though concentrating on economic relationships, has always considered itself a complete approach to human society. In effect, a new belief system and thus a world rather than a national movement.

In this respect as well, it owes much to Great Britain for it was in London in 1864 that the first *Socialist International* was organized by Karl Marx. This radical leftist organization died off after limping along for twelve years, by which time its headquarters had moved to New York.

After the passage of about another twelve years, the *Second Socialist International* met in Paris to celebrate the anniversary of the fall of the Bastille in the French Revolution. By this time, serious factions were developing. There were the Anarchists, who wanted to tear down everything, Communists who wanted to tear down the established order and build another in its place, and the Democratic-Socialist majority who favored peaceful political action.

Struggling for internal peace and cohesion right up to the First World War, socialism would remain largely ineffectual at this critical international time. Peace brought them all together again in Bern, Switzerland, but by this time the Soviet Union had been created, and the Russian Communists refused to attend the meeting on the ground that the Second Socialist International opposed the type of dictatorship it saw as necessary in order to achieve revolutions. Thus the *Communist International* was created in direct opposition to the Socialist International. While the socialists went on to advocate the "triumph of democracy, firmly rooted in the principles of liberty". The main objective of this new Socialist International was to maintain the peace, an ironic and very elusive goal in the period between the two world wars.

The Nazi attack on Poland in September, 1939, completely shattered the organization. In 1946, however a new *Socialist Information and Liaison Office* was set up to reestablish old contacts, and in 1951 the Communist International was revived with a conference in Frankfurt, Germany. At which time, it adopted a document entitled "Aims and Tasks of Democratic Socialism". A summary of these objectives gives a good picture of modern Democratic-Socialism as it exists on paper in its ideal form.

As always, the first principle is nationalized ownership of the major means of production and distribution. Usually public ownership is deemed appropriate for the strategically important services, public utilities, banking and resource industries such as coal, iron, lumber and oil. Farming has never been considered well adapted to public administration and has usually been excluded from nationalization. From this takeover of the free enterprise system, socialists expect a more perfect freedom to evolve. Offering equal opportunity for all, the minimizing of class conflict, better products for less cost, and security from physical want or need.

At the international level, socialism seeks a world of free peoples living together in peace and harmony for the mutual benefit of all. That freedom, at least from colonial rule, has largely been won. Peace throughout the world, however, is still as far off in most respects as it has ever been. According to the socialist doctrine, putting an end to capitalism will do much to reduce the likelihood of war. Armies and business are seen to need each other in a marriage of the weapons-mentality and devotion to private profit through the economic exploitation of weaker countries.

The United States remains the bastion of the free enterprise system. Socialism in the United States has long been regarded historically as a "menace" to the "American way". There is no doubt that socialists argue for change. Capitalism in their opinion makes for unfair distribution of wealth, causing private affluence and public squalor. They also hold it responsible for environmental pollution and economic inflation. By curbing the absolute freedom of the private businessman or corporation, socialism hopes to satisfy all human necessities at the price of individual self-indulgence. Anti-trust legislation, the graduated income tax, and Social Security have all moved the United States toward the idea of the "welfare state", which recognizes as its prime objective full employment and a minimum living standard for all, whether employed or not.

While communism and socialism arose in reaction to the excesses of 19th century capitalism, all three have matured in the past 100 years. Capitalism has mellowed, while a sibling rivalry may continue to exist between communism and socialism. Officially, communism clings to the idea of revolution and the seizing of capitalist property by the state without compensation socialism accepts gradualism, feeling that a revolution, particularly in an industrial society would be ruinous. In fact, socialists and in some situations even communists, have come to realize that not all economic institutions function better in public hands. Private responsibility frequently offers benefits that go to the public good. This is particularly true in the agricultural sector, where personal ownership and cultivation of land have always been deeply ingrained.

All socialism denies certain freedoms, sometimes hidden in what it considers favorable terms. It deprives the minority of special economic privileges for the benefit of majority. The more left-wing, communistic socialism may deny the democratic process entirely. Traditionally defined, democracy holds to the idea that the people, exercising their majority opinion at the polls, will arrive at the common good by electing representative individuals to govern them. Communists would interpret this to mean the tyranny of an uneducated majority obliged to decide between a politically selected group of would-be leaders.

There is no question that the democratic process has its limitations, but for want of a better method, contemporary socialism accepts democracy as a major principle.

The expressed goals of modern socialism are commendable, but goals of course are easy to state, especially when there is no real opportunity to carry them out. The gulf between theory and practice is often insurmountable, the situation thus remains whether given the chance socialism can bring about a better world than now exists. Nowhere today does socialism exist in a pure and unchallenged form, but in many nations it has made impressive gains.

Communism –In 1848, Karl Marx (with Freidrich Engels) began his *Communist Manifesto* with the prophetic sentence "*a specter is haunting Europe, the specter of communism".* Little more than a century later, nearly one third of the world's population would live under governments professing communism. Even with the collapse of the Soviet Union and the Eastern Communist Block, China with nearly one fourth of the world's population, not to mention North Korea and Cuba, still claim to follow the communist ideal. Yet, in these societies, not one of them could say that they have achieved, (through massive toil, treachery and bloodshed), the ideal state that communism was supposed to create.

Marx took the name for his ideal society from the *French Communes*, feudal villages that held land and produce in common. But he was not satisfied with villages. His dream was of newly industrialized Europe shaped into a communist world. As he saw it, other systems would give way, or if they fought back, would be destroyed. With the birth of the industrial age in the early 19th century, privately owned factories employed larger and larger work forces. The owners of these factories made vast profits, which they plowed back into building more factories. The workers were becoming mere tools in a huge anonymous crowd, alienated from the product of their toil. Labor was hard, often dangerous, and poorly rewarded.

This was the economic system of capitalism in its formative years, and Marx saw it leading only to increased enrichment of the owners of great businesses and to the eventual enslavement of the working class. Marx exhorted the workers to revolt. He urged them in his writings to seize the factories from the capitalists, not in order to become capitalist themselves, but in order to place the means of production in the hands of the community for the benefit of all its citizens. This intermediate society controlling the means of production is called the "*Dictatorship of the Proletariat"*. It is what the Soviet Union and other so-called communist nations achieved, but it is not communism. True communism comes only with the further step of the state giving ownership back to the people who then continue to live together in abundance without supervision from a ruling class.

So, despite endless writing on the subject of communism, almost all of its verbiage has been devoted to the struggle to achieve socialism. Today for the commissar who drives the worker, and the peasant who pulls the load, communism still remains the goal, the end of the struggle. Though Marx and his disciples have insisted and continue to insist that socialism is only a stop on the way to communism, they have not dared to describe this final paradise on Earth except in the haziest of ways.

With the final achievement of communism, greed and competition will presumably cease. Each person will contribute according to their ability and receive according to their need. There will be no cause for crime or vice of any kind, no race or class rivalry, no grounds for war, and no reason for government.

Perfection indeed, but unhappily not yet of this world. In fact, it is not measurably nearer today anywhere than when Marx first conceived it.

Fascism – The last important historical economic system to arise. It has been called a reaction against the last two ideologies discussed. It can, at times cooperate with a Monarchy if it has to.

In general, Fascism is the effort to create, by dictatorial means, a viable national society in which competing interests were to be adjusted to each other by being entirely subordinated to the service of the state. The following features have been characteristic of Fascism in its various manifestations: (1) An origin at a time of serious economic disruption and of rapid and bewildering social change. (2) A philosophy that rejects democratic and humanitarian ideals and glorifies the absolute sovereignty of the state, the unity and destiny of the people, and their unquestioning loyalty and obedience to the dictator. (3) An aggressive nationalism which calls for the mobilization and regimentation of every aspect of national life and makes open use of violence and intimidation. (4) The simulation of mass popular support, accomplished by outlawing all but a single political party and by using suppression, censorship, and propaganda. (5) A program of vigorous action including economic reconstruction, industrialization, pursuit of economic self-sufficiency, territorial expansion and war which is dramatized as bold, adventurous, and promising a glorious future.

Fascist movements often had socialists origins. For example, in Italy, where fascism first arose in place of socialism, Benito Mussolini, sought to impose what he called "*corporativism*". A fascist "*corporate*" state, would in theory run the economy for the benefit of the whole country like a corporation. It would be centrally controlled and managed by an elite who would see that its benefits would go to everyone.

Fascism has always declared itself the uncompromising enemy of communism, with which, however, fascist actions have much in common. (In fact, many of the methods of organization and of propaganda used by fascists were taken from the experience of the early Russian communists. This along with the belief in a single strong political party, secret police, etc.) The propertied interests and the upper classes, fearful of revolution, often gave their support to fascism on the basis of promises by the fascist leaders to maintain the status quo and safeguard property. (In effect, accomplishing a revolution from above with their help as opposed from below against them.

However, fascism did consider itself a revolutionary movement of a different type). Once established, a fascist regime ruthlessly crushes communist and socialist parties as well as all democratic opposition. It regiments the propertied interests to its national goals and wins the potentially revolutionary masses to fascist programs by substituting a rabid nationalism for class conflict. Thus fascism may be regarded as an extreme defensive expedient. Adopted by a nation faced with the sometimes illusionary threat of communist subversion or revolution. Under fascism, capital is regulated as much as labor and fascist contempt for legal or constitutional guarantees effectively destroyed whatever security the capitalistic system had enjoyed under pre-fascist governments.

In addition, fascist or similar regimes are at times anti-Communist. This is evidenced by the Soviet-German treaty of 1939. During the period of alliance created by the treaty, Italy and Germany and their satellite countries ceased their anti-Communist propaganda. They emphasized their own revolutionary and proletarian origins and attacked the so-called plutocratic western democracies.

The fact that fascist countries sought to control national life by methods identical to those of communist governments make such nations vulnerable to communism after the fascist regime is destroyed.

In theory at least, the chief distinction between fascism and communism is that fascism is *nationalist*, exalted the interests of the state and glorified war between nations. Whereas, communism is *internationalist,* exalting the interests of a specific economic class (the proletariat) and glorifying world wide class warfare. In practice, however, this fundamental distinction loses some of its validity. For in its heyday, fascism was also an internationalist movement. A movement dedicated to world conquest, (like communism), as evidenced by the events prior to and during the Second World War. At the same time, many elements in communism as it evolved came to be very nationalistic as well.

A "market" is an economic term to describe the places and situations in which goods and services are bought and sold. In a capitalistic free enterprise economy, the market prices of goods and services rise and fall according to decreases and increases in the supply and demand and the degree of competition.

In an economic system, there is also a "market" for land, capital, and labor. The labor market, for example, is studied by economists in order to understand trends in jobs, productivity of workers, activities of labor unions, and patterns of employment. Potential customers for a product or service are called a market and are the subject of market research to determine who would possibly make use of whatever is offered to customers.

Other types of markets which are parts of countries' economic systems include the following:

Stock Market
This is part of a capitalistic free enterprise system and is one of significant investment and speculation. Any changes in the prices of stocks are seriously affected by those who buy stocks when their prices are rising and sell them when their prices are falling. Business planners quite often regard the stock market as a barometer of the degree of confidence investors have in the conditions of businesses in the future. When the stock market is a rising "bull" market, economists and investors see it as the public showing confidence in the future of business. At the same time, when the market is a falling "bear" market, it is an indication of a lack of confidence. In unstable economic conditions, one or more conditions and situations can seriously affect the stock market's rise and fall. The "bottom line" is that these fluctuations are directly tied to and directly affected by investment changes.

"Black" Market
This illegal market has in the past and even today exists in countries where wage and price controls are in place and enforced by law. In these markets, goods and products are priced and sold above legal limits, especially if the maximum legal price is much less than free-market price. The black market thrives when certain products are unavailable in the regulated market and there is a demand for them, or if wage and price controls are in place for an extended period.

Common Market
This market, also known as the European Economic Community (EEC), began in 1958 and is comprised of several European nations. Its major purpose was to remove all restrictive tariffs and import quotas in order to encourage and facilitate free trade among member nations. Included were efforts to move workers and services without restrictions.

Skill 4.5 **Describe how trade generates economic development and interdependence and analyze the resulting challenges and benefits for individuals, producers, and governments.**

"Globalism" is defined as the principle of the interdependence of all the world's nations and their peoples. Within this global community, every nation, in some way to a certain degree, is dependent on other nations. Since no one nation has all of the resources needed for production, trade with other nations is required to obtain what is needed for production, to sell what is produced or to buy finished products, to earn money to maintain and strengthen the nation's economic system.

Developing nations receive technical assistance and financial aid from developed nations. Many international organizations have been set up to promote and encourage cooperation and economic progress among member nations. Through the elimination of such barriers to trade as tariffs, trade is stimulated resulting in increased productivity, economic progress, increased cooperation and understanding on diplomatic levels.

Those nations not part of an international trade organization not only must make those economic decisions of what to produce, how and for whom, but must also deal with the problem of tariffs and quotas on imports. Regardless of international trade memberships, economic growth and development are vital and affect all trading nations. Businesses, labor, and governments share common interests and goals in a nation's economic status. International systems of banking and finance have been devised to assist governments and businesses in setting the policy and guidelines for the exchange of currencies.

SUBAREA V.   INQUIRY AND PUBLIC DISCOURSE AND DECISION MAKING

Skill 5.1   Acquire information from books, maps, newspapers, data sets, and other sources; and organize and present the information in maps, graphs, charts, and timelines.

We use **illustrations** of various sorts because it is often easier to demonstrate a given idea visually instead of orally. Sometimes it is even easier to do so with an illustration than a description. This is especially true in the areas of education and research because humans are visually stimulated. It is a fact that any idea presented visually in some manner is always easier to understand and to comprehend than simply getting an idea across verbally, by hearing it or reading it. Throughout this document, there are several illustrations that have been presented to explain an idea in a more precise way. Sometimes these will demonstrate some of the types of illustrations available for use in the arena of political science. Among the more common illustrations used in political science are various types of **maps, graphs and charts**.

Photographs and globes are useful as well, but as they are limited in what kind of information that they can show, they are rarely used. Unless, as in the case of a photograph, it is of a particular political figure or a time that one wishes to visualize.

Although maps have advantages over globes and photographs, they do have a major disadvantage. This problem must be considered as well. The major problem of all maps comes about because most maps are flat and the Earth is a sphere. It is impossible to reproduce exactly on a flat surface an object shaped like a sphere. In order to put the earth's features onto a map they must be stretched in some way. This stretching is called **distortion.**

Distortion does not mean that maps are wrong, it simply means that they are not perfect representations of the Earth or its parts. **Cartographers,** or mapmakers, understand the problems of distortion. They try to design them so that there is as little distortion as possible in the maps.

The process of putting the features of the Earth onto a flat surface is called **projection**. All maps are really map projections. There are many different types. Each one deals in a different way with the problem of distortion. Map projections are made in a number of ways. Some are done using complicated mathematics. However, the basic ideas behind map projections can be understood by looking at the three most common types:

(1) **Cylindrical Projections** - These are done by taking a cylinder of paper and wrapping it around a globe. A light is used to project the globe's features onto the paper. Distortion is least where the paper touches the globe. For example, suppose that the paper was wrapped so that it touched the globe at the equator, the map from this projection would have just a little distortion near the equator. However, in moving north or south of the equator, the distortion would increase as you moved further away from the equator. The best known and most widely used cylindrical projection is the **Mercator Projection.** It was first developed in 1569 by Gerardus Mercator, a Flemish mapmaker.

(2). **Conical Projections** - The name for these maps come from the fact that the projection is made onto a cone of paper. The cone is made so that it touches a globe at the base of the cone only. It can also be made so that it cuts through part of the globe in two different places. Again, there is the least distortion where the paper touches the globe. If the cone touches at two different points, there is some distortion at both of them. Conical projections are most often used to map areas in the **middle latitudes**. Maps of the United States are most often conical projections. This is because most of the country lies within these latitudes.

(3). **Flat-Plane Projections** - These are made with a flat piece of paper. It touches the globe at one point only. Areas near this point show little distortion. Flat-plane projections are often used to show the areas of the north and south poles. One such flat projection is called a **Gnomonic Projection**. On this kind of map all meridians appear as straight lines, Gnomonic projections are useful because any straight line drawn between points on it forms a **Great-Circle Route**.

Great-Circle Routes can best be described by thinking of a globe and when using the globe the shortest route between two points on it can be found by simply stretching a string from one point to the other. However, if the string was extended in reality, so that it took into effect the globe's curvature, it would then make a great-circle. A great-circle is any circle that cuts a sphere, such as the globe, into two equal parts. Because of distortion, most maps do not show great-circle routes as straight lines, Gnomonic projections, however, do show the shortest distance between the two places as a straight line, because of this they are valuable for navigation. They are called Great-Circle Sailing Maps.

To properly analyze a given map one must be familiar with the various parts and symbols that most modern maps use. For the most part, this is standardized, with different maps using similar parts and symbols, these can include:

The Title - All maps should have a title, just like all books should. The title tells you what information is to be found on the map.

The Legend - Most maps have a legend. A legend tells the reader about the various symbols that are used on that particular map and what the symbols represent, (also called a *map key*).

The Grid - A grid is a series of lines that are used to find exact places and locations on the map. There are several different kinds of grid systems in use, however, most maps do use the longitude and latitude system, known as the **Geographic Grid System**.

Directions - Most maps have some directional system to show which way the map is being presented. Often on a map, a small compass will be present, with arrows showing the four basic directions, north, south, east, and west.

The Scale - This is used to show the relationship between a unit of measurement on the map versus the real world measure on the Earth. Maps are drawn to many different scales. Some maps show a lot of detail for a small area. Others show a greater span of distance, whichever is being used one should always be aware of just what scale is being used. For instance the scale might be something like 1 inch = 10 miles for a small area or for a map showing the whole world it might have a scale in which 1 inch = 1,000 miles. The point is that one must look at the map key in order to see what units of measurements the map is using.

Maps have four main properties. They are (1) the size of the areas shown on the map. (2) The shapes of the areas, (3) Consistent scales, and (4) Straight line directions. A map can be drawn so that it is correct in one or more of these properties. No map can be correct in all of them.

Equal areas - One property which maps can have is that of equal areas, In an equal area map, the meridians and parallels are drawn so that the areas shown have the same proportions as they do on the Earth. For example, Greenland is about 118th the size of South America, thus it will be show as 118th the size on an equal area map. The **Mercator projection** is an example of a map that does not have equal areas. In it, Greenland appears to be about the same size of South America. This is because the distortion is very bad at the poles and Greenland lies near the North Pole.

Conformality - A second map property is conformality, or correct shapes. There are no maps which can show very large areas of the earth in their exact shapes. Only globes can really do that, however Conformal Maps are as close as possible to true shapes. The United States is often shown by a Lambert Conformal Conic Projection Map.

Consistent Scales - Many maps attempt to use the same scale on all parts of the map. Generally, this is easier when maps show a relatively small part of the earth's surface. For example, a map of Florida might be a Consistent Scale Map. Generally maps showing large areas are not consistent-scale maps. This is so because of distortion. Often such maps will have two scales noted in the key. One scale, for example, might be accurate to measure distances between points along the Equator. Another might be then used to measure distances between the North Pole and the South Pole.

Maps showing physical features often try to show information about the elevation or *relief* of the land. *Elevation* is the distance above or below the sea level. The elevation is usually shown with colors, for instance, all areas on a map which are at a certain level will be shown in the same color.

Relief Maps - Show the shape of the land surface, flat, rugged, or steep. Relief maps usually give more detail than simply showing the overall elevation of the land's surface. Relief is also sometimes shown with colors, but another way to show relief is by using *contour lines*. These lines connect all points of a land surface which are the same height surrounding the particular area of land.

Thematic Maps - These are used to show more specific information, often on a single *theme,* or topic. Thematic maps show the distribution or amount of something over a certain given area. Things such as population density, climate, economic information, cultural, political information, etc ...

Political science would be almost impossible without maps. Information can be gained looking at a map that might take hundreds of words to explain otherwise. Maps reflect the great variety of knowledge covered by political science. To show such a variety of information maps are made in many different ways. Because of this variety, maps must be understood in order to make the best sense of them. Once they are understood, maps provide a solid foundation for political science studies.

To apply information obtained from *graphs* one must understand the two major reasons why graphs are used:

1. *To present a model or theory visually in order to show how two or more variables interrelate.*

2. *To present real world data visually in order to show how two or more variables interrelate.*

Most often used are those known as *bar graphs* and *line graphs*. (Charts are often used for similar reasons and are explained in the next section).

Graphs themselves are most useful when one wishes to demonstrate the sequential increase, or decrease of a variable or to show specific correlations between two or more variables in a given circumstance.

Most common is the *bar graph*. Because it has an easy to see and understand way of visually showing the difference in a given set of variables. However it is limited in that it can not really show the actual proportional increase, or decrease, of each given variable to each other. (In order to show a decrease, a bar graph must show the "bar" under the starting line, thus removing the ability to really show how the various different variables would relate to each other).

Thus in order to accomplish this one must use a **line graph**. Line graphs can be of two types a *linear* or *non-linear* graph. A linear line graph uses a series of straight lines a non-linear line graph uses a curved line. Though the lines can be either straight or curved, all of the lines are called *curves*.

A line graph uses a number line or *axis.* The numbers are generally placed in order, equal distances from one another, the number line is used to represent a number, degree or some such other variable at an appropriate point on the line. Two lines are used, intersecting at a specific point. They are referred to as the X-axis and the Y-axis. The Y-axis is a vertical line the X-axis is a horizontal line. Together they form a *coordinate system.* The difference between a point on the line of the X-axis and the Y-axis is called the *slope* of the line, or the change in the value on the vertical axis divided by the change in the value on the horizontal axis. The Y-axis number is called the *rise* and the X-axis number is called the *run*, thus the equation for slope is:

> *SLOPE* = *RISE* - (*Change in value on the vertical axis*)
> *RUN* - (*Change in value on the horizontal axis*)

The slope tells the amount of increase or decrease of a given *specific* variable. When using two or more variables one can plot the amount of difference between them in any given situation. This makes presenting information on a line graph more involved. It also makes it more informative and accurate than a simple bar graph. Knowledge of the term slope and what it is and how it is measured helps us to describe verbally the pictures we are seeing visually. For example, if a curve is said to have a slope of "zero", you should picture a flat line. If a curve has a slope of "one", you should picture a rising line that makes a 45-degree angle with the horizontal and vertical axis lines.

The preceding examples are of *linear* (straight line) curves. With *non-linear* curves (the ones that really do curve) the slope of the curve is constantly changing, so as a result, we must then understand that the slope of the non-linear curved line will be at *a* specific point. How is this done? The slope of a non-linear curve is determined by the slope of a straight line *that intersects the curve at that specific point.*

In all graphs, an upward sloping line represents a direct relationship between the two variables. A downward slope represents an inverse relationship between the two variables. In reading any graph, one must always be very careful to understand what is being measured, what can be deduced and what cannot be deduced from the given graph.

To use *charts* correctly, one should remember the reasons one uses graphs. The general ideas are similar. It is usually a question as to which, a graph or chart, is more capable of adequately portraying the information one-wants to illustrate. One can see the difference between them and realize that in many ways graphs and charts are interrelated. One of the most common types, because it is easiest to read and understand, even for the lay person, is the *Pie-chart*.

You can see pie-charts used often, especially when one is trying to illustrate the differences in percentages among various items, or when one is demonstrating the divisions of a whole.

Realistically, one can make a chart out of almost any multiple set of variables. Remember to properly show the differences between them, what you are trying to prove and keep it clear enough to read and understand with a minimum of effort. The usefulness of a chart is wasted if too much time is taken in order to understand it. Charts are always used to simplify an idea, NEVER to complicate it.

As stated before, in political science and related fields, all type of illustrations, maps, graphs and charts are useful tools for both education and research. As such, they quite often are used to better demonstrate an idea than simply stating it since there are some problems and situations that are easier to understand visually than verbally. They are also better in trying to show relationships between any given set of variables or circumstances. However one must always remember that though a picture may "be worth a thousand words", it still can't say everything and one should always be aware of the limits of any diagrammatic model. In other words," *seeing is not always, necessarily, believing"*.

Skill 5.2   Interpret the meaning and significance of information and use a variety of technologies to assist in accessing and managing information.

Demography is the branch of science of statistics most concerned with the social well being of people. **Demographic tables** may include: (1) Analysis of the population on the basis of age, parentage, physical condition, race, occupation and civil position, giving the actual size and the density of each separate area. (2) Changes in the population as a result of birth, marriage, and death. (3) Statistics on population movements and their effects and their relations to given economic, social and political conditions. (4) Statistics of crime, illegitimacy and suicide. (5) Levels of education and economic and social statistics.

Such information is also similar to that area of science known as **vital statistics** and as such is indispensable in studying social trends and making important legislative, economic, and social decisions. Such demographic information is gathered from census, and registrar reports and the like, and by state laws such information, especially the vital kind, is kept by physicians, attorneys, funeral directors, member of the clergy, and similar professional people. In the United States such demographic information is compiled, kept and published by the Public Health Service of the United States Department of Health, Education, and Welfare.

The most important element of this information is the so-called **rate**, which customarily represents the average of births and deaths for a unit of 1000 population over a given calendar year. These general rates are called **crude rates**, which are then sub-divided into *sex, color, age, occupation, locality, etc.* They are then known as **refined rates**.

In examining **statistics** and the sources of statistical data one must also be aware of the methods of statistical information gathering. For instance, there are many good sources of raw statistical data. Books such as *The Statistical Abstract of the United States,* published by the United States Chamber of Commerce, *The World Fact Book,* published by the Central Intelligence Agency or *The Monthly Labor Review* published by the United States Department of Labor are excellent examples that contain much raw data. Many such yearbooks and the like on various topics are readily available from any library, or from the government itself. However, knowing how that data and information was gathered is at least equally as important as the figures themselves. Because only by having knowledge of statistical language and methodology, can one really be able to gauge the usefulness of any given piece of data presented. Thus we must first understand just what statistics are and what they can and cannot, tell us.

Simply put, statistics is the mathematical science that deals with the collection, organization, presentation, and analysis of various forms of numerical data and with the problems such as interpreting and understanding such data. The raw materials of statistics are sets of numbers obtained from enumerations or measurements collected by various methods of extrapolation, such as census taking, interviews, and observations.

In collecting any such statistical information and data, care and adequate precautions must always be taken in order to assure that the knowledge obtained is complete and accurate. It is also important to be aware of just how much data is necessary to collect in order to establish the idea that is attempting to be formulated. One important idea to understand is that statistics usually deal with a specific **model**, **hypothesis**, or **theory** that is being attempted to be proven.

Though one should be aware that a theory can never actually be proved correct it can only really be corroborated. (**Corroboration** meaning that the data presented is more consistent with this theory than with any other theory, so it makes sense to use this theory.) One should also be aware of what is known as **correlation** (the joint movement of various data points) does not infer **causation** (the change in one of those data points caused the other data points to change). It is important that one take these aspects into account so that one can be in a better position to appreciate what the collected data is really saying

Once collected, data must then be arranged, tabulated, and presented to permit ready and meaningful analysis and interpretation. Often tables, charts or graphs will be used to present the information in a concise easy to see manner, with the information sometimes presented in raw numerical order as well. **Tests of reliability** are used, bearing in mind the manner in which the data has been collected and the inherent biases of any artificially created model to be used to explain real world events. Indeed the methods used and the inherent biases and reasons actually for doing the study by the individual(s) involved, must never be discounted.

So one should always remember that statistical methods can and have been used to prove or disprove historically just about anything. While statistics are a good and important empirical research tool, too much reliance on them alone, without any other information or data, can be misleading and statistics should only be used with other empirical methods of research. As the famous saying goes, *"Figures don't lie, but liars always figure. "*

Libraries of all sorts are valuable when conducting research and nowadays almost all have digitized search systems to assist in finding information on almost any subject. Even so, the Internet with powerful search engines like Google readily available can retrieve information that doesn't exist in libraries or if it does exist, is much more difficult to retrieve.

Conducting a research project once involved the use of punch cards, microfiche and other manual means of storing the data in a retrievable fashion. No more. With high-powered computers available to anyone who chooses to conduct research, the organizing of the data in a retrievable fashion has been revolutionized. Creating multi-level folders, copying and pasting into the folders, making ongoing additions to the bibliography at the very time that a source is consulted, and using search-and-find functions make this stage of the research process go much faster with less frustration and a decrease in the likelihood that important data might be overlooked.

Serious research requires high-level analytical skills when it comes to processing and interpreting data. A degree in statistics or at least a graduate-level concentration is very useful. However, a team approach to a research project will include a statistician in addition to those members who are knowledgeable in the social sciences.

Skill 5.3 **Apply methods of conducting investigations by formulating a clear statement of a question, gathering and organizing information from a variety of sources, analyzing and interpreting information, formulating and testing hypotheses, and reporting results.**

The scientific method is the process by which researchers over time endeavor to construct an accurate (that is, reliable, consistent and non-arbitrary) representation of the world. Recognizing that personal and cultural beliefs influence both our perceptions and our interpretations of natural phenomena, standard procedures and criteria minimize those influences when developing a theory.

The scientific method has four steps:

1. Observation and description of a phenomenon or group of phenomena.
2. Formulation of a hypothesis to explain the phenomena.
3. Use of the hypothesis to predict the existence of other phenomena or to predict quantitatively the results of new observations.
4. Performance of experimental tests of the predictions by several independent experimenters and properly performed experiments.

While the researcher may bring certain biases to the study, it's important that bias not be permitted to enter into the interpretation. It's also important that data that doesn't fit the hypothesis not be ruled out. This is unlikely to happen if the researcher is open to the possibility that the hypothesis might turn out to be null. Another important caution is to be certain that the methods for analyzing and interpreting are flawless. Abiding by these mandates is important if the discovery is to make a contribution to human understanding.

The phenomena that interest social scientists are usually complex. Capturing that complexity more fully requires the assessment of simultaneous co-variations along the following dimensions: the units of observation, their characteristics, and time. This is how behavior occurs. For example, to obtain a richer and more accurate picture of the progress of school children means measuring changes in their attainment over time together with changes in the school over time. This acknowledges that changes in one arena of behavior are usually contingent on changes in other areas. Models used for research in the past were inadequate to handle the complexities suggested by multiple co-variations. However, the evolution of computerized data processing has taken away that constraint.

While descriptions of the research project and presentation of outcomes along with analysis must be a part of every report, graphs, charts, and sometimes maps are necessary to make the results clearly understandable.

Skill 5.4   Recognize an issue as a question of public policy, trace the origins of the issue, analyze various perspectives people bring to the issue, and evaluate possible ways to resolve the issue.

The struggle over what is to be the fair method to ensure equal political representation for all different groups in the United States continues to dominate the national debate. This has revolved around the problems of trying to ensure proper racial and minority representation. Various civil rights acts, notably the Voting Rights Act of 1965, sought to eliminate the remaining features of unequal suffrage in the United States.

Most recently, the question has revolved around the issue of what is called "**gerrymandering**", which involves the adjustment of various electoral districts in order to achieve a predetermined goal. Usually this is used in regards to the problem of minority political representation. The fact that gerrymandering sometimes creates odd and unusual looking districts (this is where the practice gets its name) and most often the sole basis of the adjustments is racial. This has led to the questioning of this practice being a fair, let alone a constitutional, way for society to achieve its desired goals. This promises to be the major issue in national electoral politics for some time to come. The debate has centered on those of the "left" (Liberals), who favor such methods, and the "right" (Conservatives), who oppose them. Overall, most Americans would consider themselves in the "middle" (Moderates).

How best to move forward with ensuring civil liberties and civil rights for all continues to dominate the national debate. In recent times, issues seem to revolve not around individual rights, but what has been called "group rights" has been raised. At the forefront of the debate is whether some specific remedies like affirmative action, quotas, gerrymandering and various other forms of preferential treatment are actually fair or just as bad as the ills they are supposed to cure. At the present, no easy answers seem to be forthcoming. It is a testament to the American system that it has shown itself able to enter into these debates, to find solutions and tended to come out stronger.

A synthesis of information from multiple sources requires an understanding of the content chosen for the synthesis, first of all. The writer of the synthesis will, no doubt, wish to incorporate his/her own ideas, particularly in any conclusions that are drawn, and show relationships to those of the chosen sources. That can only happen if the writer has a firm grip on what others have said or written. The focus is not so much on documentary methods but on techniques of critically examining and evaluating the ideas of others. Even so, careful documentation is extremely important in this type of presentation, particularly with regard to which particular edition is being read in the case of written sources; and date, location, etc., of online sources. The phrase "downloaded from such-and-such a website on such-and-such a date" is useful. If the conversation, interview, or speech is live, date, circumstances, and location must be indicated.

The purpose of a synthesis is to understand the works of others and to use that work in shaping a conclusion. The writer or speaker must clearly differentiate between the ideas that come from a source and his/her own.

Skill 5.5   Analyze constructive conversation about matters of public concern.

From the earliest days of political expression in America, efforts were a collaborative affair. One of the first of the democratic movements was the Sons of Liberty, an organization that made its actions known but kept the identity of its members a secret. Famous members of this group included John and Samuel Adams. Other patriotic movements sprang up after the success of the Sons of Liberty was assured, and the overall struggle against British oppression was a collaborative effort involving thousands of people throughout the American colonies.

American political discussion built on the example of the British Parliament, which had two houses of its legislative branch of government containing representatives who had great debates on public policy before making laws. Although this process isn't anywhere near as wide open and public and spirited as it is today, the lawmakers nonetheless had their chance to make their views known on the issues of the day. Some laws like those implementing the infamous taxes following the British and American victory in the French and Indian War, required relatively little debate, since they were so popular and were obviously wanted by the Prime Minister and other heads of the government. Other laws enjoyed spirited debate and took months to pass.

The Assemblies of the American colonies inherited this tradition and enjoyed spirited debate as well, even though they met just one or a few times a year. One of the most famous examples of both collaboration and deliberation was the Stamp Act Congress, a gathering of fed-up Americans who drafted resolutions demanding that Great Britain repeal the unpopular tax on paper and documents. The Americans who met at both of the Continental Congresses and the Constitutional Convention built on this tradition as well.

Thanks to the voluminous notes taken diligently by James Madison, we have a clear record of just how contentious at times the debate over the shape and scope of the American federal government was. Still, every interest was advanced, every argument put forward, and every chance given to repeal the main points of the government document. The result was a blueprint for government approved by the vast majority of the delegates and eventually approved by people in all of the American colonies. This ratification process has continued throughout the history of the country, through passage by both houses of Congress to ratification by state legislatures and finally to approval by a majority of the people of a majority of states.

With this sometimes spirited and sometimes virulent debate have come countless opportunities to influence that debate. Even in the earliest times, people having special interests were trying to influence political debates in their favor. Plenty of people who favored a strong central government or its opposite, a weak central government, could be found who were not delegates to the Constitutional Convention. No doubt these people were in communication with the delegates.

Also developing at this time were the nation's first political parties, the Federalists and the Democratic-Republicans. It wasn't elected officials who were members of these political parties, although those elected officials were the most famous members. The people who joined these political parties wanted to see their political interests protected and were sometimes very effective in making sure that the people that they voted for did the things that they were elected to do. As the nation grew, so did the number of political parties and so did the number of people who were pursuing the so-called "special interests." Actually, a special interest is nothing more than a subject that a person or people who pursue one issue above all others. As more and more people gained more and more money, they began to pressure their lawmakers more and more to pass laws that favored their interests. Exporters of goods from ports to destinations overseas would not want to see heavy taxes on such exports. People who owned large amounts of land wouldn't want to see a sharp increase in property taxes. The list goes on and on. These special interests can be found today. These days, it's just more money and more ways to influence lawmakers that distinguish special interest pursuits from those made in years past. So, too, can we draw a straight line from the deliberative-collaborative traditions of today to the secret meetings and political conventions of colonial days.

Bibliography

Adams, James Truslow. (2006). "The March of Democracy," Vol 1. "The Rise of the Union". New York: Charles Scribner's Sons, Publisher.

Barbini, John & Warshaw, Steven. (2006). "The World Past and Present." New York: Harcourt, Brace, Jovanovich, Publishers.

Berthon, Simon & Robinson, Andrew. (2006. "The Shape of the World." Chicago: Rand McNally, Publisher.

Bice, David A. (2006). "A Panorama of Florida II". (Second Edition). Marceline, Missouri: Walsworth Publishing Co., Inc.

Bram, Leon (Vice-President and Editorial Director). (2006). "Funk and Wagnalls New Encyclopedia." United States of America.

Burns, Edward McNall & Ralph, Philip Lee. (2006. "World Civilizations Their History and Culture" (5th ed.). New York: W.W. Norton & Company, Inc., Publishers.

Dauben, Joseph W. (2006). "The World Book Encyclopedia." Chicago: World Book Inc. A Scott Fetzer Company, Publisher.

De Blij, H.J. & Muller, Peter O. (2006). "Geography Regions and Concepts" (Sixth Edition). New York: John Wiley & Sons, Inc., Publisher.

Encyclopedia Americana. (2006). Danbury, Connecticut: Grolier Inc, Publisher.

Heigh, Christopher (Editor). (2006). "The Cambridge Historical Encyclopedia of Great Britain and Ireland." Cambridge: Cambridge University Press, Publisher.

Hunkins, Francis P. & Armstrong, David G. (2006). "World Geography People and Places." Columbus, Ohio: Charles E. Merrill Publishing Co. A Bell & Howell Company, Publishers.

Jarolimek, John; Anderson, J. Hubert & Durand, Loyal, Jr. (2006). "World Neighbors." New York: Macmillan Publishing Company. London: Collier Macmillan Publishers.

McConnell, Campbell R. (2006). "Economics-Principles, Problems, and Policies" (Tenth Edition). New York: McGraw-Hill Book Company, Publisher.

Millard, Dr. Anne & Vanags, Patricia. (2006). "The Usborne Book of World History." London: Usborne Publishing Ltd., Publisher.

Novosad, Charles (Executive Editor). (2006). "The Nystrom Desk Atlas." Chicago: Nystrom Division of Herff Jones, Inc., Publisher.

Patton, Clyde P.; Rengert, Arlene C.; Saveland, Robert N.; Cooper, Kenneth S. & Cam, Patricia T. (2006). "A World View." Morristown, N.J.: Silver Burdette Companion, Publisher.

Schwartz, Melvin & O'Connor, John R. (2006). "Exploring A Changing World." New York: Globe Book Company, Publisher.

"The Annals of America: Selected Readings on Great Issues in American History 1620-1968." (2006). United States of America: William Benton, Publisher.

Tindall, George Brown & Shi, David E. (2006). "America-A Narrative History" (Fourth Edition). New York: W.W. Norton & Company, Publisher.

Todd, Lewis Paul & Curti, Merle. (2006). "Rise of the American Nation" (Third Edition). New York: Harcourt, Brace, Jovanovich, Inc., Publishers.

Tyler, Jenny; Watts, Lisa; Bowyer, Carol; Trundle, Roma & Warrender, Annabelle (2006) 'The Usbome Book of World Geography." London: Usbome Publishing Ltd., Publisher.

Willson, David H. (2006). "A History of England." Hinsdale, Illinois: The Dryder Press, inc., Publisher

Sample Test

1. **Which one of the following is not a reason why Europeans came to the New World?**

   A. To find resources in order to increase wealth

   B. To establish trade

   C. To increase a ruler's power and importance

   D. To spread Christianity

2. **The study of human origins has been a major contribution of:**

   A. Evans

   B. Schliemann

   C. Margaret Mead

   D. The Leakeys

3. **Downstream for the flow of the Yangtze River is primarily:**

   A. North

   B. South

   C. East

   D. West

4. **The results of the Renaissance, Enlightenment, Commercial and Industrial Revolutions were more unfortunate for the people of:**

   A. Asia

   B. Latin America

   C. Africa

   D. Middle East

5. **Government regulation of economic activities for favorable balance of trade was the first major economic theory. It was called:**

   A. Laissez-faire

   B. Globalism

   C. Mercantilism

   D. Syndicalism

6. **The first ancient civilization to introduce and practice monotheism was the:**

   A. Sumerians

   B. Minoans

   C. Phoenicians

   D. Hebrews

7. **Which one of the following does not affect climate?**

   A. Elevation or altitude

   B. Ocean currents

   C. Latitude

   D. Longitude

8. **The foundation of modern constitutionalism is embodied in the idea that government is limited by law. This was stated by:**

   A. John Locke

   B. Rousseau

   C. St. Thomas Aquinas

   D. Montesquieu

9. **The only colony not founded and settled for religious, political or business reasons was:**

   A. Delaware

   B. Virginia

   C. Georgia

   D. New York

10. **The "father of political science" is considered to be:**

    A. Aristotle

    B. John Locke

    C. Plato

    D. Thomas Hobbes

11. **Bathtubs, hot and cold running water, and sewage systems with flush toilets were developed by the:**

    A. Minoans

    B. Mycenaeans

    C. Phoenicians

    D. Greeks

12. **In Western Europe, the achievements of the Renaissance were unsurpassed and made these countries outstanding cultural centers on the continent. All of the following were accomplishments except:**

   A. Investment of the printing press

   B. A rekindling of interest in the learning of classical Greece and Rome

   C. Growth in literature, philosophy and art

   D. Better military tactics

13. **Of the thirteen English colonies, the greatest degree of religious toleration was found in:**

   A. Maryland

   B. Rhode Island

   C. Pennsylvania

   D. Delaware

14. **The chemical process of radiocarbon dating would be most useful and beneficial in the field of:**

   A. Archaeology

   B. Geography

   C. Sociology

   D. Anthropology

15. **Which one of the following is not an important legacy of the Byzantine Empire?**

   A. It protected Western Europe from various attacks from the East by such groups as the Persians, Ottoman Turks, and Barbarians

   B. It played a part in preserving the literature, philosophy, and language of ancient Greece

   C. Its military organization was the foundation for modern armies

   D. It kept the legal traditions of Roman government, collecting and organizing many ancient Roman laws

16. **In the United States, federal investigations into business activities are handled by the:**

A. Department of Treasury

B. Security & Exchange Commission

C. Government Accounting Office

D. Federal Trade Commission

17. **The makeup of today's modern newspapers including comics, puzzles, sports, and columnists was a technique first used by:**

A. William Randolph Hearst

B. Edward W. Scripps

C. Joseph Pulitzer

D. Charles A. Dana

18. **Which French Renaissance writer wrote about the dangers of absolute powers and later examined himself in an effort to make inquiries into humankind and nature?**

A. Francois Rabelais

B. Desiderius Erasmus

C. Michel de Montaigne

D. Sir Francis Bacon

19. **Which of the following contributed to the severity of the Great Depression in California?**

A. An influx of Chinese immigrants.

B. The dust bowl drove people out of the cities.

C. An influx of Mexican immigrants.

D. An influx of Oakies.

20. **Downstream for the flow of the Nile River is:**

A. North

B. South

C. East

D. West

21. **The year 1619 was a memorable year for the colony of Virginia. Three important events occurred resulting in lasting effects on US history. Which one of the following is not one of the events?**

A. Twenty African slaves arrived.

B. The London Company granted the colony a charter making it independent.

C. The colonists were given the right by the London Company to govern themselves through representative government in the Virginia House of Burgesses

D. The London Company sent to the colony 60 women who were quickly married, establishing families and stability in the colony.

22. **Of all the major causes of both World Wars I and II, the most significant one is considered to be:**

A. Extreme nationalism

B. Military buildup and aggression

C. Political unrest

D. Agreements and alliances

23. **The end to hunting, gathering, and fishing of prehistoric people was due to:**

A. Domestication of animals

B. Building crude huts and houses

C. Development of agriculture

D. Organized government in villages

24. **In the United States government, power or control over public education, marriage, and divorce is:**

A. Implied or suggested

B. Concurrent or shared

C. Delegated or expressed

D. Reserved

25. **The principle of "popular sovereignty" allowing people in any territory to make their own decision concerning slavery was stated by;**

A. Henry Clay

B. Daniel Webster

C. John C. Calhoun

D. Stephen A. Douglas

26. **Under the brand new Constitution, the most urgent of the many problems facing the new federal government was that of:**

A. Maintaining a strong army and navy

B. Establishing a strong foreign policy

C. Raising money to pay salaries and war debts

D. Setting up courts, passing federal laws, and providing for law enforcement officers

27. **Which one of the following was not a reason why the United States went to war with Great Britain in 1812?**

A. Resentment by Spain over the sale exploration, and settlement of the Louisiana Territory

B. The westward movement of farmers because of the need for more land

C. Canadian fur traders were agitating the northwestern Indians to fight American expansion

D. Britain continued to seize American ships on the high seas and force American seamen to serve aboard British ships

28. **"Participant observation" is a method of study most closely associated with and used in:**

A. Anthropology

B. Archaeology

C. Sociology

D. Political Science

29. **The early ancient civilizations developed systems of government:**

A. To provide for defense against attack

B. To regulate trade

C. To regulate and direct the economic activities of the people as they worked together in groups

D. To decide on the boundaries of the different fields during planting seasons

30. **The "divine right" of kings was the key political characteristic of:**

A. The Age of Absolutism

B. The Age of Reason

C. The Age of Feudalism

D. The Age of Despotism

31. **The principle of zero in mathematics is the discovery of the ancient civilization found in:**

A. Egypt

B. Persia

C. India

D. Babylon

32. **The Ganges River empties into the:**

A. Bay of Bengal

B. Arabian Sea

C. Red Sea

D. Arafura Sea

33. **One South American country quickly and easily gained independence in the 19th century from European control; was noted for the uniqueness of its political stability and gradual orderly changes. This most unusual Latin American country is:**

A. Chile

B. Argentina

C. Venezuela

D. Brazil

34. **In which of the following disciplines would the study of physical mapping, modern or ancient, and the plotting of points and boundaries be least useful?**

A. Sociology

B. Geography

C. Archaeology

D. History

35. **US foreign minister Robert R. Livingstone said, "From this day the United States takes their place among the greatest powers." He was referring to the action taken by President Thomas Jefferson:**

A. Who had authorized the purchase of the Louisiana Purchase

B. Who sent the US Marines and naval ships to fight the Barbary pirates

C. Who had commissioned the Lewis and Clark expedition

D. Who repealed the Embargo Act

36. **The only Central American country with no standing army, a freely elected government, and considered the oldest democracy in the region is:**

A. Costa Rica

B. Belize

C. Honduras

D. Guatemala

37. **During the 1920s, the United States almost completely stopped all immigration. One of the reasons was:**

A. Plentiful cheap unskilled labor was no longer needed by industrialists

B. War debts from World War I made it difficult to render financial assistance

C. European nations were reluctant to allow people to leave since there was a need to rebuild populations and economic stability

D. The United States did not become a member of the League of Nations

38. **Seventeen sixty-three was the year of Great Britain's total victory over her European rivals and the establishment of a global empire. Of the American colonies, a European statesman accurately prophesied that these colonies no longer needed English protection and would soon gain independence. He was:**

A. Edmund Burke

B. Comte de Rochambeau

C. Count Vergennes

D. William Pitt

39. **Colonial expansion by Western European powers in the 18th and 19th centuries was due primarily to:**

A. Building and opening the Suez Canal

B. The Industrial Revolution

C. Marked improvements in transportation

D. Complete independence of all the Americas and loss of European domination and influence

40. **America's weak foreign policy and lack of adequate diplomacy during the 1870s and 1880s led to the comment that "a special Providence takes care of fools, drunkards, and the United States" is attributed to:**

A. Otto von Bismarck

B. Benjamin Disraeli

C. William Gladstone

D. Paul von Hindenburg

41. **It can be reasonably stated that the change in the United States from primarily an agricultural country into an industrial power was due to all of the following except:**

A. Tariffs on foreign imports

B. Millions of hardworking immigrants

C. An increase in technological developments

D. The change from steam to electricity for powering industrial machinery

42. **Many American authors were noted for "local Color" writings about the way of life in certain regions. Which one of the following was not associated with the other three in writing about life in the mining camps of the West?**

A. Hamlin Garland

B. Joaquin Miller

C. Bret Harte

D. Mark Twain

43. **There is no doubt of the vast improvement of the US Constitution over the weak Articles of Confederation. Which one of the four accurate statements below is a unique yet eloquent description of the document?**

A. The establishment of a strong central government in no way lessened or weakened the individual states.

B. Individual rights were protected and secured.

C. The Constitution is the best representation of the results of the American genius for compromise.

D. Its flexibility and adaptation to change gives it a sense of timelessness.

44. **The study of a people's language and writing would be part of all of the following except:**

    A. Sociology

    B. Archaeology

    C. History

    D. Geography

45. **The changing focus during the Renaissance when artists and scholars were less concerned with religion but centered their efforts on a better understanding of people and the world was called:**

    A. Realism

    B. Humanism

    C. Individualism

    D. Intellectualism

46. **The "father of anatomy" is considered to be:**

    A. Vesalius

    B. Servetus

    C. Galen

    D. Harvey

47. **In the US government, the power of coining money is:**

    A. Implied or suggested

    B. Concurrent or shared

    C. Delegated or expressed

    D. Reserved

48. **The source of authority for national, state, and local governments in the US is:**

    A. The will of the people

    B. The US Constitution

    C. Written laws

    D. The Bill of Rights

49. **India's greatest ruler is considered to be:**

    A. Akbar

    B. Asoka

    C. Babur

    D. Jahan

50. **"Poverty is the parent of revolution and crime" was from the writings of:**

    A. Plato

    B. Aristotle

    C. Cicero

    D. Gaius

51. **Geography was first studied in an organized manner by:**

    A. The Egyptians

    B. The Greeks

    C. The Romans

    D. The Arabs

52. **From about 1870 to 1900 the settlement of America's "last frontier", the West, was completed. One attraction for settlers was free land but it would have been to no avail without:**

    A. Better farming methods and technology

    B. Surveying to set boundaries

    C. Immigrants and others to seek new land

    D. The railroad to get them there

53. **Meridians, or lines of longitude, not only help in pinpointing locations but are also used for:**

    A. Measuring distance from the Poles

    B. Determining direction of ocean currents

    C. Determining the time around the world

    D. Measuring distance on the equator

54. **Historians state that the West helped to speed up the Industrial Revolution. Which one of the following statements was not a reason for this?**

   A. Food supplies for the ever increasing urban populations came from farms in the West

   B. A tremendous supply of gold and silver from western mines provided the capital needed to built industries

   C. Descendants of western settlers, educated as engineers, geologists, and metallurgists in the East, returned to the West to mine the mineral resources needed for industry

   D. Iron, copper, and other minerals from western mines were important resources in manufacturing products

55. **In the United States government, the power of taxation and borrowing is:**

   A. Implied or suggested

   B. Concurrent or shared

   C. Delegated or expressed

   D. Reserved

56. **The post-Civil War years were a time of low public morality, a time of greed, graft, and dishonesty. Which one of the reasons listed would not be accurate?**

   A. The war itself because of the money and materials needed to carry on the War

   B. The very rapid growth of industry and big business after the War

   C. The personal example set by President Grant

   D. Unscrupulous heads of large impersonal corporations

57. **Studies in astronomy, skills in mapping, and other contributions to geographic knowledge came from:**

   A. Galileo

   B. Columbus

   C. Eratosthenes

   D. Ptolemy

58. **Which one of the following would not be considered a result of World War II?**

    A. Economic depressions and slow resumption of trade and financial aid

    B. Western Europe was no longer the center of world power

    C. The beginnings of new power struggles not only in Europe but in Asia as well

    D. Territorial and boundary changes for many nations, especially in Europe

59. **The study of the ways in which different societies around the world deal with the problems of limited resources and unlimited needs and wants is in the area of:**

    A. Economics

    B. Sociology

    C. Anthropology

    D. Political Science

60. **Nineteenth century imperialism by Western European nations had important and far-reaching effects on the colonial peoples they ruled. All four of the following are the result of this. Which one was most important and had lasting effects on key 20th century events?**

    A. Local wars were ended

    B. Living standards were raised

    C. Demands for self government and feelings of nationalism surfaced

    D. Economic developments occurred

61. **After the War of 1812, Henry Clay and others proposed economic measures, including raising tariffs to protect American farmers and manufacturers from foreign competition. These measures were proposed in the period known as:**

    A. Era of Nationalism

    B. American Expansion

    C. Era of Good Feeling

    D. American System

62. "These are the times that try men's souls" were words penned by:

A. Thomas Jefferson

B. Samuel Adams

C. Benjamin Franklin

D. Thomas Paine

63. The Age of Exploration begun in the 1400s was led by:

A. The Portuguese

B. The Spanish

C. The English

D. The Dutch

64. Which one of the following is not a function or responsibility of the US political parties?

A. Conducting elections or the voting process

B. Obtaining funds needed for election campaigns

C. Choosing candidates to run for public office

D. Making voters aware of issues and other public affairs information

65. The economist who disagreed with the idea that free markets lead to full employment and prosperity and suggested that increasing government spending would end depressions was:

A. Keynes

B. Malthus

C. Smith

D. Friedman

66. The study of social behavior of minority groups would be in the area of:

A. Anthropology

B. Psychology

C. Sociology

D. Cultural Geography

67. An extensive knowledge of surgery and medicine as well as principles of irrigation, fertilization and terrace farming was unique to:

A. The Mayans

B. The Atacamas

C. The Incas

D. The Tarapacas

68. **The idea of universal peace through world organization was a philosophy of:**

A. Rousseau

B. Immanuel Kant

C. Montesquieu

D. John Locke

69. **Which ancient civilization is credited with being the first to develop irrigation techniques through the use of canals, dikes, and devices for raising water?**

A. The Sumerians

B. The Egyptians

C. The Babylonians

D. The Akkadians

70. **The study of past human cultures based on physical artifacts is:**

A. History

B. Anthropology

C. Cultural Geography

D. Archaeology

71. **The "father" of modern economics is considered by most economists to be:**

A. Thomas Robert Malthus

B. John Stuart Mill

C. Adam Smith

D. John Maynard Keynes

72. **The ideas and innovations of the period of the Renaissance were spread throughout Europe mainly because of:**

A. Extensive exploration

B. Craft workers and their guilds

C. The invention of the printing press

D. Increased travel and trade

73. **The American labor union movement started gaining new momentum:**

A. During the building of the railroads

B. After 1865 with the growth of cities

C. With the rise of industrial giants such as Carnegie and Vanderbilt

D. During the war years of 1861-1865

74. Soil erosion is most likely to occur in large amounts in:

A. Mountain ranges

B. Deserts

C. Tropical rainforests

D. River valleys

75. Who is considered to be the most important figure in the spread of Protestantism across Switzerland?

A. Calvin

B. Zwingli

C. Munzer

D. Leyden

76. The principle that "men entrusted with power tend to abuse it" is attributed to:

A. Locke

B. Rousseau

C. Aristotle

D. Montesquieu

77. After 1783, the largest "land owner" in the Americas was:

A. Britain

B. Spain

C. France

D. United States

78. The purchase of goods or services on one market for immediate resale on another market is:

A. Output

B. Enterprise

C. Arbitrage

D. Mercantile

79. After the Civil War, the US adapted an attitude of isolation from foreign affairs. But the turning point marking the beginning of the US becoming a world power was:

A. World War I

B. Expansion of business and trade overseas

C. The Spanish-American War

D. The building and financial of the Panama Canal

80. The programs such as unemployment insurance and health insurance for the elderly are the responsibility of:

A. Federal government

B. Local government

C. State government

D. Communal government

81. The English explorer who gave England its claim to North American was:

A. Raleigh

B. Hawkins

C. Drake

D. Cabot

82. The three day Battle of Gettysburg was the turning point of the Civil War for the North leading to ultimate victory. The battle in the West reinforcing the North's victory and sealing the South's defeat was the day after Gettysburg at:

A. Perryville

B. Vicksburg

C. Stones River

D. Shiloh

83. The study of the exercise of power and political behavior in human society today would be conducted by experts in:

A. History

B. Sociology

C. Political Science

D. Anthropology

84. During the period of Spanish colonialism, which of the following was not a key to the goal of exploiting, transforming and including the native people?

A. Missions

B. Ranchos

C. Presidios

D. Pueblos

85. Potential customers for any product or service are not only called consumers but can also be called a:

A. Resource

B. Base

C. Commodity

D. Market

86. **An early cultural group was so skillful in navigating on the seas that they were able to sail at night guided by stars. They were the:**

   A. Greeks

   B. Persians

   C. Minoans

   D. Phoenicians

87. **One method of trade restriction used by some nations is:**

   A. Limited treaties

   B. Floating exchange rate

   C. Bill of exchange

   D. Import quotas

88. **A political system in which the laws and traditions put limits on the powers of government is:**

   A. Federalism

   B. Constitutionalism

   C. Parliamentary system

   D. Presidential system

89. **Which one of the following did not contribute to the early medieval European civilization?**

   A. The heritage from the classical cultures

   B. The Christian religion

   C. The influence of the German Barbarians

   D. The spread of ideas through trade and commerce

90. **The Roman Empire gave so much to the world, especially the Western world. Of the legacies below, the most influential, effective and lasting is:**

   A. The language of Latin

   B. Roman law, justice, and political system

   C. Engineering and building

   D. The writings of its poets an historians

91. Charlemagne's most important influence on Western civilization is seen today in:

A. Relationship of church and state

B. Strong military for defense

C. The criminal justice system

D. Education of women

92. Public administration, such as public officials in the areas of budget, accounting, distribution of public funds, and personnel management, would be part of the field of:

A. Anthropology

B. Sociology

C. Law and Taxation

D. Political Science and Economics

93. "Marbury vs Madison (1803)" was an important Supreme Court case which set the precedent for:

A. The elastic clause

B. Judicial review

C. The supreme law of the land

D. Popular sovereignty in the territories

94. Which one of the following is not a use for a region's wetlands?

A. Produces fresh clean water

B. Provides habitat for wildlife

C. Provides water for hydroelectric power

D. Controls floods

95. The philosopher who coined the term "sociology" also stated that social behavior and events could be measured scientifically. He is identified as:

A. Auguste Comte

B. Herbert Spencer

C. Rousseau

D. Kant

96. The belief that the United States should control all of North America was called:

A. Westward Expansion

B. Pan Americanism

C. Manifest Destiny

D. Nationalism

97. **A well-known World War II figure who said that democracy was like a rotting corpse that had to be replaced by a superior way of life and more efficient government was:**

A. Hitler

B. Stalin

C. Tojo

D. Mussolini

98. **The Radical Republicans who pushed the harsh Reconstruction measures through Congress after Lincoln's death lost public and moderate Republican support when they went too far:**

A. In their efforts to impeach the President

B. By dividing ten southern states into military-controlled districts

C. By making the ten southern states give freed African Americans the right to vote

D. Sending carpetbaggers into the South to build up support for Congressional legislation

99. **The economic system promoting individual ownership of land, capital, and businesses with minimal governmental regulations is called:**

A. Macro-economy

B. Micro-economy

C. Laissez-faire

D. Free enterprise

100. **A political philosophy favoring or supporting rapid social changes in order to correct social and economic inequalities is called:**

A. Nationalism

B. Liberalism

C. Conservatism

D. Federalism

101. **China's last imperial ruling dynasty was one of its most stable and successful and, under its rule, Chinese culture made an outstanding impression on Western nations. This dynasty was:**

A. Min

B. Manchu

C. Han

D. Chou

102. Development of a solar calendar, invention of the decimal system, and contributions to the development of geometry and astronomy are all the legacy of:

A. The Babylonians

B. The Persians

C. The Sumerians

D. The Egyptians

103. The study of "spatial relationships and interaction" would be done by people in the field of:

A. Political Science

B. Anthropology

C. Geography

D. Sociology

104. The circumference of the earth, which greatly contributed to geographic knowledge was calculated by:

A. Ptolemy

B. Eratosthenes

C. Galileo

D. Strabo

105. The first European to see Florida and sail along its coast was:

A. Cabot

B. Columbus

C. Ponce de Leon

D. Narvaez

106. Which one of the following events did not occur during the period known as the "Era of Good Feeling?"

A. President Monroe issued the Monroe Doctrine

B. Spain ceded Florida to the United States

C. The building of the National Road

D. The charter of the second Bank of the United States

107. Native communities in early California are commonly divided into several cultural areas. How many cultural areas?

A. 4

B. 5

C. 6

D. 7

108. The world religion which includes a caste system is:

A. Buddhism

B. Hinduism

C. Sikhism

D. Jainism

109. The idea that continued population growth would, in future years, seriously affect a nation's productive capabilities was stated by:

A. Keynes

B. Mill

C. Malthus

D. Friedman

110. After World War II, the United States:

A. Limited its involvement in European affairs

B. Shifted foreign policy emphasis from Europe to Asia

C. Passed significant legislation pertaining to aid to farmers and tariffs on imports

D. Entered the greatest period of economic growth in its history

111. France decided in 1777 to help the American colonies in their war against Britain. This decision was based on:

A. The naval victory of John Paul Jones over the British ship Serapis"

B. The survival of the terrible winter at Valley Forge

C. The success of colonial guerilla fighters in the South

D. The defeat of the British at Saratoga

112. What event sparked a great migration of people from all over the world to California?

A. The birth of Labor Unions

B. California statehood

C. The invention of the automobile

112. Which individual was responsible for promoting "welfare capitalism" in the formation of Michigan's economy?

A. Gerald Ford

B. Antoine de la Mothe Cadillac

C. Robert Cavelier Sieur de la Salle

D. Henry Ford

114. A number of women worked hard in the first half of the 19th century for women's rights but decisive gains did not come until after 1850. The earliest accomplishments were in:

A. Medicine

B. Education

C. Writing

D. Temperance

115. Nineteenth century German

unification was the result of the hard work of:

A. Otto von Bismarck

B. Kaiser William II

C. Von Moltke

D. Hindenburg

116. The geographical drought stricken region of Africa south of the Sahara and extending east and west from Senegal to Somalia is:

A. The Kalahari

B. The Namib

C. The Great Rift Valley

D. The Sahel

117. The idea or proposal for more equal division of profits among employers and workers was put forth by:

A. Karl Marx

B. Thomas Malthus

C. Adam Smith

D. John Stuart Mill

118. The term that best describes how the Supreme Court can block laws that may be unconstitutional from being enacted is:

A. Jurisprudence

B. Judicial Review

C. Exclusionary Rule

D. Right of Petition

119. On the spectrum of American politics, the label that most accurately describes voters to the "right of center" is:

A. Moderates

B. Liberals

C. Conservatives

D. Socialists

120. Marxism believes which two groups are in continual conflict?

A. Farmers and landowners

B. Kings and the nobility

C. Workers and owners

D. Structure and superstructure

121. The United States legislature is bi-cameral, this means:

A. It consists of several houses

B. It consists of two houses

C. The Vice-President is in charge of the legislature when in session

D. It has an upper and lower house

122. What Supreme Court ruling established the principal of judicial review?

A. Jefferson vs Madison

B. Lincoln vs Douglas

C. Marbury vs Madison

D. Marbury vs Jefferson

123. To be eligible to be elected President one must:

A. Be a citizen for at least five years

B. Be a citizen for seven years

C. Have been born a citizen

D. Be a naturalized citizen

124. **The international organization established to work for world peace at the end of the Second World War is the:**

   A. League of Nations

   B. United Federation of Nations

   C. United Nations

   D. United World League

125. **Which of the following is an example of a direct democracy?**

   A. Elected representatives

   B. Greek city-states

   C. The United States Senate

   D. The United States House of Representative

Answer Key

1. B	41. A	81. D	121. B
2. D	42. A	82. B	122. C
3. C	43. C	83. C	123. C
4. C	44. A	84. B	124. C
5. C	45. B	85. D	125. B
6. D	46. A	86. D	
7. D	47. C	87. D	
8. C	48. A	88. B	
9. C	49. A	89. D	
10. A	50. B	90. B	
11. A	51. B	91. A	
12. D	52. D	92. D	
13. B	53. C	93. B	
14. A	54. C	94. C	
15. C	55. B	95. A	
16. D	56. C	96. C	
17. C	57. D	97. D	
18. C	58. A	98. A	
19. D	59. A	99. D	
20. A	60. C	100. B	
21. B	61. D	101. B	
22. A	62. D	102. D	
23. C	63. A	103. C	
24. D	64. A	104. B	
25. D	65. A	105. A	
26. C	66. C	106. A	
27. A	67. C	107. C	
28. A	68. B	108. B	
29. C	69. A	109. C	
30. A	70. D	110. D	
31. C	71. C	111. D	
32. A	72. C	112. D	
33. D	73. B	113. D	
34. A	74. C	114. B	
35. A	75. A	115. A	
36. A	76. D	116. D	
37. A	77. B	117. D	
38. C	78. C	118. B	
39. B	79. C	119. C	
40. A	80. A	120. C	

Rationales with Sample Questions

1. Which one of the following is not a reason why Europeans came to the New World?

    A. To find resources in order to increase wealth

    B. To establish trade

    C. To increase a ruler's power and importance

    D. To spread Christianity

Answer:

B. To establish trade

The Europeans came to the New World for a number of reasons; often they came to find new natural resources to extract for manufacturing. The Portuguese, Spanish and English were sent over to increase the monarch's power and spread influences such as religion (Christianity) and culture. Therefore, the only reason given that Europeans didn't come to the New World was to establish trade.

2. The study of human origins has been a major contribution of:

A. Evans

B. Schliemann

C. Margaret Mead

D. The Leakeys

Answer:

D. The Leakeys

Although each of the above-mentioned people made significant contributions   to the study of people's history, (A) English archeologist Sir Arthur Evans (1851-1941) has been primarily associated with the excavation of the Knossos on the island of Crete. (B) Heinrich Schliemann (1922-1890) was the German archeologist most well known for the excavation of the ruins of Troy. (C) Margaret Mead (1901-1978) was a cultural anthropologist most acclaimed for her 1928 book *Coming of Age in Samoa*, besides authoring numerous books, she was also the curator of ethnology at the American Museum of Natural History in New York City. (D) The Leakeys, Louis (1903-1972), Mary (1913-1976) and son Richard (1944-), discovered fossils in East Africa that changed the world consensus about the age of humans and also discovered ancient fossils in Olduvai Gorge, Tanzania. The Leakeys, however, were most concerned with the study of early human origins.

3. **Downstream for the flow of the Yangtze River is primarily:**

   A. North

   B. South

   C. East

   D. West

Answer:

 C. East

The Yangtze River runs from Tibet through China and flows eastward to the Pacific Ocean. The Yangtze River is an important travel and trade route through China and meets the Pacific at Shanghai.

4. The results of the Renaissance, Enlightenment, Commercial and the Industrial Revolutions were more unfortunate for the people of:

A. Asia

B. Latin America

C. Africa

D. Middle East

Answer:

C. Africa

The results of the Renaissance, Enlightenment, Commercial and Industrial Revolutions were quite beneficial for many people in much of the world. New ideas of humanism, religious tolerance, and secularism were spreading. Increased trade and manufacturing were surging economies in much of the world. The people of Africa, however, suffered during these times as they became largely left out of the developments. Also, the people of Africa were stolen, traded, and sold into slavery to provide a cheap labor force for the growing industries of Europe and the New World.

5. **Government regulation of economic activities for favorable balance of trade was the first major economic theory. It was called:**

   A. Laissez-faire

   B. Globalism

   C. Mercantilism

   D. Syndicalism

Answer:

C. Mercantilism

(A) Laissez-faire is the doctrine that calls for no government interference in economic and political policy. (B) Globalism is not an economic or political theory, nor is it an actual word in the English language. Globalization is the idea that we are all increasingly connected in a worldwide system. (D) Syndicalism is similar to anarchism claiming that workers should control and govern economic policies and regulations as opposed to state control. Therefore, (C) mercantilism is the best regulation of economic activities for a favorable balance of trade.

6. **The first ancient civilization to introduce and practice monotheism was the:**

   A. Sumerians

   B. Minoans

   C. Phoenicians

   D. Hebrews

Answer:

D. Hebrews

The (A) Sumerians and (C) Phoenicians both practiced religions in which many gods and goddesses were worshipped. Often these Gods/Goddesses were based on a feature of nature such as a sun, moon, weather, rocks, water, etc. The (B) Minoan culture shared many religious practices with the Ancient Egyptians. It seems that the king was somewhat of a god figure and the queen, a goddess. Much of the Minoan art point to worship of multiple gods. Therefore, only the (D) Hebrews introduced and fully practiced monotheism, or the belief in one god.

7. **Which one of the following does not affect climate?**

   A. Elevation and altitude

   B. Ocean currents

   C. Latitude

   D. Longitude

Answer:

D. Longitude

Latitude is the primary influence of earth climate as it determines the climatic region in which an area lies. Elevation or altitude and ocean currents are considered to be secondary influences on climate. Longitude is considered to have no important influence over climate.

8. The foundation of modern constitutionalism is embodied in the idea that government is limited by law. This law was stated by:

    A. John Locke

    B. Rousseau

    C. St. Thomas Aquinas

    D. Montesquieu

Answer:

C. St. Thomas Aquinas

(A) John Locke (1632-1704), whose book *Two Treatises of Government* has long been considered a founding document on the rights of people to rebel against an unjust government, was an important figure in the founding of the US Constitution and on general politics of the American Colonies. (D) Montesquieu (1689-1755) and (B) Rousseau (1712-1778) were political philosophers who explored the idea of what has come to be known as liberalism. They pushed the idea that through understanding the interconnectedness of economics, geography, climate and psychology, that changes could be made to improve life. Therefore, it was St. Thomas Aquinas (1225-1274) who merged Aristotelian ideas with Christianity, who helped lay the ideas of modern constitutionalism and the limiting of government by law.

9. The only colony not founded and settled for religious, political, or business reasons was:

A. Delaware

B. Virginia

C. Georgia

D. New York

Answer:

C. Georgia

The Swedish and the Dutch established Delaware and New York as Middle Colonies. They were established with the intention of growth by economic prosperity from farming across the countryside. The English, with the intention of generating a strong farming economy settled Virginia, a Southern Colony. Georgia was the only one of these colonies not settled for religious, political or business reasons as it was started as a place for debtors from English prisons.

10. The "father of political science" is considered to be:

A. Aristotle

B. John Locke

C. Plato

D. Thomas Hobbes

Answer:

A. Aristotle

(D) Thomas Hobbes (1588-1679) wrote the important work *Leviathan* in which he pointed out that people are by all means selfish, individualistic animals that will always look out for themselves and therefore, the state must combat this nature desire. (B) John Locke (1632-1704) whose book *Two Treatises of Government* has long been considered a founding document on the rights of people to rebel against an unjust government was an important figure in the founding of the US Constitution and on general politics of the American Colonies. (C) Plato (427-347 B.C.) and Aristotle (384-322 B.C.) both contributed to the field of political science. Both believed that political order would result in the greatest stability. In fact, Aristotle studied under Plato. Both Plato and Aristotle studied the ideas of causality and the Prime Mover, but their conclusions were different. Aristotle, however, is considered to be "the father of political science" because of his development of systems of political order the true development, a scientific system to study justice and political order.

11. Bathtubs, hot and cold running water, and sewage systems with flush toilets were developed by the:

A. Minoans

B. Mycenaeans

C. Phoenicians

D. Greeks

Answer:

A. Minoans

The (A) Minoans were one of the earliest Greek cultures and existed on the island of Crete and flourished from about 1600 B.C. to about 1400 B.C. During this time, the (B) Mycenaean were flourishing on the mainland of what is now Greece. However, it was the Minoans on Crete that are best known for their advanced ancient civilization in which such advances as bathtubs, hot and cold running water, sewage systems and flush toilets were developed. The (C) Phoenicians also flourished around 1250 B.C., however, their primary development was in language and arts. The Phoenicians created an alphabet that has still considerable influence in the world today. The great developments off the (D) Greeks were primarily in the fields of philosophy, political science, and early ideas of democracy.

12. In Western Europe, the achievements of the Renaissance were unsurpassed and made these countries outstanding cultural centers on the continent. All of the following were accomplishments except:

A. Invention of the printing press

B. A rekindling of interest in the learning of classical Greece & Rome

C. Growth in literature, philosophy, and art

D. Better military tactics

Answer:

D. Better military tactics

The Renaissance in Western Europe produced many important achievements that helped push immense progress among European civilization. Some of the most important developments during the Renaissance were Gutenberg's invention of the printing press in Germany and a reexamination of the ideas and philosophies of classical Greece and Rome that eventually helped Renaissance thinkers to approach more modern ideas. Also important during the Renaissance was the growth in literature (Petrarch, Boccaccio, Erasmus), philosophy (Machiavelli, More, Bacon) and art (Van Eyck, Giotto, da Vinci). Therefore, improved military tactics is the only possible answer as it was clearly not a characteristic of the Renaissance in Western Europe.

13. Of the thirteen English colonies, the greatest degree of religious toleration was found in:

    A. Maryland

    B. Rhode Island

    C. Pennsylvania

    D. Delaware

Answer:

B. Rhode Island
The greatest degree of religious tolerance in all of the colonies was found in Rhode Island. Roger Williams, founder of Providence and Rhode Island, had objected to the Massachusetts colonial seizure of Indian lands and settlements and the relationship between these seizures and the Church of England. Williams was banished from Massachusetts and purposely set up Rhode Island as the first colony with a true separation of church and state.

14. The chemical process of radiocarbon dating would be most useful and beneficial in the field of:

    A. Archaeology

    B. Geography

    C. Sociology

    D. Anthropology

Answer:

A. Archaeology

Radiocarbon dating is a chemical process that helps generate a more absolute method for dating artifacts and remains by measuring the radioactive materials present in them today and calculating how long it takes for certain materials to decay. Since geographers mainly study locations and special properties of earth's living things and physical features, sociologists mostly study human society and social conditions and anthropologists generally study human culture and humanity, the answer is archaeology because archeologists study past human cultures by studying their remains.

15. Which one of the following is not an important legacy of the Byzantine Empire?

A. It protected Western Europe from various attacks from the East by such groups as the Persians, Ottoman Turks, and Barbarians

B. It played a part in preserving the literature, philosophy, and language of ancient Greece

C. Its military organization was the foundation for modern armies

D. It kept the legal traditions of Roman government, collecting and organizing many ancient Roman laws.

Answer:

C. Its military organization was the foundation for modern armies
The Byzantine Empire (1353-1453) was the successor to the Roman Empire in the East and protected Western Europe from invaders such as the Persians and Ottomans. The Byzantine Empire was a Christian incorporation of Greek philosophy, language, and literature along with Roman government and law. Therefore, although regarded as having a strong infantry, cavalry, and Engineering corps along with excellent morale amongst its soldiers, the Byzantine Empire is not particularly considered a foundation for modern armies.

16. In the United States, federal investigations into business activities are handled by the:

    A. Department of Treasury

    B. Security and Exchange Commission

    C. Government Accounting Office

    D. Federal Trade Commission

Answer:

D. Federal Trade Commission

The Department of Treasury (A), established in 1789, is an executive government agency that is responsible for advising the president on fiscal policy. There is no such thing as a Government Accounting Office. In the United States, Federal Trade Commission or FTC handles federal investigations into business activities. The establishment of the FTC in 1915 as an independent government agency was done so as to assure fair and free competition among businesses.

17. The makeup of today's modern newspapers – including comics, puzzles, sports, and columnists – was a technique first used by:

    A. William Randolph Hearst

    B. Edward W. Scripps

    C. Joseph Pulitzer

    D. Charles A. Dana

Answer:
C. Joseph Pulitzer
(A) William Randolph Hearst (1863-1951) was better known for his vast "empire" of publications, mostly newspapers and magazines. (B) Edward W. Scripps (1854-1926) set up the first chain of newspapers in the United States called the Scripps-McRae League and later set up the Scripps-Howard chain. (D) Charles A. Dana (1819-1897) was a newspaper editor most well known for his strong stance on the Civil War and his relentless pursuit of exposing corruption in the post-Civil War administration of Grant. The answer is, therefore, Joseph Pulitzer (1847-1911). His papers, *New York World* and *Evening World*, were the first to include such modern techniques as comics, puzzles, columnists, illustrations, and sports.

18. Which French Renaissance writer wrote about the dangers of absolute powers and later examined himself in an effort to make inquiries into humankind and nature?

A. Francois Rabelais

B. Desiderius Erasmus

C. Michel de Montaigne

D. Sir Francis Bacon

Answer:

C. Michel de Montaigne

(A) Francois Rabelais (1490-1553) was a French writer and physician who was both a practicing monk (first Franciscan then later Benedictine) and a respected humanist thinker of the Renaissance. (B) Desiderius Erasmus (1466-1536) was a Dutch humanist who was very critical of the Catholic Church but was equally conflicted with Luther's Protestant Reformation. Although Luther had once considered him an ally, Erasmus opposed Luther's break from the church and favored a more internal reform to corruption, he never left the Catholic Church. (D) Sir Francis Bacon (1561-1626) was an English philosopher and writer who pushed the idea that knowledge must come from thorough scientific knowledge and experiment, and insufficient data must not be used in reaching conclusions. (C) Michel de Montaigne (1533-1592), a French essayist from a mixed background, half Catholic and half Jewish, did write some about the dangers of absolute powers, primarily monarchs but also of the Church. His attitude changed as his examination of his own life developed into a study of mankind and nature.

19. Which of the following contributed to the severity of the Great Depression in California?

 A. An influx of Chinese immigrants.

 B. The dust bowl drove People out of the cities.

 C. An influx of Mexican immigrants.

 D. An influx of Oakies.

Answer:

D. An influx of Oakies

The answer is "An influx of Oakies" (D). The Dust Bowl of the Great Plains destroyed agriculture in the area. People living in the plains areas lost their livelihood and many lost their homes and possessions in the great dust storms that resulted from a period of extended drought. People from all of the states affected by the Dust Bowl made their way to California in search of a better life. Because the majority of the people were from Oklahoma, they were all referred to as "Oakies." These migrants brought with them their distinctive plains culture. The great influx of people seeking jobs exacerbated the effects of the Great Depression in California.

20. Downstream for the flow of the Nile River is:

 A. North

 B. South

 C. East

 D. West

Answer:

A. North

The Nile River flows from Central Africa, north to the Mediterranean Sea. The Nile River Delta is in Egypt.

21. The year 1619 was a memorable year for the colony of Virginia. Three important events occurred resulting in lasting effects on US history. Which one of the following was not one of the events?

    A. Twenty African slaves arrived.

    B. The London Company granted the colony a charter making it independent.

    C. The colonists were given the right by the London Company to govern themselves through representative government in the Virginia House of Burgesses.

    D. The London Company sent to the colony 60 women who were quickly married, establishing families and stability in the colony.

Answer:

B. The London Company granted the colony a charter making it independent.

In the year 1619, the Southern colony of Virginia had an eventful year including the first arrival of twenty African slaves, the right to self-governance through representative government in the Virginia House of Burgesses (their own legislative body), and the arrival of sixty women sent to marry and establish families in the colony. The London Company did not, however, grant the colony a charter in 1619.

22. Of all the major causes of both World Wars I and II, the most significant one is considered to be:

    A. Extreme nationalism

    B. Military buildup and aggression

    C. Political unrest

    D. Agreements and alliances

Answer:

A. Extreme nationalism

Although military buildup and aggression, political unrest, and agreements and alliances were all characteristic of the world climate before and during World War I and World War II, the most significant cause of both wars was extreme nationalism. Nationalism is the idea that the interests and needs of a particular nation are of the utmost and primary importance above all else. Some nationalist movements could be liberation movements while others were oppressive regimes, much depends on their degree of nationalism. The nationalism that sparked WWI included a rejection of German, Austro-Hungarian, and Ottoman imperialism by Serbs, Slavs and others culminating in the assassination of Archduke Ferdinand by a Serb nationalist in 1914. Following WWI and the Treaty of Versailles, many Germans and others in the Central Alliance Nations, malcontent at the concessions and reparations of the treaty started a new form of nationalism. Adolf Hitler and the Nazi regime led this extreme nationalism. Hitler's ideas were an example of extreme, oppressive nationalism combined with political, social and economic scapegoating and was the primary cause of WWII.

23. The end to hunting, gathering, and fishing of prehistoric people was due to:

   A. Domestication of animals

   B. Building crude huts and houses

   C. Development of agriculture

   D. Organized government in villages

Answer:

C. Development of agriculture

Although the domestication of animals, the building of huts and houses and the first organized governments were all very important steps made by early civilizations, it was the development of agriculture that ended the once dominant practices of hunting, gathering, and fishing among prehistoric people. The development of agriculture provided a more efficient use of time and for the first time a surplus of food. This greatly improved the quality of life and contributed to early population growth.

24. In the United States government, power or control over public education, marriage, and divorce is:

   A. Implied or suggested

   B. Concurrent or shared

   C. Delegated or expressed

   D. Reserved

Answer:

D. Reserved

In the United States government, power or control over public education, marriage, and divorce is reserved. This is to say that these powers are reserved for the people of the states to decide for themselves.

25. The principle of "popular sovereignty", allowing people in any Territory to make their own decision concerning slavery was stated by:

A. Henry Clay

B. Daniel Webster

C. John C. Calhoun

D. Stephen A. Douglas

Answer:

D. Stephen A. Douglas

(A) Henry Clay (1777-1852) and (B) Daniel Webster (1782-1852) were prominent Whigs whose main concern was keeping the United States one nation. They opposed Andrew Jackson and his Democratic party around the 1830s in favor of promoting what Clay called "the American System". (C) John C. Calhoun (1782-1850) served as Vice-President under John Quincy Adams and Andrew Jackson, and then as a state senator from South Carolina. He was very pro-slavery and a champion of states' rights. The principle of "popular sovereignty", in which people in each territory could make their own decisions concerning slavery, was the doctrine of (D) Stephen A. Douglas (1813-1861). Douglas was looking for a middle ground between the abolitionists of the North and the pro-slavery Democrats of the South. However, as the polarization of pro- and anti-slavery sentiments grew, he lost the presidential election to Republican Abraham Lincoln, who later abolished slavery.

26. Under the brand new Constitution, the most urgent of the many problems facing the new federal government was that of:

A. Maintaining a strong army and navy

B. Establishing a strong foreign policy

C. Raising money to pay salaries and war debts

E. Setting up courts, passing federal laws, and providing for law enforcement officers

Answer:

C. Raising money to pay salaries and war debts

Maintaining strong military forces, establishment of a strong foreign policy, and setting up a justice system were important problems facing the United States under the newly ratified Constitution. However, the most important and pressing issue was how to raise money to pay salaries and war debts from the Revolutionary War. Alexander Hamilton (1755-1804) then Secretary of the Treasury proposed increased tariffs and taxes on products such as liquor. This money would be used to pay off war debts and to pay for internal programs. Hamilton also proposed the idea of a National Bank.

27. Which one of the following was not a reason why the United States went to war with Great Britain in 1812?

    A. Resentment by Spain over the sale, exploration, and settlement of the Louisiana Territory

    B. The westward movement of farmers because of the need for more land

    C. Canadian fur traders were agitating the northwestern Indians to fight American expansion

    D. Britain continued to seize American ships on the high seas and force American seamen to serve aboard British ships

Answer:

A. Resentment by Spain over the sale, exploration, and settlement of the Louisiana Territory

The United States went to war with Great Britain in 1812 for a number of reasons including the expansion of settlers westward and the need for more land, the agitation of Indians by Canadian fur traders in eastern Canada, and the continued seizures of American ships by the British on the high seas. Therefore, the only statement given that was not a reason for the War of 1812 was the resentment by Spain over the sale, exploration and settlement of the Louisiana Territory. In fact, the Spanish continually held more hostility towards the British than towards the United States. The War of 1812 is often considered to be the second American war for independence.

28. **"Participant observation" is a method of study most closely associated with and used in:**

   A. Anthropology

   B. Archaeology

   C. Sociology

   D. Political science

Answer:

A. Anthropology

"Participant observation" is a method of study most closely associated with and used in (A) anthropology or the study of current human cultures. (B) Archaeologists typically the study of the remains of people, animals or other physical things. (C) Sociology is the study of human society and usually consists of surveys, controlled experiments, and field studies. (D) Political science is the study of political life including justice, freedom, power and equality in a variety of methods.

29. The early ancient civilizations developed systems of government:

   A. To provide for defense against attack

   B. To regulate trade

   C. To regulate and direct the economic activities of the people as they worked together in groups

   D. To decide on the boundaries of the different fields during planting seasons

Answer:

C. To regulate and direct the economic activities of the people as they worked together in groups

Although ancient civilizations were concerned with defense, trade regulation and the maintenance of boundaries in their fields, they could not have done any of them without first regulating and directing the economic activities of the people as they worked in groups. This provided for a stable economic base from which they could trade and actually had something worth providing defense for.

30. The "divine right" of kings was the key political characteristic of:

   A. The Age of Absolutism

   B. The Age of Reason

   C. The Age of Feudalism

   D. The Age of Despotism

Answer:

A. The Age of Absolutism

The "divine right" of kings was the key political characteristic of The Age of Absolutism and was most visible in the reign of King Louis XIV of France, as well as during the times of King James I and his son, Charles I. The divine right doctrine claims that kings and absolute leaders derive their right to rule by virtue of their birth alone. They see this both as a law of God and of nature.

31. The principle of zero in mathematics is the discovery of the ancient civilization found in:

    A. Egypt

    B. Persia

    C. India

    D. Babylon

Answer:

C. India

Although the Egyptians practiced algebra and geometry, the Persians developed an alphabet, and the Babylonians developed Hammurabi's Code, which would come to be considered among the most important contributions of the Mesopotamian civilization, it was the Indians that created the idea of zero in mathematics changing drastically our ideas about numbers.

32. The Ganges River empties into the:

    A. Bay of Bengal

    B. Arabian Sea

    C. Red Sea

    D. Arafura Sea

Answer:

A. Bay of Bengal

The Ganges River runs 1,560 miles, northeast through India across the plains to the Bay of Bengal in Bangladesh. The Ganges is considered to be the most sacred river in India according to the Hindus.

33. One South American country quickly and easily gained independence in the 19th century from European control; was noted for the uniqueness of its political stability and gradual orderly changes. This most unusual Latin American country is:

A. Chile

B. Argentina

C. Venezuela

D. Brazil

Answer:

D. Brazil

While Chile, Argentina, and Venezuela all have had histories marred by civil wars, dictatorships, and numerous violent coups during their quests for independence, Brazil experienced a more rapid independence. Independence was gained quickly and more easily than the other countries due to a bloodless revolution in 1889 that officially made Brazil a republic and the economic stability they had in place from a strong coffee and rubber based economy.

34. In which of the following disciplines would the study of physical mapping, modern or ancient, and the plotting of points and boundaries be least useful?

A. Sociology

B. Geography

C. Archaeology

D. History

Answer:

A. Sociology

In geography, archaeology, and history, the study of maps and plotting of points and boundaries is very important as all three of these disciplines hold value in understanding the spatial relations and regional characteristics of people and places. Sociology, however, mostly focuses on the social interactions of people and while location is important, the physical location is not as important as the social location such as the differences between studying people in groups or as individuals.

35. U.S. foreign minister Robert R. Livingstone said, "From this day the United States take their place among the greatest powers." He was referring to the action taken by President Thomas Jefferson:

A. Who had authorized the purchase of the Louisiana Territory

B. Who sent the US Marines and naval ships to fight the Barbary pirates

C. Who had commissioned the Lewis and Clark expedition

D. Who repealed the Embargo Act

Answer:

A. Who had authorized the purchase of the Louisiana Territory

Livingstone's claim that "from this day, the United States takes their place among the greatest powers" was a reference to Jefferson's authorization and acquisition of the Louisiana Territory. What he meant was that now the United States was beginning to fulfill what would later become known as "Manifest Destiny", and it would be this growth of physical size and political power that put the United States on course to be a world super power.

36. The only Central American country with no standing army, a freely elected government, and considered the oldest democracy in the region is:

A. Costa Rica

B. Belize

C. Honduras

D. Guatemala

Answer:

A. Costa Rica

Belize, Guatemala, and Honduras have all struggled over the past few hundred years. Efforts for independence from colonial powers such as Spain and Great Britain proved difficult and brought up many difficult issues such as the violent border disputes between Guatemala and Belize as late as the 1980s and 1990s that created strong tensions and almost all out war. Honduras experienced many bloody civil wars since its quest for independence began in the early 19th century. Even today, Honduras struggles as one of the poorest nations in the world and has continued to experience serious exploitation and abuses of workers by first world multinational corporations. Since the late 18th century, Costa Rica on the other hand, has experienced longstanding democracy and stability. They have no army and despite a couple of breakdowns in the political system, most notably in 1917 and 1948, it is considered the longest standing democracy in Central America.

37. During the 1920s, the United States almost completely stopped all immigration. One of the reasons was:

A. Plentiful cheap, unskilled labor was no longer needed by industrialists

B. War debts from World War I made it difficult to render financial assistance

C. European nations were reluctant to allow people to leave since there was a need to rebuild populations and economic stability

D. The United States did not become a member of the League of Nations

Answer:

A. Plentiful cheap, unskilled labor was no longer needed by industrialists

The primary reason that the United States almost completely stopped all immigration during the 1920s was because their once, much needed, cheap, unskilled labor jobs, made available by the once booming industrial economy, were no longer needed. This has much to do with the increased use of machines to do the work once done by cheap, unskilled laborers.

38. 1763 was the year of Great Britain's total victory over her European rivals and the establishment of a global empire. Of the American colonies, a European statesman accurately prophesied that these colonies no longer needed English protection and would soon gain independence. He was:

    A. Edmund Burke

    B. Comte de Rochambeau

    C. Count Vergennes

    D. William Pitt

Answer:

C. Count Vergennes

Edmund Burke (1729-1797) was a British statesman that did believe in some political reforms in Great Britain's dealing with the American colonies but still believed in the needed guidance and power of the crown in maintaining order. He supported the Declaratory Acts that reasserted Great Britain's control over the colonies in 1766. Burke was important in both the American and French Revolutions. Comte de Rochambeau (1725-1807) was a French marshal who helped George Washington during the American Revolution. William Pitt (1759-1806) was a British statesman who was also a liberal in terms of his ideas for change in economic policy but he never speculated about the future independence of the American colonies. Count Vergennes or Charles Gravier Vergennes (1717-1787) was the French statesman who made the accurate prophecy that the American Colonies would soon be independent from Great Britain. Vergennes not only supported the American Revolution but also helped negotiate the Treaty of Paris in 1783 that secured independence for the colonies.

39. Colonial expansion by Western European powers in the 18th and 19th centuries was due primarily to:

A. Building and opening the Suez Canal

B. The Industrial Revolution

C. Marked improvements in transportation

D. Complete independence of all the Americas and loss of European domination and influence

Answer:

B. The Industrial Revolution

Colonial expansion by Western European powers in the late 18th and 19th centuries was due primarily to the Industrial Revolution in Great Britain that spread across Europe and needed new natural resources and therefore, new locations from which to extract the raw materials needed to feed the new industries.

40. America's weak foreign policy and lack of adequate diplomacy during the 1870s and 1880s led to the comment that "a special Providence takes care of fools, drunkards, and the United States" is attributed to:

A. Otto von Bismarck

B. Benjamin Disraeli

C. William Gladstone

D. Paul von Hindenburg

Answer:

A. Otto Von Bismarck

Benjamin Disraeli (1804-1881), a conservative, and William Gladstone (1809-1898), a liberal, were political rivals in Great Britain. Gladstone was greatly disliked by both his rival Disraeli and his Queen for being such a staunch political and economic reformer. Paul von Hindenberg (1847-1934) was a German field marshal and president (1925-1934) who fought against the Americans in World War I.

However, it was Otto von Bismarck (1815-1898), the German statesman who came to be known as the Iron Chancellor, who once said "a special Providence takes care of fools, drunkards, and the United States". Bismarck was saying that despite the United States' shortcomings in foreign policy, leadership and military strength, they continued to grow and gained power in the face of much better run governments, armies and foreign policy makers.

41. It can be reasonably stated that the change in the United States from primarily an agricultural country into an industrial power was due to all of the following except:

A. Tariffs on foreign imports

B. Millions of hardworking immigrants

C. An increase in technological developments

D. The change from steam to electricity for powering industrial machinery

Answer:

A. Tariffs on foreign imports

It can be reasonably stated that the change in the United States from primarily an agricultural country into an industrial power was due to a great degree of three of the reasons listed above. It was a combination of millions of hard-working immigrants, an increase in technological developments, and the change from steam to electricity for powering industrial machinery. The only reason given that really had little effect was the tariffs on foreign imports.

42. Many American authors were noted for "local color" writings about the way of life in certain regions. Which one of the following was not associated with the other three in writing about life in the mining camps of the West?

    A. Hamlin Garland

    B. Joaquin Miller

    C. Bret Harte

    D. Mark Twain

Answer:

A. Hamlin Garland

Hamlin Garland (1860-1940), unlike the other three authors mentioned, grew up in the mid-western farmlands and wrote stories that were bitter pictures of the difficulties of farm life. He also wrote political critiques. Joaquin Miller (1839-1913), an American poet, moved in 1852 to the Oregon frontier where he wrote about life in gold-mining camps, experiences with Native Americans, and painted an overall energetic and pleasant picture of frontier life. Bret Harte (1836-1902) moved to California at age 19 and wrote local-color short stories of life in mining camps and on the western frontiers of California. Mark Twain (1835-1910), however, was perhaps the most well known and celebrated novelist of early American. Twain, also known as Samuel Langhorne Clemens, was born in Missouri and lived in a variety of places before making it out West, first to Carson City, Nevada, and then later to Sacramento. Twain would return to Hartford, Connecticut, where he spent his later years and wrote *Roughing It* in 1887, about the difficult lives he saw lived on the Western frontier. Twain is best known for his books *The Adventures of Huckleberry Finn* and *The Adventures of Tom Sawyer*, the former of which is considered by many to be the first truly great American novel.

43. There is no doubt of the vast improvement of the U.S. Constitution over the weak Articles of Confederation. Which one of the four statements below is not a description of the document?

    A. The establishment of a strong central government in no way lessened or weakened the individual states

    B. Individual rights were protected and secured

    C. The Constitution demands unquestioned respect and subservience to the federal government by all states and citizens

    D. Its flexibility and adaptation to change gives it a sense of timelessness

Answer:

C. The Constitution demands unquestioned respect and subservience to the federal government by all states and citizens.

The U.S. Constitution was indeed a vast improvement over the Articles of Confederation and the authors of the document took great care to assure longevity. It clearly stated that the establishment of a strong central government in no way lessened or weakened the individual states. In the Bill of Rights, citizens were assured that individual rights were protected and secured. Possibly the most important feature of the new Constitution was its flexibility and adaptation to change which assured longevity.

Therefore, the only statement made that doesn't describe some facet of the Constitution is "The Constitution demands unquestioned respect and subservience to the federal government by all states and citizens". On the contrary, the Constitution made sure that citizens could critique and make changes to their government and encourages such critiques and changes as necessary for the preservation of democracy.

44. The study of a people's language and writing would be part of all of the following except:

A. Sociology

B. Archaeology

C. History

D. Geography

Answer:

A. Sociology

The study of a people's language and writing would be a part of studies in the disciplines of sociology (study of social interaction and organization), archaeology, (study of ancient artifacts including written works), and history (the study of the past). Language and writing would be less important to geography that tends to focus more on locations and spatial relations than on the people in those regions and their languages or writings.

45. The changing focus during the Renaissance when artists and scholars were less concerned with religion but centered their efforts on a better understanding of people and the world was called:

    A. Realism

    B. Humanism

    C. Individualism

    D. Intellectualism

Answer:

B. Humanism

Realism is a medieval philosophy that contemplated independence of existence of the body, the mind, and God. The idea of individualism is usually either a reference to an economic or political theory. Intellectualism is the placing of great importance and devotion to the exploring of the intellect. Therefore, the changing focus during the Renaissance when artists and scholars were less concerned with religion but centered their efforts on a better understanding of people and the world was called humanism.

46. The "father of anatomy" is considered to be:

    A. Vesalius

    B. Servetus

    C. Galen

    D. Harvey

Answer:

A. Vesalius

Andreas Vesalius (1514-1564) is considered to be the "father of anatomy" as a result of his revolutionary work on the human anatomy based on dissections of human cadavers. Prior to Vesalius, men such as Galen, (130-200) had done work in the field of anatomy, but they had based the majority of their work on animal studies.

47. In the United States government, the power of coining money is:

A. Implied or suggested

B. Concurrent or shared

C. Delegated or expressed

D. Reserved

Answer:

C. Delegated or expressed

In the United States government, the power of coining money is delegated or expressed. Therefore, only the United States government may coin money, the states may not coin money for themselves.

48. The source of authority for national, state, and local governments in the United States is:

A. The will of the people

B. The United States Constitution

C. Written laws

D. The Bill of Rights

Answer:

A. The will of the people

The source of authority for national, state, and local governments in the United States is the will of the people. Although the United States Constitution, the Bill of Rights, and the other written laws of the land are important guidelines for authority, they may ultimately be altered or changed by the will of the people.

49. India's greatest ruler is considered to be:

   A. Akbar

   B. Asoka

   C. Babur

   D. Jahan

Answer:

A. Akbar

Akbar (1556-1605) is considered to be India's greatest ruler. He combined a drive for conquest with a magnetic personality and went so far as to invent his own religion, Dinillahi, a combination of Islam, Christianity, Zoroastrianism, and Hinduism. Asoka (273 B.C.-232 B.C.) was also an important ruler as he was the first to bring together a fully united India. Babur (1483-1540) was both considered to be a failure as he struggled to maintain any power early in his reign, but later to be somewhat successful in his quest to reunite Northern India. Jahan's (1592-1666) rule of India is considered to be the golden age of art and literature in the region.

50. "Poverty is the parent of revolution and crime" was from the writings of:

   A. Plato

   B. Aristotle

   C. Cicero

   D. Gaius

Answer:

B. Aristotle

Aristotle once wrote "Poverty is the parent of revolution and crime", a comment that is probably as relevant today as it was in Aristotle's day. It showed his true insight as one of the great political and social commentators and philosophers of all time.

51. Geography was first studied in an organized manner by the:

A. Egyptians

B. Greeks

C. Romans

D. Arabs

Answer:

B. Greeks

The Greeks were the first to study geography, possibly because of the difficulties they faced as a result of geographic conditions. Greece had difficulty uniting early on as their steep, treacherous, mountainous terrain made it difficult for the city-states to be united. As the Greeks studied their geography, it became possible to defeat more powerful armies on their home turf, such as the great victory over the Persians at Marathon.

52. From about 1870 to 1900, the last settlement of America's "last frontier", the West, was completed. One attraction for settlers was free land but it would have been to no avail without:

A. Better farming methods and technology

B. Surveying to set boundaries

C. Immigrants and others to see new lands

D. The railroad to get them there

Answer:

D. The railroad to get them there

From about 1870 to 1900, the settlement for America's "last frontier" in the West was made possible by the building of the railroad. Without the railroad, the settlers never could have traveled such distances in an efficient manner.

53. Meridians, or lines of longitude, not only help in pinpointing locations, but are also used for:

    A. Measuring distance from the Poles

    B. Determining direction of ocean currents

    C. Determining the time around the world

    D. Measuring distance on the Equator

Answer:

C. Determining the time around the world

Meridians, or lines of longitude, are the determining factor in separating time zones and determining time around the world.

54. Historians state that the West helped to speed up the Industrial Revolution. Which one of the following statements was not a reason for this?

    A. Food supplies for the ever-increasing urban populations came from farms in the West.

    B. A tremendous supply of gold and silver from western mines provided the capital needed to build industries.

    C. Descendants of western settlers, educated as engineers, geologists, and metallurgists in the East, returned to the West to mine the mineral resources needed for industry.

    D. Iron, copper, and other minerals from western mines were important resources in manufacturing products.

Answer:

C. Descendants of western settlers, educated as engineers, geologists, and metallurgists in the East, returned to the West to mine the mineral resources needed for industry.

The West helped to speed up the Industrial Revolution in a number of important and significant ways. First, the land yielded crops for the growing urban populations. Second, the gold and silver supplies coming out of the Western mines provided the capital needed to build industries. Also, resources such as iron and copper were extracted from the mines in the West and provided natural resources for manufacturing. The descendants of western settlers typically didn't become educated and then returned to the West as miners. The miners were typically working class with little or no education.

55. In the United States government, the power of taxation and borrowing is:

A. Implied or suggested

B. Concurrent or shared

C. Delegated or expressed

D. Reserved

Answer:

B. Concurrent or shared

In the United States government, the power of taxation is concurrent or shared with the states. An example of this is the separation of state and federal income tax and the separate filings of tax returns for each.

56. The post-Civil War years were a time of low public morality, a time of greed, graft, and dishonesty. Which one of the reasons listed would not be accurate?

A. The war itself because of the money and materials needed to carry on war

B. The very rapid growth of industry and big business after the war

C. The personal example set by President Grant

D. Unscrupulous heads of large impersonal corporations

Answer:

C. The personal example set by President Grant

The post-Civil War years were a particularly difficult time for the nation and public morale was especially low. The war had plunged the country into debt and ultimately into a recession by the 1890s. Racism was rampant throughout the South and the North where freed Blacks were taking jobs for low wages. The rapid growth of industry and big business caused a polarization of rich and poor, workers and owners. Many people moved into the urban centers to find work in the new industrial sector, jobs were typically low-wage, long hours, and poor working conditions. The heads of large impersonal corporations were arrogant in treating their workers inhumanely and letting morale drop to a record low. The heads of corporations showed their greed and malice towards the workingman by trying to prevent and disband labor unions.

57. Studies in astronomy, skills in mapping, and other contributions to geographic knowledge came from:

    A. Galileo

    B. Columbus

    C. Eratosthenes

    D. Ptolemy

Answer:

D. Ptolemy

Ptolemy (2nd century AD) was important in the fields of astronomy and geography. His theory stated that the earth was the center of the universe and all the other planets rotated around it, a theory that was later proven false. Ptolemy, however, was important for his contributions to the fields of mapping, mathematics, and geography. Galileo (1564-1642) was also important in the field of astronomy but did not make the mapping and geographic contributions of Ptolemy. He invented and used the world's first telescope and advanced Copernicus' theory that the earth revolved around the sun, much to the dismay of the Church.

58. Which one of the following would not be considered a result of World War II?

A. Economic depressions and slow resumption of trade and financial aid

B. Western Europe was no longer the center of world power

C. The beginnings of new power struggles not only in Europe but in Asia as well

D. Territorial and boundary changes for many nations, especially in Europe

Answer:

A. Economic depressions and slow resumption of trade and financial aid

Following World War II, the economy was vibrant and flourished from the stimulant of war and an increased dependence of the world on United States industries. Therefore, World War II didn't result in economic depressions and slow resumption of trade and financial aid. Western Europe was no longer the center of world power. New power struggles arose in Europe and Asia and many European nations underwent changing territories and boundaries.

59. The study of ways in which different societies around the world deal with the problems of limited resources and unlimited needs and wants is in the area of:

A. Economics

B. Sociology

C. Anthropology

D. Political Science

Answer:

A. Economics

The study of the ways in which different societies around the world deal with the problems of limited resources and unlimited needs and wants is a study of Economics. Economists consider the law of supply and demand as fundamental to the study of the economy. However, Sociology and Political Science also consider the study of economics and its importance in understanding social and political systems.

60. Nineteenth century imperialism by Western Europe nations had important and far-reaching effects on the colonial peoples they ruled. All four of the following are the results of this. Which one was the most important and had lasting effects on key 20th century events?

    A. Local wars were ended

    B. Living standards were raised

    C. Demands for self-government and feelings of nationalism surfaced

    D. Economic developments occurred

Answer:

C. Demands for self-government and feelings of nationalism surfaced

The 19th century imperialism by Western European nations had some very serious and far-reaching effects. The most important and lasting effect on events of the 20th century is the demands for self-government and the rise of nationalism. Both World War I and World War II were caused to a large degree by the rise of nationalist sentiment across Europe and Asia. Nationalism has also fueled numerous liberation movements and revolutionary movements across the globe from Central and South America to the South Pacific to Africa and Asia.

61. After the War of 1812, Henry Clay and others proposed economic measures, including raising tariffs to protect American farmers and manufacturers from foreign competition. These measures were proposed in the period known as:

A. Era of Nationalism

B. American Expansion

C. Era of Good Feeling

D. American System

Answer:

D. American System

Although there is no official (A) "Era of Nationalism", it could be used to describe the time leading up to and including the First and Second World Wars, as nationalism was on the rise. (B) American Expansion describes the movement of American settlers across the frontier towards the West. The so-called (C) "Era of Good Feeling" is the period after the War of 1812 but doesn't describe the policies proposed by Clay. The economic measures, including raising tariffs to protect American farmers and manufacturers from foreign competition, was known as the (D) American System.

62. "These are the times that try men's souls" were words penned by:

A. Thomas Jefferson

B. Samuel Adams

C. Benjamin Franklin

D. Thomas Paine

Answer:

D. Thomas Paine

Thomas Paine (1737-1809), the great American political theorist, wrote "these are the times that try men's souls" in his 16 part pamphlet *The Crisis*. Paine's authoring of *Common Sense* was an important step in spreading information to the American colonists about their need for independence from Great Britain.

63. The Age of Exploration begun in the 1400s was led by:

A. The Portuguese

B. The Spanish

C. The English

D. The Dutch

Answer:

A. The Portuguese

Although the Age of Exploration had many important players among them, the Dutch, Spanish and English, it was the Portuguese who sent the first explorers to the New World.

64. Which one of the following is not a function or responsibility of the US political parties?

    A. Conducting elections or the voting process

    B. Obtaining funds needed for election campaigns

    C. Choosing candidates to run for public office

    D. Making voters aware of issues and other public affairs information

Answer:

A. Conducting elections or the voting process

The US political parties have numerous functions and responsibilities. Among them are obtaining funds needed for election campaigns, choosing the candidates to run for office, and making voters aware of the issues. The political parties, however, do not conduct elections or the voting process, as that would be an obvious conflict of interest.

65. The economist who disagreed with the idea that free markets lead to full employment and prosperity and suggested that increasing government spending would end depressions was:

A. Keynes

B. Malthus

C. Smith

D. Friedman

Answer:

A. Keynes

John Maynard Keynes (1883-1946) advocated an economic system in which government regulations and spending on public works would stimulate the economy and lead to full employment. This broke from the classical idea that free markets would lead to full employment and prosperity. He was still a firm believer in capitalism, but in a less classical sense than Adam Smith (1723-1790), whose *Wealth of Nations* advocated for little or no government interference in the economy.
Smith claimed that an individual's self-interest would bring about the public's welfare. It is important to note that Smith was firmly against the free market systems of monopoly power and warned that the private sector, particularly large manufacturers, if left unregulated could potentially stand in opposition to the public welfare.

66. The study of the social behavior of minority groups would be in the area of:

      A. Anthropology

      B. Psychology

      C. Sociology

      D. Cultural Geography

Answer:

C. Sociology

The study of social behavior in minority groups would be primarily in the area of Sociology, as it is the discipline most concerned with social interaction and being. However, it could be argued that Anthropology, Psychology, and Cultural Geography could have some interest in the study as well.

67. An extensive knowledge of surgery and medicine as well as principles of irrigation, fertilization and terrace farming was unique to:

      A. The Mayans

      B. The Atacamas

      C. The Incas

      D. The Tarapacas

Answer:

C. The Incas

The Incas of Peru had an extensive knowledge of surgery and medicine as well as principles of irrigation, fertilization, and terrace farming. These were unique achievements for an ancient civilization.

68. The idea of universal peace through world of organization was a philosophy of:

    A. Rousseau

    B. Immanuel Kant

    C. Montesquieu

    D. John Locke

Answer:

B. Immanuel Kant

Immanuel Kant (1724-1804) was the German metaphysician and philosopher, who was a founding proponent of the idea that world organization was the means for achieving universal peace. Kant's ideas helped to found such world peace organizations as the League of Nations in the wake of World War I.

69. Which ancient civilization is credited with being the first to develop irrigation techniques through the use of canals, dikes, and devices for raising water?

    A. The Sumerians

    B. The Egyptians

    C. The Babylonians

    D. The Akkadians

Answer:

A. The Sumerians

The ancient (A) Sumerians of the Fertile Crescent of Mesopotamia are credited with being the first to develop irrigation techniques through the use of canals, dikes, and devices for raising water. The (B) Egyptians also practiced controlled irrigation but that was primarily through the use of the Nile's predictable flooding schedule. The (C) Babylonians were more noted for their revolutionary systems of law than their irrigation systems.

70. The study of past human cultures based on physical artifacts is:

A. History

B. Anthropology

C. Cultural Geography

D. Archaeology

Answer:

D. Archaeology

Archaeology is the study of past human cultures based on physical artifacts such as fossils, carvings, paintings, and engraved writings.

71. The "father" of modern economics is considered by most economists today to be:

A. Thomas Robert Malthus

B. John Stuart Mill

C. Adam Smith

D. John Maynard Keynes

Answer:

C. Adam Smith

Adam Smith (1723-1790) is considered by many to be the "father" of modern economics. In the *Wealth of Nations,* Smith advocated for little or no government interference in the economy. Smith claimed that individuals' self-interest would bring about the public's welfare. It is important to note that Smith was firmly against the free market systems of monopoly power and warned that the private sector, particularly large manufacturers, if left unregulated could potentially stand in opposition to the public welfare. John Maynard Keynes 1883-1946) was also an important economist. He advocated an economic system in which government regulations and spending on public works would stimulate the economy and lead to full employment. John Stuart Mill (1806-1873) was a progressive British philosopher and economist, whose ideas came closer to socialism than to the classical capitalist ideas of Adam Smith. Mill constantly advocated for political and social reforms, including emancipation for women, labor organizations, and farming cooperatives. Thomas Malthus (1766-1834) was a British economist who introduced the study of population and early on considered famine, war, and disease to be the primary checks on world population. He later modified his views and recognized his early theoretical shortcomings and shifted his focus to the causes of unemployment.

72. The ideas and innovations of the period of the Renaissance were spread throughout Europe mainly because of:

    A. Extensive exploration

    B. Craft workers and their guilds

    C. The invention of the printing press

    D. Increased travel and trade

Answer:

C. The invention of the printing press

The ideas and innovations of the Renaissance were spread throughout Europe for a number of reasons. While exploration, increased travel, and spread of craft may have aided the spread of the Renaissance to small degrees, nothing was as important to the spread of ideas as Gutenberg's invention of the printing press in Germany.

73. The American labor union movement started gaining new momentum:

    A. During the building of the railroads

    B. After 1865 with the growth of cities

    C. With the rise of industrial giants such as Carnegie and Vanderbilt

    D. During the war years of 1861-1865

Answer:

B. After 1865 with the growth of cities

The American Labor Union movement had been around since the late 18th and early 19th centuries. The Labor movement began to first experience persecution by employers in the early 1800s. The American Labor Movement remained relatively ineffective until after the Civil War. In 1866, the National Labor Union was formed, pushing such issues as the eight-hour workday and new policies of immigration. This gave rise to the Knights of Labor and eventually the American Federation of Labor (AFL) in the 1890s and the Industrial Workers of the World (1905). Therefore, it was the period following the Civil War that empowered the labor movement in terms of numbers, militancy, and effectiveness.

74. Soil erosion is most likely to occur in large amounts in:

A. Mountain ranges

B. Deserts

C. Tropical rainforests

D. River valleys

Answer:

C. Tropical rainforests

Soil erosion is most likely to occur in tropical rainforests as the large amount of constant rainfall moves the soil at a greater rate across a greater area. Mountain ranges and river valleys experience some soil erosion but don't have the levels of precipitation found in a tropical rainforest. Deserts have virtually no soil erosion due to their climate.

75. Who is considered to be the most important figure in the spread of Protestantism across Switzerland?

    A. Calvin

    B. Zwingli

    C. Munzer

    D. Leyden

Answer:

A. Calvin
While Huldreich Zwingli (1484-1531) was the first to spread the Protestant Reformation in Switzerland around 1519, it was John Calvin (1509-1564), whose less radical approach to Protestantism who really made the most impact in Switzerland. Calvin's ideas separated from the Lutherans over the "Lord's Supper" debate over the sacrament, and his branch of Protestants became known as Calvinism. Calvin certainly built on Zwingli's early influence but really made the religion widespread throughout Switzerland. Thomas Munzer (1489-1525) was a German Protestant reformer whose radical and revolutionary ideas about God's will to overthrow the ruling classes and his siding with the peasantry got him beheaded. Munzer has since been studied and admired by Marxists for his views on class. Leyden (or Leiden) was a founder of the University of Leyden, a Protestant place for study in the Netherlands.

76. The principle that "men entrusted with power tend to abuse it" is attributed to:

   A. Locke

   B. Rousseau

   C. Aristotle

   D. Montesquieu

Answer:

D. Montesquieu

The principle that "men entrusted with power tend to abuse it" is attributed to Montesquieu (1689-1755), the great French philosopher whose ideas based much on Locke's ideas, along with Rousseau, had a strong influence on the French Revolution of 1789. Although it would be reasonable to assume that Locke, Rousseau, and Aristotle would probably agree with the statement, all four of these men had profound impacts on the ideas of the Enlightenment, from humanism to constitutionals.

77. After 1783, the largest "land owner" in the Americas was:

   A. Britain

   B. Spain

   C. France

   D. United States

Answer:

A.   Spain

Despite the emergence of the United States as an independent nation in control of the colonies over the British, and the French control of Canada, Spain remained the largest "land owner" in the Americas controlling much of the southwest as well as much of Central and South America.

78. The purchase of goods or services on one market for immediate resale on another market is:

A. Output

B. Enterprise

C. Arbitrage

D. Mercantile

Answer:

C. Arbitrage

Output is an amount produced or manufactured by an industry. Enterprise is simply any business organization. Mercantile is one of the first systems of economics in which goods were exchanged. Therefore, arbitrage is an item or service that an industry produces. The dictionary definition of arbitrage is the purchase of securities on one market for immediate resale on another market in order to profit from a price discrepancy.

79. After the Civil War, the United States adapted an attitude of isolation from foreign affairs. But the turning point marking the beginning of the US becoming a world power was:

A. World War I

B. Expansion of business and trade overseas

C. The Spanish-American War

D. The building and financing of the Panama Canal

Answer:

C. The Spanish-American War

The turning point marking the beginning of the United States becoming a super power was the Spanish-American War. This was seen as an extension of the Monroe doctrine, calling for United States dominance in the Western Hemisphere and removal of European powers in the region. The United States' relatively easy defeat of Spain in the Spanish-American War marked the beginning of a continuing era of dominance for the United States. In addition, in the post-Civil War era, Spain was the largest land owner in the Americas. Their easy defeat at the hands of the United States in Cuba, the Philippines, and elsewhere showed the strength of the United States across the globe.

80. The programs such as unemployment insurance and health insurance for the elderly are the responsibility of:

A. Federal Government

B. Local Government

C. State Government

D. Communal Government

Answer:

A. Federal Government

Assistance programs, such as unemployment insurance and health insurance for the elderly is the responsibility of the federal government.

81. The English explorer who gave England its claim to North America was:

A. Raleigh

B. Hawkins

C. Drake

D. Cabot

Answer:

D. Cabot

Sir Walter Raleigh (1554-1618) was an English explorer and navigator, who was sent to the New World in search of riches. He founded the lost colony on Roanoke Island, North Carolina, and was later imprisoned for a supposed plot to kill the King for which he was later released. Sir John Hawkins (1532-1595) and Sir Francis Drake (1540-1596) were both navigators who worked in the slave trade, made some voyages to the New World, and commanded ships against and defeated the Spanish Armada in 1588. John Cabot (1450-1498) was the English explorer who gave England claim to North America.

82. The three-day Battle of Gettysburg was the turning point of the Civil War for the North leading to ultimate victory. The battle in the West reinforcing the North's victory and sealing the South's defeat was the day after Gettysburg at:

A. Perryville

B. Vicksburg

C. Stones River

D. Shiloh

Answer:

B. Vicksburg

The Battle of Vicksburg was crucial in reinforcing the North's victory and sealing the south's defeat for a couple of reasons. First, the Battle of Vicksburg potentially gave the Union full control of the Mississippi River. More importantly, the battle split the Confederate Army and allowed General Grant to reach his goal of restoring commerce to the important northwest area.

83. The study of the exercise of power and political behavior in human society today would be conducted by experts in:

A. History

B. Sociology

C. Political Science

D. Anthropology

Answer:

C. Political Science

Experts in the field of political science today would likely conduct the study of exercise of power and political behavior in human society. However, it is also reasonable to suggest that such studies would be important to historians (study of the past, often in an effort to understand the present), sociologists (often concerned with power structure in the social and political worlds), and even some anthropologists (study of culture and their behaviors).

84. **During the period of Spanish colonialism, which of the following was not a key to the goal of exploiting, transforming and including the native people?**

   A. Missions

   B. Ranchos

   C. Presidios

   D. Pueblos

Answer:

B. Ranchos

The goal of Spanish colonialism was to exploit, transform and include the native people of California. The Spanish empire sought to do this first by gathering the native people into communities where they could both be taught Spanish culture and be converted to Roman Catholicism and its value system. The social institutions by which this was accomplished was the encouragement of the Mission System, which established a number of Catholic missions a day's journey apart. Once the native people were brought to the missions, they were incorporated into a mission society and indoctrinated in the teachings of Catholicism. The Presidios were fortresses that were constructed to protect Spanish interests and the communities from invaders. The Pueblos were small civilian communities that attracted settlers with the gift of land, seed, and farming equipment. The function of the Pueblos was to produce food for the missions and for the presidios.

85. Potential customers for any product or service are not only called consumers but can also be called a:

    A. Resource

    B. Base

    C. Commodity

    D. Market

Answer:

D. Market

Potential customers for any product or service are not only customers but can also be called a market. A resource is a source of wealth; natural resources are the basis for manufacturing goods and services. A commodity is anything that is bought or sold, any product.

86. An early cultural group was so skillful in navigating on the sea that they were able to sail at night guided by starts. They were the:

    A. Greeks

    B. Persians

    C. Minoans

    D. Phoenicians

Answer:

D. Phoenicians

Although the Greeks were quite able sailors and developed a strong navy in their defeat of the Persians at sea in the Battle of Marathon, it was the Eastern Mediterranean culture of the Phoenicians that had first developed the astronomical skill of sailing at night with the starts as their guide. The Minoans were an advanced early civilization off the Greek coast on Crete more noted for their innovations in terms of sewage systems, toilets, and running water.

87. One method of trade restriction used by some nations is:

   A. Limited treaties

   B. Floating exchange rate

   C. Bill of exchange

   D. Import quotas

Answer:

D. Import quotas

One method of trade restriction used by some nations is import quotas. The amounts of goods imported are regulated in an effort to protect domestic enterprise and limit foreign competition. Both the United States and Japan, two of the world's most industrialized nations have import quotas to protect domestic industries.

88. A political system in which the laws and traditions put limits on the powers of government is:

   A. Federalism

   B. Constitutionalism

   C. Parliamentary system

   D. Presidential system

Answer:

B. Constitutionalism

Constitutionalism is a political system in which laws and traditions put limits on the powers of government. Federalism is the idea of a strong, centralized national government to hold together the nation. The parliamentary system, such as the governments of Great Britain and Israel, are systems in which a group of representatives are led by a prime minister contrasting with a presidential system which is run by a head of state, the elected (or sometimes self-appointed) president.

89. Which one of the following did not contribute to the early medieval European civilization?

    A. The heritage from the classical cultures

    B. The Christian religion

    C. The influence of the German Barbarians

    D. The spread of ideas through trade and commerce

Answer:

D. The spread of ideas through trade and commerce
The heritage of the classical cultures such as Greece, the Christian religion which became dominant, and the influence of the Germanic Barbarians (Visigoths, Saxons, Ostrogoths, Vandals and Franks) were all contributions to early medieval Europe and its plunge into feudalism. During this period, lives were often difficult and lived out on one single manor, with very little travel or spread of ideas through trade or commerce. Civilization seems to have halted progress during these years.

90. The Roman Empire gave so much to the world, especially the Western world. Of the legacies below, the most influential, effective and lasting is:

A. The language of Latin

B. Roman law, justice, and political system

C. Engineering and building

D. The writings of its poets and historians

Answer:

B. Roman law, justice, and political system
Of the lasting legacies of the Roman Empire, it is their law, justice, and political system that has been the most effective and influential on our Western world today. The idea of a Senate and different houses is still maintained by our United States government and their legal justice system is also the foundation of our own. We still use many Latin words in our justice system, terms such as *habeas corpus* and *voir dire*. English, Spanish, Italian, French, and others are all based on Latin. The Roman language, Latin itself has died out. The Roman engineering and building and their writings and poetry have also been influential but not nearly to the degree that their governmental and justice systems have been.

91. Charlemagne's most important influence on Western civilization is seen today in:

A. Relationship of church and state

B. Strong military for defense

C. The criminal justice system

D. Education of women

Answer:

A. Relationship of church and state

Charlemagne was the leader of the Germanic Franks responsible for the promotion of the Holy Roman Empire across Europe. Although he unified governments and aided the Pope, he re-crowned himself in 802 A.D. to demonstrate that his power and right to rule was not a grant from the Pope, but rather a secular achievement. Therefore, although he used much of the Church's power in his rise to power, the Pope in turn used Charlemagne to ascend the Church to new heights. Thus, Charlemagne had an influence on the issues between Church and state.

92. Public administration, such as public officials in the areas of budgets, accounting, distribution of public funds, and personnel management, would be a part of the field of:

A. Anthropology

B. Sociology

C. Law and Taxation

D. Political Science and Economics

Answer:

D. Political Science and Economics

Public administration, such as public officials in the areas of budgets, accounting, distribution of public funds, and personnel management, would be parts of the fields of Economics and Political Science. While political scientists would be concerned with public administration, economists would also be concerned with the distribution of public funds, budgets, and accounting and their effects on the economy.

93. "Marbury vs Madison (1803)" was an important Supreme Court case which set the precedent for:

    A. The elastic clause

    B. Judicial review

    C. The supreme law of the land

    D. Popular sovereignty in the territories

Answer:

B. Judicial review

Marbury vs Madison (1803) was an important case for the Supreme Court as it established judicial review. In that case, the Supreme Court set precedence to declare laws passed by Congress as unconstitutional. Popular sovereignty in the territories was a failed plan pushed by Stephen Davis to allow states to decide the slavery question for themselves. In his attempt to appeal to the masses in the pre-Civil War elections. The supreme law of the land is just that, the law that rules. The elastic clause is not a real term.

94. Which one of the following is not a use for a region's wetlands?

A. Produces fresh clean water

B. Provides habitat for wildlife

C. Provides water for hydroelectric power

D. Controls floods

Answer:

C. Provides water for hydroelectric power

A region's wetlands provide a number of uses and services not limited to but including production of fresh water, habitat and natural preserve of wildlife, and flood control. Wetlands are not used in the production of hydroelectric power the way dams or other power structures do.

95. The philosopher who coined the term "sociology" also stated that social behavior and events could be measured scientifically. He is identified as:

A. Auguste Comte

B. Herbert Spencer

C. Rousseau

D. Immanuel Kant

Answer:

A. Auguste Comte

Auguste Comte (1798-1857) was a French philosopher and social reformer who founded the school of positivism. Comte identified the uses of different scientific applications as dependent on the preceding science in the order of mathematics, astronomy, physics, chemistry, biology, and finally his coined term, sociology. Herbert Spencer (1820-1903) also helped spread sociology, although his evolutionary theory was more practical and popular than it was scientific. Rousseau (1712-1778) was a political philosopher who explored the idea of what has come to be known as liberalism. Immanuel Kant (1724-1804) was the German metaphysician and philosopher who was a founding proponent of the idea that world organization was the means for achieving universal peace.

96. **The belief that the United States should control all of North America was called:**

A. Westward Expansion

B. Pan Americanism

C. Manifest Destiny

D. Nationalism

Answer:

C. Manifest Destiny

The belief that the United States should control all of North America was called Manifest Destiny. This idea fueled much of the violence and aggression towards those already occupying the lands such as the Native Americans. Manifest Destiny was certainly driven by sentiments of (D) nationalism and gave rise to (A) westward expansion.

97. A well known World War II figure who said that democracy was like a rotting corpse that had to be replaced by a superior way of life and more efficient government was:

A. Hitler

B. Stalin

C. Tojo

D. Mussolini

Answer:

D. Mussolini

(A) Adolf Hitler (1889-1945), the Nazi leader of Germany, and (C) Hideki Tojo (1884-1948), the Japanese General and Prime Minister, were well known World War II figures who led Axis forces into war on a quest of spreading fascism. (B) Joseph Stalin (1879-1953) was the Communist Russian head of state during World War II. Although all three were repressive in their actions, it was (D) Benito Mussolini (1883-1945), the Fascist and widely-considered incompetent leader of Italy during World War II, who once said "democracy was like a rotting corpse that had to be replaced by a superior way of life and more efficient government".

98. The Radical Republicans who pushed the harsh Reconstruction measures through Congress after Lincoln's death lost public and moderate Republican support when they went too far:

A. In their efforts to impeach the President

B. By dividing ten southern states into military-controlled districts

C. By making the ten southern states give freed African-Americans the right to vote

D. Sending carpetbaggers into the South to build up support for Congressional legislation

Answer:

A. In their efforts to impeach the President

The public support and the moderate Republicans were actually being drawn towards the more radical end of the Republican spectrum following Lincoln's death during Reconstruction. Because many felt as though Andrew Johnson's policies towards the South were too soft and were running the risk of rebuilding the old system of white power and slavery. Even moderate Republicans in the North felt as though it was essential to rebuild the South but with the understanding that they must be abide by the Fourteenth and Fifteenth Amendments assuring Blacks freedom and the right to vote. The radical Republicans were so frustrated that the President would make concessions to the old Southerners that they attempted to impeach him. This turned back the support that they had received from the public and from moderates.

99. **The economic system promoting individual ownership of land, capital, and businesses with minimal governmental regulations is called:**

   A. Macro-economy

   B. Micro-economy

   C. Laissez-faire

   D. Free enterprise

Answer:

D. Free Enterprise

(D) Free enterprise or capitalism is the economic system that promotes private ownership of land, capital, and business with minimal government interference. (C) Laissez-faire is the idea that an "invisible hand" will guide the free enterprise system to the maximum potential efficiency.

100. **A political philosophy favoring or supporting rapid social changes in order to correct social and economic inequalities is called:**

   A. Nationalism

   B. Liberalism

   C. Conservatism

   D. Federalism

Answer:

B. Liberalism

A political philosophy favoring rapid social changes in order to correct social and economic inequalities are called Liberalism. Liberalism was a theory that could be said to have started with the great French philosophers Montesquieu (1689-1755) and Rousseau (1712-1778). It is important to understand the difference between political, economic, and social liberalism, as they are different and how they sometimes contrast one another in the modern world.

101. China's last imperial ruling dynasty was one of its most stable and successful and under its rule, Chinese culture made an outstanding impression on Western nations. This dynasty was:

A. Ming

B. Manchu

C. Han

D. Chou

Answer:

B. Manchu

The (A) Ming Dynasty lasted from 1368-1644 and was among the more successful dynasties but focused attention towards foreign trade and encouraged growth in the arts. Therefore, it was the (B) Manchu Dynasty, the last imperial ruling dynasty, which came to power in the 1600s and expanded China's power in Asia greatly that was and still is considered to be among the most important, most stable, and most successful of the Chinese dynasties. The (C) Han and (D) Chou Dynasties were part of the "ancient" dynasties of China and while important in Chinese History, their influence did not hold impression on Western nations as the Manchu.

102. Development of a solar calendar, invention of the decimal system, and contributions to the development of geometry and astronomy are all the legacy of:

A. The Babylonians

B. The Persians

C. The Sumerians

D. The Egyptians

Answer:

D. The Egyptians

The (A) Babylonians of ancient Mesopotamia flourished for a time under their great contribution of organized law and code, called Hammurabi's Code (1750 B.C.), after the ruler Hammurabi. The fall of the Babylonians to the Persians in 539 B.C. made way for the warrior-driver Persian Empire that expanded from Pakistan to the Mediterranean Sea until the conquest of Alexander the Great in 331 B.C. The Sumerians of ancient Mesopotamia were most noted for their early advancements as one of the first civilizations and their contributions towards written language known as cuneiform. It was the (D) Egyptians who were the first true developers of a solar calendar, the decimal system, and made significant contributions to the development of geometry and astronomy.

103. The Study of "spatial relationships and interaction" would be done by people in the field of:

A. Political Science

B. Anthropology

C. Geography

D. Sociology

Answer:

C. Geography

Geography is the discipline within Social Science that most concerns itself with the study of "spatial relationships and interaction".

104. The circumference of the earth, which greatly contributed to geographic knowledge, was calculated by:

A. Ptolemy

B. Eratosthenes

C. Galileo

D. Strabo

Answer:

B. Eratosthenes

There is no doubt to Ptolemy and Galileo's influence as astronomers. (A) Ptolemy as an earlier theorist and (C) Galileo as a founder of modern scientific knowledge of astronomy and our place in the galaxy. However, it was (B) Eratosthenes (275 B.C. – 195 B.C.), the Greek writer, philosopher, and astronomer, who is credited with measuring the earth's circumference as well as the distances between Earth, sun, and moon. (D) Strabo was more concerned with geography and history than astronomy.

105. The first European to see Florida and sail along its coast was:

    A. Cabot

    B. Columbus

    C. Ponce de Leon

    D. Narvaez

Answer:

A. Cabot

(A) John Cabot (1450-1498) was the English explorer who gave England claim to North American and the first European to see Florida and sail along its coast. (B) Columbus (1451-1506) was sent by the Spanish to the New World and has received false credit for "discovering America" in 1492, although he did open up the New World to European expansion, exploitation, and Christianity. (C) Ponce de Leon (1460-1521), the Spanish explorer, was the first European to actually land on Florida. (D) Panfilo de Narvaez (1470-1528) was also a Spanish conquistador, but he was sent to Mexico to force Cortes into submission. He failed and was captured.

106. Which one of the following events did not occur during the period known as the "Era of Good Feeling"?

A. President Monroe issued the Monroe Doctrine

B. Spain ceded Florida to the United States

C. The building of the National Road

D. The charter of the second Bank of the United States

Answer:

A. President Monroe issued the Monroe Doctrine

The so-called "Era of Good Feeling" describes the period following the War of 1812. This was during the Presidency of James Madison and focused the nation on internal national improvements such as the building of the second national bank (Charter for Bank of United States), construction of new roads (National Road), and the Treaty of Ghent, which ended the War of 1812 by forcing Spain to cede Florida to the United States. Of the possible answers, only the Monroe Doctrine (1823), which called for an end to any European occupation and colonization in the Americas, was not a part of the "Era of Good Feeling", it came a bit after.

107. Native communities in early California are commonly divided into several cultural areas. How many cultural areas?

A. 4

B. 5

C. 6

D. 7

Answer:

C. 6

The answer is 6 (C). Due to the great diversity of the native communities, the state is generally divided into six "culture areas." The culture areas are: (1) the Southern Culture Area, (2) the Central Culture Area, (3) the Northwestern Culture Area, (4) the Northeastern Culture Area, (5) the Great Basin Culture Area, and (6) the Colorado River Culture Area. These areas are geographically distinct and supported different sorts of cultures depending upon the availability of an adequate water supply, the ability to cultivate the land, and the availability of game.

108. The world religion, which includes a caste system, is:

A. Buddhism

B. Hinduism

C. Sikhism

D. Jainism

Answer:

B. Hinduism

Buddhism, Sikhism, and Jainism all rose out of protest against Hinduism and its practices of sacrifice and the caste system. The caste system, in which people were born into castes, would determine their class for life including who they could marry, what jobs they could perform, and their overall quality of life.

109. **The idea that continued population growth would, in future years, seriously affect a nation's productive capabilities was stated by:**

A. Keynes

B. Mill

C. Malthus

D. Friedman

Answer:

C. Malthus

(C) John Maynard Keynes (1883-1946) advocated an economic system in which government regulations and spending on public works would stimulate the economy and lead to full employment. (C) Thomas Malthus (1766-1834) was the English economist who had the idea that population growth would seriously affect a nation's productive capabilities. Malthus' ideas also included predictions about running out of food and a natural selection-like process brought about by population that would maintain balance. His theory was proven wrong long ago. (B) Mill (1806 -1973), an English economist and (D) Friedman (1912-) an American economist contrasted one another greatly. Mill was almost a Socialist and wrote the early work in Political Economy while Friedman was a financial advisor in the arch conservative government of President Ronald Reagan.

110. After World War II, the United States:

A. Limited its involvement in European affairs

B. Shifted foreign policy emphasis from Europe to Asia

C. Passed significant legislation pertaining to aid to farmers and tariffs on imports

D. Entered the greatest period of economic growth in its history

Answer:

D. Entered the greatest period of economic growth in its history

After World War II, the United States did not limit or shift its involvement in European affairs. In fact, it escalated the Cold War with the Soviet Union at a swift pace and attempted to contain Communism to prevent its spread across Europe. There was no significant legislation pertaining to aid to farmers and tariffs on imports. In fact, since World War II, trade has become more liberal than ever. Free trade, no matter how risky or harmful to the people of the United States or other countries, has become the economic policy of the United States called neo-liberalism. Due to this, the United States after World War II entered the greatest period of economic growth in its history and remains a world superpower.

111. France decided in 1777 to help the American colonies in their war against Britain. This decision was based on:

A. The naval victory of John Paul Jones over the British ship "Serapis"

B. The survival of the terrible winter at Valley Forge

C. The success of colonial guerilla fighters in the South

D. The defeat of the British at Saratoga

Answer:

D. The defeat of the British at Saratoga

The defeat of the British at Saratoga was the overwhelming factor in the Franco-American alliance of 1777 that helped the American colonies defeat the British. Some historians believe that without the Franco-American alliance, the American Colonies would not have been able to defeat the British and American would have remained a British colony.

112. What event sparked a great migration of people from all over the world to California?

A. The birth of Labor Unions

B. California statehood

C. The invention of the automobile

D. The gold rush

The answer is "The Gold Rush" (D). The discovery of gold in California created a lust for gold that quickly brought immigrants from the eastern United States and many parts of the world. To be sure, there were struggles and conflicts, as well as the rise of nativism. Yet this vast migration of people from all parts of the world began the process that has created California's uniquely diverse culture.

113. **Which individual was responsible for promoting "welfare capitalism" in the formation of Michigan's economy?**

A. Gerald Ford

B. Antoine de la Mothe Cadillac

C. Robert Cavelier Sieur de la Salle

D. Henry Ford

Answer: D. Henry Ford

Henry Ford's idea of "welfare capitalism" was a winner as his workers were consistently the highest-paid and the happiest workers in the country. Ford wanted his workers to come to work happy and go home satisfied, and he believed that a higher than normal wage and more than adequate working conditions could help create the workplace ideal that would create more products of a higher quality than could his competitors. The famous Frenchman, Robert Cavelier Sieur de la Salle (C) explored the Michigan area, including the adjoining Great Lake. Detroit was the result of the efforts of yet another Frenchman, Antoine de la Mothe Cadillac (B), angling to protect French efforts against both Native Americans and British. (A) Gerald Ford was the 38th and 40th President of the United States.

114. A number of women worked hard in the first half of the 19th century for women's rights but decisive gains did not come until after 1850. The earliest accomplishments were in:

A. Medicine

B. Education

C. Writing

D. Temperance

Answer:

B. Education

Although women worked hard in the early 19th century to make gains in medicine, writing, and temperance movements, the most prestigious accomplishments of the early women's movement was in the field of education. Women such as Mary Wollstonecraft (1759-1797), Alice Palmer(1855-1902), and of course Elizabeth Blackwell (1821-1910), led the way for women, particularly in the area of higher education.

115. Nineteenth century German unification was the result of the hard work of:

A. Otto von Bismarck

B. Kaiser William II

C. von Moltke

D. Hindenburg

Answer:

A. Otto von Bismarck

(A) Otto von Bismarck is the man most often credited with the unification of Germany. Bismarck became the first Chancellor of a unified Germany. He ultimately lost power to his successor Kaiser William II, who ultimately led Germany into World War I, when nationalist sentiment proved too strong for the united Germany. Ultimately, Germany's concessions in the Treaty of Versailles to end World War I, and Adolf Hitler's Nazi regime's defeat at the hands of Allied forces in World War II had destroyed the unified Germany that Bismarck had achieved in the mid to late 1800s.

116. The geographical drought-stricken region of Africa south of the Sahara and extending east and west from Senegal to Somalia is:

A. The Kalahari

B. The Namib

C. The Great Rift Valley

D. The Sahel

Answer:

D. The Sahel

The (A) Kalahari is located between the Orange and Zambezi Rivers and has an annual rainfall of about 5 to 20 inches. The (B) Namib is a desert, rocky plateau along the coast of Namibia in Southwest Africa that receives less than .5 inches of rainfall annually. The (C) Great Rift Valley is a fault system that runs 3000 miles from Syria to Mozambique and has great variations in elevation. Therefore, it is the (D) Sahel, the region of Africa South of the Sahara and extending East and West from Senegal to Somalia. The Sahel experienced a serious drought in the 1960s and then again in the 1980s and 1990s. International relief efforts have been focused there in an effort to keep the region alive.

117. The idea or proposal for more equal division of profits among employers and workers was put forth by:

A. Karl Marx

B. Thomas Malthus

C. Adam Smith

D. John Stuart Mill

Answer:

D. John Stuart Mill

(A) Karl Marx (1818-1883) was the German social philosopher and economist who wrote *The Communist Manifesto* and numerous other landmark works in his goal to help the world understand the inability of capitalism to provide for the workers, the idea of class struggle, and the central role of economy. (B) Thomas Malthus (1766-1834) was a British economist who introduced the study of population and early on considered famine, war, and disease to be the primary checks on world population. He later modified his views and recognized his early theoretical shortcoming and shifted his focus to the causes of unemployment. (C) Adam Smith (1723-1790) is considered by many to be the "father" of modern capitalist economics. In the *Wealth of Nations*, Smith advocated for little or no government interference in the economy. Smith claimed that an individual's self-interest would bring about the public's welfare.

It is important to note that Smith was firmly against the free market systems of monopoly power and warned that the private sector, particularly large manufacturers, if left unregulated could potentially stand in opposition to the public welfare. (D) John Stuart Mill (1806-1873) was the progressive British philosopher and economist whose ideas came closer to socialism than to the classical capitalist ideas of Adam Smith. Mill constantly advocated for political and social reforms, including emancipation for women, labor organizations, farming cooperatives, and most importantly a more equal division of profits among employers and workers.

118. The term that best describes how the Supreme Court can block laws that may be unconstitutional from being enacted is:

    A. Jurisprudence

    B. Judicial Review

    C. Exclusionary Rule

    D. Right of Petition

Answer:

B. Judicial Review

(A) Jurisprudence is the study of the development and origin of law. (B) Judicial review is the term that best describes how the Supreme Court can block laws that they deem as unconstitutional as set forth in Marbury vs Madison. The (C) "exclusionary rule" is a reference to the Fourth Amendment of the Constitution and says that evidence gathered in an illegal manner or search must be thrown out and excluded from evidence. There is nothing called the (D) "Right of Petition", however the Petition of Right is a reference to a statement of civil liberties sent by the English Parliament to Charles I in 1628.

119. On the spectrum of American politics the label that most accurately describes voters to the "right of center" is:

    A. Moderates

    B. Liberals

    C. Conservatives

    D. Socialists

Answer:

C. Conservatives

(A) Moderates are considered voters who teeter on the line of political centrality or drift slightly to the left or right. (B) Liberals are voters who stand on the left of center. (C) Conservative voters are those who are "right of center". (D) Socialist would land far to the left on the political spectrum of America.

120. Marxism believes which two groups are in continual conflict:

    A. Farmers and landowners

    B. Kings and the nobility

    C. Workers and owners

    D. Structure and superstructure

Answer:

C. Workers and owners

Marxism believes that the workers and owners are in continual conflict. Marxists refer to these two groups as the proletariat and the bourgeoisie. The proletariat is exploited by the bourgeoisie and will, according to Marxism, rise up over the bourgeoisie in class warfare in an effort to end private control over the means of production.

121. The United States legislature is bi-cameral, this means:

    A. It consists of several houses

    B. It consists of two houses

    C. The Vice-President is in charge of the legislature when in session

    D. It has an upper house and a lower house

Answer:

B. It consists of two houses

The bi-cameral nature of the United States legislature means that it has two houses, the Senate and the House of Representatives, that make up the Congress. The Vice-President is part of the Executive branch of government but presides over the Senate and may act as a tiebreaker. An upper and lower house would be parts of a Parliamentary system of government such as the governments of Great Britain and Israel.

122. What Supreme Court ruling established the principal of Judicial Review?

    A. Jefferson vs Madison

    B. Lincoln vs Douglas

    C. Marbury vs Madison

    D. Marbury vs Jefferson

Answer:

C. Marbury vs Madison

Marbury vs Madison established the principal of judicial review. The Supreme Court ruled that it held no authority in making the decision (regarding Marbury's commission as Justice of the Peace in District of Columbia) as the Supreme Court's jurisdiction (or lack thereof) in the case, was conflicted with Article III of the Constitution.

123. To be eligible to be elected President one must:

    A. Be a citizen for at least five years

    B. Be a citizen for seven years

    C. Have been born a citizen

    D. Be a naturalized citizen

Answer:

C. Have been born a citizen

Article II, Section 1 of the United States Constitution clearly states, "No person except a natural-born citizen, or citizen of the United States at the time of the adoption of this Constitution, shall be eligible to the office of President, neither shall any person be eligible to that office who shall not have attained to the age of thirty-five years, and been fourteen years a resident within the United States.

124. The international organization established to work for world peace at the end of the Second World War is the :

  A. League of Nations

  B. United Federation of Nations

  C. United Nations

  D. United World League

Answer:

C. United Nations

The international organization established to work for world peace at the end of the Second World War was the United Nations. From the ashes of the failed League of Nations, established following World War I, the United Nations continues to be a major player in world affairs today.

125. Which of the following is an example of a direct democracy?

  A. Elected representatives

  B. Greek city-states

  C. The Constitution

  D. The Confederate States

Answer:

B. Greek city-states

The Greek city-states are an example of a direct democracy as their leaders were elected directly by the citizens and the citizens themselves were given voice in government. (A) Elected representatives in the United States as in the case of the presidential elections are actually elected by an electoral college that is supposed to be representative of the citizens. As we have learned from the elections of 2000, this is a flawed system. The United States Congress, the Senate, and the House of Representatives are also examples of indirect democracy as they represent the citizens in the legislature as opposed to having citizens represent themselves.

XAMonline, INC. 21 Orient Ave. Melrose, MA 02176

Toll Free number 800-509-4128

TO ORDER Fax 781-662-9268 OR www.XAMonline.com

MICHIGAN TEST FOR TEACHER EXAMINATION - MTTC - 2007

PO#   Store/School:

Address 1:

Address 2 (Ship to other):

City, State Zip

Credit card number_____-_____-_____-_____   expiration_____

EMAIL _____

PHONE   **FAX**

13# ISBN 2007	TITLE	Qty	Retail	Total
978-1-58197-968-8	MTTC Basic Skills 96			
978-1-58197-954-1	MTTC Biology 17			
978-1-58197-955-8	MTTC Chemistry 18			
978-1-58197-957-2	MTTC Earth-Space Science 20			
978-1-58197-966-4	MTTC Elementary Education 83			
978-1-58197-967-1	MTTC Elementary Education 83 Sample Questions			
978-1-58197-950-3	MTTC English 02			
978-1-58197-961-9	MTTC Family and Consumer Sciences 40			
978-1-58197-959-6	MTTC French Sample Test 23			
978-1-58197-965-7	MTTC Guidance Counselor 51			
978-1-58197-964-0	MTTC Humanities& Fine Arts 53, 54			
978-1-58197-972-5	MTTC Integrated Science (Secondary) 94			
978-1-58197-973-2	MTTC Emotionally Impaired 59			
978-1-58197-953-4	MTTC Learning Disabled 63			
978-1-58197-963-3	MTTC Library Media 48			
978-1-58197-958-9	MTTC Mathematics (Secondary) 22			
978-1-58197-962-6	MTTC Physical Education 44			
978-1-58197-956-5	MTTC Physics Sample Test 19			
978-1-58197-952-7	MTTC Political Science 10			
978-1-58197-951-0	MTTC Reading 05			
978-1-58197-960-2	MTTC Spanish 28			
978-158197-970-1	MTTC Social Studies 84			
			SUBTOTAL	
	FOR PRODUCT PRICES GO TO WWW.XAMONLINE.COM		Ship	$8.25
			TOTAL	

CPSIA information can be obtained at www.ICGtesting.com
Printed in the USA
BVOW05s0700200913

331535BV00002B/55/A